With the Conquering Turk: confessions of a Bashi-Bazouk, etc. An account of the campaign in Thessaly in 1897

George Warrington Steevens

With the Conquering Turk: confessions of a Bashi-Bazouk, etc. [An account of the campaign in Thessaly in 1897.]
Steevens, George Warrington
British Library, Historical Print Editions
British Library
1897
vi, 315 p. ; 8º.
9136.ee.9.

WITH THE CONQUERING TURK

WITH THE CONQUERING TURK

CONFESSIONS OF A BASHI-BAZOUK

BY

G. W. STEEVENS

AUTHOR OF
'THE LAND OF THE DOLLAR,' ETC.

WITH FOUR MAPS

WILLIAM BLACKWOOD AND SONS
EDINBURGH AND LONDON
MDCCCXCVII

CONTENTS.

LIST OF MAPS.

WITH THE CONQUERING TURK.

DOWN THE VARDAR.

It was something of a physical relief to emerge
on the Turkish side of the frontier, and exchange
the squat, flat-faced Servian for the long-limbed,
big - featured Turk. Sharp nosed, bold eyed,
bushy browed, a little heavy in the mouth and
cheek, slouching a little in his walk, a little
slow in movement, but always powerful in
build and masterful in bearing—he is the stuff
which either heroes or devils might be made
of. But he is primarily and beyond all mis-
taking a man.

The rambling little frontier station is called
Zibeftche, or rather it is so transliterated for
convenience of pronunciation, and one wonders

respectfully how inconvenient it may have been before. Leave Zibeftche and at once you are in the East. Immediately there is the dash of colour: the fez in all shades of red, from joyous scarlet to sad plum-colour, runs through every-thing like a thread of red embroidery. This is the one note of uniformity. Otherwise the Turk, or his subject, draws no rein upon the fancy in the matter of colours. He clothes himself spon-taneously in rainbows, and groups himself with-out affectation into spectroscopes. A blue shirt or a magenta jersey, a buff open waistcoat or a green fur-lined cloak, or a black or a white sheepskin, a sash of scarlet touched with gold and green, either six inches wide or a generous two feet swathing all the body—you see them all in any knot of half a dozen. You will see breeches that recall the Western groom, bags that recall a bicycle skirt, violet skin-tights or the white kilt and high, white, braided gaiters of the Albanian. If a man fancies the gold embroidery on his socks, he wears them outside his trousers; if he does not, they will do inside; if he has no socks at all, why, he does not pretend to have any, and gets on just as well.

All this and more you may see as you joggle not too hurriedly down the valley of the Vardar. The sight is not without its serious import, for

are we not in Macedonia? For all the curious
stranger knows, each costume stands for one of
the jarring races whose feuds and clashing
ambitions have made Macedonia the infernal
machine of Europe. The gaiters of the Albanian and the knee-boots of the Servian, the
dark-blue kilt of the Wallach and the shoddy
reach-me-downs of the Greek, the sheepskin cap
of the Bulgar and the fez of the Turk—from
head to foot these people express in their very
garments the elements of the problem of Macedonia. "Macedonia for the Macedonians," cried
Mr Gladstone in the generosity of his uninstructed ardour; but which are the Macedonians?
There are at least six kinds of Macedonians.
Each insists that it is the true and only heir,
and must enter into the whole inheritance; and
that is the beginning and end, and the perpetual imminent peril of the Macedonian question.
Because of this the factious claimants establish
consulates and endow bishoprics and provoke
outrages. Because of this each is ready to rush
into war at any moment, to swallow up the
whole cake before anybody else can have a bite
at it. Many have been the proposed medicines
for Macedonia; but one that will cure all dis-
contents there never has been yet. And until
six into one goes one there never will be.

In this kaleidoscope of nationalities and national dresses appeared the uniform of the Turkish soldier with a steadily increasing insistence. Soldiers there were, of course, from the first — at the frontier and at the little guard-houses along the line. At first they were few. Here and there a reservist, his Martini slung over his shoulder and his belt of cartridges round his waist, smoked stolidly by the side of the line or at a wayside station. But they were less stolid than usual. When a few were gathered together they seemed more alert than is the Turkish wont; they joked and were not above a little horseplay. Their behaviour in the train was that of all other soldiers in trains. They laughed and shouted; they did not sit still for a minute on end; whenever the train stopped a minute—and first and last it stopped a good many — they got out, and devoted great energy to doing things of no importance. At every station there were the same loitering, chibook-puffing Martinis and cartridge belts; the same unusual animation, yet animation always without excitement. No screams of "*Zeto Hellas!*" or "*Zeto ho polemos!*" or "*A Berlin!*" But at one station, where some forty men embarked, they gave one cheer. Their cheer was neither enthusiastic nor joyous. It was deep and hoarse and grim, like the growl of a beast that scents blood. It was the sort of cheer that you wake up at night to remember.

The uniform of these soldiers was peculiar, but not extensive. Uniform, indeed, is the unhappiest possible word for it, for there was nothing uniform about it except the fez, and even over that one gallant fellow wore a crimson shawl muffling his face and tied under his chin, as if he were an old lady with toothache. Still almost all the reservists had one military garment—usually a coat. Shabby it may have been, and usually was, but still it was a coat, generally blue or black, and not without a trace here and there of red or blue facings. But to infer from the disorder of their apparel that the Turks are unfitted for heavy campaigning was even now absurd. The first hour in Turkey was enough to teach that lesson to any man with eyes in his head. To talk about an army in rags and barefooted, as was being busily done in English newspapers, was merely twaddle. What if they were in rags? The Turkish peasant lives in rags; and the shrill wind from the mountains does not move him to a single shiver. His uniform coat may be old, but it is one more garment than usual, and therefore

all to the good. As for his feet, certainly he
has no boots. But then he never has boots;
he doesn't want boots, and they would make
him profoundly uncomfortable if he were made
to wear them. Only soldiers in garrison in
towns ever wear boots in this country. There
were waiting at the front for each of these
men a couple of pairs of sandals or canvas
slippers. A gentleman who was in the Crimea
told me that with these the Turks would march
on for ever when our men were falling out by
the dozen, because their boots galled them. The
sandal is good enough for the Turk to plough
his land and herd his sheep in; it would presumably be good enough for him to fight the
Greeks in.

As we crept further down the Vardar, nearer
to Salonica, the sea, and the front, we took on
board no more soldiers. Those we had were only
small detachments, often only twos or threes—
men from the remote mountain valleys, it appeared, who had received the call to arms late
and were late in getting to the railway. The
main force of the third Army Corps, which stands
for the fighting strength of Macedonia, had
poured itself long ago down to Salonica, to pass
thence slowly to the frontier mountains. So as
we still crept south the country became silent

and somnolent. The valley became at many points a gorge with just room for the train to cling to the foot of a cliff as it wound through the deepening shadows. Villages and stations were few and distant. A poor country—though as the light fell the valley opened out again, and fields of wheat and opium poppies spread themselves out dimly on either hand. By now the train was very silent : the soldiers, like good Turks, began to go to sleep as soon as it began to grow dark. And I for one was fast asleep when there rose up the sound of riot about my ears, and a score of yelling dishevelled porters were fighting for my bags. I got a dusky impression of a fair gravelled platform planted with laburnums. I mechanically produced my passport, which a polite gentleman in a fez seemed to be asking for, and fondly I hoped I had seen the last of the thing. I had a vision of being driven rapidly between high-walled court-yards and clinging desperately to one side of the landau to save myself from being dropped out of the other. Then I was in the first hotel in Salonica, so they told me, with a large, dingy hall and a naked-looking cocoanut-matted dining-room, with an orchestra in the café and a mob of bellowing carriage-drivers in the street fit to wake the dead. But they didn't wake me.

II.

A CITY OF JEWS.

THE two men in the bare dining-room of the first
hotel in Salonica were talking bad Spanish. It
was curious; but were we not in the Levant,
where you may expect to hear bad anything
under heaven? It became more curious when I
went into the bazaar, and heard two ancient Jews
—quite unmistakable grey-bearded, eagle-nosed,
shiny-eyed, gaberdined Jews—also talking bad
Spanish. There must be a large Spanish colony
in Salonica, I told myself. Then I went to the
telegraph office. Here was another Jew handing
in a telegram; nothing strange in that. But he,
too, was talking bad Spanish, and—wonder of
wonders!—the staid Turk at the receipt of telegrams was answering him in bad Spanish too.
What on earth did it all mean? Could I possibly have taken the wrong train somewhere, and
got to Spain instead of Macedonia?

On inquiry I found that this was Salonica after all. But Salonica is principally populated by Spanish Jews, and Spanish is its staple tongue. The Jews have been there some four hundred years—since the days of Ferdinand and Isabella. Persecuted out of Spain, they came to Salonica, and the Turk, as always, received them with toleration. And there they have been ever since, preserving the rites and speaking the language of their fathers. In a way it is a purer, because an older, Spanish than that of Spain to-day. The Spaniards have worn the Latin *filius* down to *hijo* by now; the Jews are still at *fijo* with a *j* sound nearer that of France than that of Spain. On the rock of Jewish tenacity the storms of time and cataclysm have beaten in vain. They talk as they talked when they left Spain; they dress much as they dressed; they keep themselves to themselves, and are proud to call themselves Spaniards. The less educated are convinced that they are the only Spaniards in the world. Even those who know Spanish ports well would never dream of trying to talk as the Spaniards do. To them "Español" means Jew, and so it does to the rest of Salonica. Out of the 120,000 people of the city it is computed that over one half are Jews; Greeks are perhaps 25,000, and Turks a trifle less. There can hardly be another city of this size in the world where the majority of the population are Jews; there are more Jews here than in Jerusalem. Salonica is the greatest, and surely the most romantic, ghetto in the world.

But the irony of it, in this principal city of Macedonia! Here is the province which all covet, wherein all are feverishly struggling to create or to simulate a preponderance of their own nationality. Here is the city which Greeks, Bulgars, Servians, and Wallachs claim, which Turkey refuses to yield, which Austria and Russia will fight for to the death. And the majority of its inhabitants are Jewish, and its reigning speech is old Spanish! Macedonia for the Macedonians? Cry rather Jewry for the Jews.

This is all strange, but there is yet stranger to come. Salonica has also a large colony of Mussulman Jews. We have heard from time to time of a solitary Jew converted to Christianity, but who ever heard before of a Jew turned Turk? Here there is a whole tribe of them. Originally they were followers of a false Messiah, who arose many generations ago. The Jews rejected him, whereupon he embraced Islam with all his disciples. The Turks received the converts and despised them; the faithful Jews spat them out of their mouths. Neither Turk nor Jew would marry them or give to them in marriage. So there they have been ever since—clinging with all the steadfast obstinacy of their old race to their new faith, marrying each other in and in till they are said to have bred into themselves weird, superhuman attributes—second-sight and prophecy. As to that I know nothing. But these Jewish Turks are the only Mussulmans—with here and there an Arab or two—who trade in the bazaar; and from their manner of trading you may see that whatever they have gained or lost they are Jews yet.

The Jews of Salonica are not of the black, Polish cast, which to most Englishmen is the type of the race. They came from Spain, and Spain under the Moors grew the flower of all Judaism. Their faces are less fleshy and finer than those of the Eastern breed; their foreheads and temples high; their silky beards often almost blonde, their noses thin and often almost straight. They move with a grave dignity, and though their faces express something of the weary pathos of their history, there is yet something of the patriarch and the philosopher in the look of the best of them.

Except for the fez, the garments of the Salonica Jew can have changed but little since his fathers were driven from beside the Guadalquivir. He wears a long open surtout, black or indigo or bottle-green, with a lining of fur; inside that, down to the heel, is a kind of dressing-gown, with a sash round the waist. Underneath he condescends to the Gentile trousers; but it is part of his stubborn Jewish steadfastness that even under the hottest suns of summer he never quits his fur.

His women are the most gorgeous of Salonica. Their gala skirts are a wonder of stiff silk, embroidered with every flower that grows in a queen's garden. Above this it must be owned that they have very little more than an open bodice and an open lace chemise. But on the head elaboration begins again. They must not show their hair; they conceal it, therefore, under a flat silk cap, rather like that of a German student, only with a yellow ribbon under the chin. The cap is all green and white, blue and yellow, and cunning needlework; behind it falls a bag for the hair, likewise of green silk, its drooping end embroidered with pearls. It sounds magnificent, but it looks ungraceful, destroying all the contours of the head. It is drawn so tight over the hair that it pulls up the eyebrows till they become almost circles. These women are said to be the most educated and cultivated of Salonica; some of them are also, in their youth, the most beautiful. But the costume is not one which I should recommend to my grandmother.

There are more than Jews in Salonica; indeed, what are there not? All the civilisations of the Levant have left their mark upon it. Here is a building which was once, so they say, the Temple of Venus. Here, chipped and defaced, stand the sculptured relics of what was once a Roman arch, side by side with a crooked hovel, wherein, sitting on the bare ground, a baker is baking his bread in an oven open to the street. Next door is a rather better shop: this one has got a floor, two or three old boxes athwart the open front for a counter, and tin pots and pans festooned about the walls; behind them the gipsy smith is cross-legged on the floor, hammering at others. Turn down a mountainous little alley—mountainous, for it is so little that nobody wants to repair it, otherwise Salonica is the best-paved town in Turkey, and its main streets, where the shabby little ponies pull shabby little tramcars, are almost up to the standard of the Caledonian Road. The sloping alley is so narrow that the jutting upper rooms of the houses hardly leave a streak of blue between. Then you come out on to the ruin of the Byzantine St Sofia. It is said to be a smaller, but exact, model of the mosque of the same name in Constantinople, though it is hard to judge by the eye. This church became a mosque; the Turks added a slender minaret, a portico, and a large court to it; it looked on all the changing fates of Salonica till the great fire of eight years ago. Then it was burned out; the wall of the court was destroyed, and so it stands to this day. It stands a bare form amid the dust and desolation all round it; charred, crumbling, maimed, blind-eyed, and solitary, surely as piteous a ruin as any in the world. This for Byzantium; for Venice speak the square battlemented walls, which enclose the town on all but the sea side, running back from the quay up the hill on which Salonica stands, to meet in the rambling citadel. Beneath these still solid monuments of the Doges there passes now the befezzed butcher, his bleeding lambs' carcasses slung from hooks on two boards, which he hangs pannierwise on his pony's back. Venetian, too, is the White Tower at the sea-front. It was built of red brick, and was once called the Bloody Tower. When the Sultan, in the tender promise of his earlier days, heard this he forbade the grisly name, and had the tower whitened. The red is wearing through again by now; which thing, say some, is a parable.

For Turkey speak the gleaming minarets, which stand sentinel over every captured mosque. Yet the whole impression of the town is not Turkish, nor Greek, nor even Jewish, but Levantine. There is the Austrian post-office, the French library, the Italian hotel. There is a beer-shop named after each battleship of the Mediterranean squadron. Under the club is a café which bears an inscription of priceless worth. The top part is defaced; beneath it you may decipher the fragment: "British naval sailors; where you will be treated as Englishmen should be; all kinds of drinks; English spoken." One of the leading inhabitants of Salonica is a Jew by race, a papal baron, and a British subject. Could such be found outside the Levant? It is a city of mixtures and mongrels, with the hardly definable influence of the Eastern Mediterranean over all. It is an influence that makes for untidiness —in dress and in ideas and in conscience. The Levantine is not sympathetic to the Briton: he is not distinguished for justice or honesty, temperance or chastity, industry or courage, though I am told he is an early riser. Such as he is, Salonica is his. For the Levantine character overspreads all races; it can almost change the unchanging Jew.

III.

A HOSPITAL'S HOSPITALITY.

EXCEPT at the extreme south-western corner a crescent of fairly high and fairly steep hills cuts off Salonica from the country inland—cuts it off also from the land-breeze in summer, as the British resident will cheerfully remind you. On the first low slopes of these hills, looking down over a quarter of a mile of dusty common, of houses half built and houses half fallen to pieces, stands the very long, white-plastered, green-shuttered, two-storeyed hospital. In front of it is a garden, with shady trees and flower-beds. Pansies and stocks were blossoming there in the last week of March, so forward was the year in that sheltered bay, though all the mountains down the Greek coast were crusted with snow, and we heard—always, of course, from Vienna, Salonica's nearest communication with the world —of terrible weather on the frontier. You walk through the garden over a kind of tesselated pavement, prettily picked out in stones of different colours — red, white, brown. Then you walk up the broad stone steps; opposite you is a clock with an inscription. An inscription in English, moreover, to the effect that it was given by the Admiralty in recognition of the kindness and skill displayed in treating petty officers and seamen for smallpox. This began to throw a new light on the Turk, that he should be equal to curing bluejackets of smallpox.

The Pasha in supreme command was away on a tour of the field-hospitals. There were depot hospitals at Serfidje, Karaveria, Elassona, and Janina, covering the whole frontier line, with nine small field-hospitals. 'Meantime the second in command received us—a small man in a very brilliant fez, bright-eyed, fair-moustached, smiling, and courteous, but with a rather strained, sad look in his eyes. The Turk, as I have said, is not naturally joyous, and I do not suppose that hard work in a hospital is likely to make a refined and sensitive man any more so.

We went into this gentleman's room. The private room of a pasha — for he, too, was a pasha — I expected to be something brilliantly coloured, something Byronic. But this was just like any other gentleman's private room. The Pasha took a seat at a table, but not till we had sat down in a row of chairs ranged along the wall. As we sat down he salaamed. We salaamed back. The theory of the salaam is that you lift up dust from the ground in your open hands, convey it to your breast, and then cast it upon your head. The practice of it is that you touch the front of your hat or head, as the case may be, with your open hand; if you are a soldier you make a moment's halt at your mouth. The other medical officers similarly ranged themselves on a row of chairs, side by side with us. They salaamed; we salaamed. Cigarettes were handed; we smoked. Then came an orderly with a tray, on which glittered gold and silver. There was a basin of jam, a stand of spoons with a bowl in the middle, a row of cups of water. You take a spoonful of jam—it was strawberry jam, and, so far as I am a judge of strawberry jam, the very best in the world — eat it — alas, for the cigarette!— put the spoon in the central basin, and take a sip of water. Next came coffee. The coffee is served in little round cups without handles. Lest you should burn your fingers, it is held in a little gold and silver stand of the shape of an egg - cup. Herewith also come glasses of

water. When you have drunk your coffee—
or eaten it, if you like, for it resembles thick
soup; and he who has not tasted Turkish coffee
does not know what coffee tastes like—you put
back the cup and the stand separately on the
tray. Which done, the Pasha salaamed; we
salaamed; the doctors salaamed; we salaamed,
and all started to make the tour of the wards.

The sick sat up in their beds as we passed—
dusky faces, mostly topped with white turbans.
They appear in this country to be ill with nearly
all their clothes on, and their favourite posture
is sitting on their heels. Some were hastily
gathering themselves into this position as we
entered; one carried his obeisance so far as to
stand on his bed at attention. On the faces of
some, who seemed to be suffering, sat a look of
stolid resignation; on those of the others, as
keen a curiosity to see what the infidel looked
like as the infidel had to see them. Not but
what there were infidels here also, for Greek,
Jew, or miscellaneous Levantine may be received
here in the civil wards, and treated as Greeks,
Jews, and Levantines should be—perhaps even a
bit better.

I am not an authority on hospitals, and, if I
were, nobody wants to hear more of them than
can reasonably be helped. But I think almost

any Englishman who only knew of the Turkish Empire by hearsay would have been astonished and disabused if he had seen what I saw. The floors, the ceilings, the sheets, and the mattresses were spotlessly clean. The case-sheet hung duly at every bed-head, with due particulars of the disease and the remedies to be applied. The pharmacy appeared provided with every drug of merit, the names written in Turkish and French on each drawer. The smell of iodoform could not have been improved upon in the most enlightened West. The operating-tables were speckless; the germs were being duly baked out of the aprons and operating apparatus in an oven. Across a court were a couple of wards for convalescents; further off, the wing reserved for the isolation of infectious maladies. In the court itself were rows on rows of trestles — a sight of some significance, for the accommodation had been brought up to a thousand beds to receive the casualties of war. So we passed out to where Salonica sweated and shivered under a summer sun and a screaming wind from the frontier mountains. There was not very much but dust in the landscape just then or afterwards, and if a peck of it in March is worth a king's ransom, Salonica was already able to buy up as many kings of Greece as could be put upon the market. At the door we shook hands with our Pasha, thanked him in French, which he spoke with mastery, salaamed, and parted. We parted again in the garden, and again at the gate; on each occasion all salaamed.

Now, this hospital, wherein many operations and cases, hazardous even in the West, have been most successfully undertaken, is entirely the work of Turks. So, at least, I understand, and in Turkey when anything is not the work of Turks — other than massacres — somebody is generally at hand to say so. Of course, one eminent surgeon does not make a civilisation, nor one excellent hospital a benevolent despotism. I dare say that this is the best hospital in the Empire; certainly there could hardly be a better. But if this hospital does not prove much, it does prove that the Turk is not the incapable savage that British fancy delights to paint him. He may not have attained much as yet, yet he is here demonstrated not incapable of attainment. But who knows? Who wants to know? You have heard, no doubt, that there are bad roads in Macedonia, but had you heard that there is a good hospital in Salonica? Of course you had not. It is nobody's interest to tell you, except, perhaps, the Turk's. And, of course, you wouldn't believe a man like him.

IV.

A WEEK OF WAITING.

SALONICA was agreeable enough, especially to a man with a taste for coffee and cigarettes by day, for beer and a café chantant by night. The sun was almost always shining, and there were endless seats to sit in it on. There was the sea to look at in front, and when you got tired of that there was a tree or two to gladden the eyes of the man who knew anybody to show him the way to them. Probably Salonica is the noisiest place in the world—a distinction the more creditable in that all its noise is made, so to speak, by hand: if it ever should be blessed with the machinery of an American city, it ought to be able to make itself distinctly heard in London. But if the last bawling driver takes home his thundering carriage at three in the morning, and the first brings out his at five minutes past, there is compensation even for that. Salonica goes to bed so late and gets up so early—revenging itself abundantly, it must be said, in the middle of the day—that you need never wait for such entertainment as it has to offer. As soon as the girls in the café had left off fiddling, the day's consignment of soldiers had begun to arrive at the railway station. While you listened to the fiddling you could sit and smoke and drink beer; while you looked at the soldiers you could sit and smoke and drink coffee. And there was generally somebody with nothing else to do quite willing to do nothing with you.

But I—could I for a moment forget it?—I had come to Salonica to be a war-correspondent. Now for a war-correspondent two things at least are indispensable—war and the possibility of corresponding about it. And Salonica offered neither. For a town of its importance and degree of civilisation, I doubt if there is any place in the world so utterly out of the world as Salonica. The newspapers in Turkey contain just what the Government wants them to contain; Salonica has but one French sheet weekly, and that devotes itself almost whole-heartedly to *la vie Salonicienne*. At Constantinople you have at least telegrams posted up in the club; you have nothing of the kind in Salonica. It is almost equidistant from every place where news could come from. You have got as far away from everywhere as you possibly can without coming near somewhere else. Go by rail, and you are getting nearer Vienna; go by sea, and you are getting nearer Athens. Stay in Salonica and you must get your news, forty-eight hours stale, from the 'Neue Freie Presse.' War might be breaking out at any moment — and the last person, the very last person in any considerable town of Europe, to hear of it might easily be the wretched man in Salonica who was expected to describe it.

Then why stay in Salonica? Elassona was the headquarters of the army; if war broke out they would be sure to hear of it sooner or later at Elassona. But to go to Elassona was the one thing it was impossible to do. The Turk has many virtues, and to these I have tried to do justice; but confidence in the casual European is not among them. He has no love for news-paper correspondents. Perhaps even, he has no cause to love them: they have let him in for three years of trouble with their blood-red pic-tures of Armenian outrages, first painted on the strength of the Prophet knows what Armenian fables. If you go to him, therefore, and say, " I am a newspaper correspondent and I wish to go to the front," he will bow and say, " It is necessary to apply in the proper quarters for permission," and probably put a special spy on you to see what you are up to next. So I applied to the Consul-General, and the Consul-General applied to the Vali, and the Vali applied to the Minister of Foreign Affairs, and to what exalted person the Minister of Foreign Affairs applied I hardly like to think. After a few days came the intelligence that there had been some slight informality. The correcter procedure would be that the Consul-General should apply to the British Ambassador at Constantinople, and that he should apply to the Minister of Foreign Affairs, and then he would apply to the necessary exalted quarters. And so the house that Jack built was duly rebuilt. It is flattering, no doubt, for a comparatively young man to become a Cabinet question, but it takes time. And here, meanwhile, was the comparatively young man growing rapidly and unprofitably older. He might stay in Salonica, and welcome; but in Salonica he must stay.

For example, it struck me one day that I should like to go to Karaveria. Karaveria is a station on the railway, from Salonica to Monastir, which formed the base of the army at the front. Troops, munitions, and stores were transported thither on the way to Elassona, and thence did the rest by road. Having risen very early in the morning, I joined a hated rival—the correspondent of another London paper —at the railway station. Briskly we stepped into the booking-office. "Two first return——" A tall officer stepped politely in front of us. "Impossible," he said. "But we only want to go to Karaveria, and come back this evening. Behold a basket of lunch as a guarantee of good faith." "Impossible without a special passport." "But it's only to Karaveria—not even outside the sandjak of Salonica." A sandjak, I gathered, is a kind of district council without the council. "No," said the ever-polite captain. "I am sorry, but I am not allowed to use my discretion. Nobody may take a ticket—nobody at all—without a special permission." To the amazement of the captain—these curious Europeans to be annoyed at having nothing to do !—we swore audibly.

Never mind, though, we will go to-morrow. We will send the Consul - General's cavass — a cavass is a kind of mixture of servant and orderly and personal Swiss Guard—to the police; he will get us a paper stating that we are not spies. In the meantime, a stroll and some coffee and cigarettes. Then some cigarettes and coffee, and a little stroll. Then lunch. On the hour of lunch comes back the cavass. The police regrets that it has no power to give such papers; application must be made to the Vali through the Consul-General for a teskere. A teskere is the document you normally require in order to be allowed to make a journey from one sandjak to another. You must get that. We swore again.

Never mind, though. The Consul-General is inexhaustible in his courtesy; let us ask him to send for a teskere. It is only a matter of a few hours; we will go the day after to-morrow. In the meantime a little—shall we say coffee and cigarettes? Then a little run in the Bay on the two-piastre steamer, with French colours floating over the rail. A couple of hours thus filled in, and then to the Consulate. The teskere? Refused? Why, certainly. Karaveria is the principal point of disentrainment for the troops going up to the front. For the present the Vali is not empowered to allow newspaper correspondents to visit it. You can go to Monastir if you like, or Uskub, or, indeed, almost anywhere where there is nothing going on. But Karaveria — for the present, no. Perhaps if an application were made to the Minister of Foreign Affairs, through the British Ambassador at Constantinople, and strongly supported in the proper quarters — but no. For the present, no!

And what will the correspondent do then,

poor thing? I do not blame the officer at the
station, nor the police, nor his Excellency the
Vali, nor his Majesty the Sultan. In their own
Turkish way they were all perfectly right, and
if I had been in their position I should have done
exactly the same as they. Karaveria, after all,
was the principal point of disentrainment, and
we were not going there to enjoy the landscape.
The Government did not want people to know
about the mobilisation; it was its own mobilisation, and it had a perfect right to keep it to
itself. Whether this was altogether wise from
its own point of view is another matter. The
Turkish Government professed itself desirous of
avoiding war, and I do not doubt that its pro-
fessions were sincere. Certainly it has gained
nothing by the war, nor will it, to outweigh the
expense and sacrifices it involved. Now it is
more than possible that if the Turks had put
fewer obstacles in the way of correspondents at
this early stage, war would have been averted.
Instead, it allowed correspondents in Thessaly,
who ought to have had a little common-sense,
but apparently had not, to proclaim to Europe
and to Greece that the Turkish army was a mob
of starving, half-naked, diseased, disorderly ruffians, who could never stand a day before the
forces of civilised Greece. It seems incredible

now, but it is indisputable, that thousands of Europeans talked glibly of Japan and China, and believed that the Greeks would have a chance against the Turks. The Greeks were glad enough to take this opinion. Of course the Turks said that they were arming. They issued daily statements from Constantinople of the number of troops that had gone up to the front. But as they let nobody go to see them, they only gave the impression that there were rather more troops in the statement than there were at the front.

As a matter of fact the statements from Constantinople were true, and the troops very decently cared for. The mobilisation worked slowly, but it worked. No doubt it could have been improved on in Germany, but it was well in advance of anything Turkey had done before. The thanks for that were due to the new direct railway from Constantinople to Salonica. Had the Sultan kept his fleet in any order this line could have been dispensed with. But the Greek fleet, trumpery as it was, commanded the Archipelago, and neither men nor stores could be sent by sea. So that, but for the Constantinople-Salonica line, the Asiatic reserves could not have been got to the front for weeks and weeks. They would have had to march to Salonica from some

point on the main line from Vienna to Constantinople, and they would have had to be fed on the
way.   In that case, with nobody at the front but
the troops from Macedonia, Albania, and Kossovo,
even the Greek army might have gained important success.

The direct line, as by comparison it is generally called, runs from a point south of Adrianople
to Dedeagatch, and thence to Salonica.   The
troops joined it from Rodosto on the Marmora,
whence runs a branch line towards Adrianople.   I
am free to admit that until I got to Salonica I did
not know that this line existed : it is shown on
no English map I have seen, although trains have
been running over it regularly once a-week for
more than a year.   Having been made principally
for strategic purposes it is supposed to stand back
from the coast, though there are two places where
it could be cut without difficulty by a landing
force.   And if the Greeks had had any decision
or enterprise, cut it certainly would have been.
If they had known their own minds they would
have cut it before the mobilisation had begun, a
couple of months before they actually went to
war.   By breaking the line of mobilisation at
Dedeagatch, at Kavalla, or at Salonica, they
might have paralysed all the armaments of
Turkey for weeks, and entered upon the war

with the heaviest conceivable odds in their
favour. But they were just as nerveless at sea,
where they had all the cards in their hand, as
they were on land. The only step they had
taken up to March 22nd, when I reached Salonica,
was to circulate a false report that they had
blown up the great bridge over the Vardar, an
hour westward of Salonica, on the railway to
Monastir. The news was duly telegraphed over
Europe, and it would have excited a vast sensa-
tion, as spelling collapse for the Turkish mobilisation, if only anybody had known where and
what the Vardar bridge was. On my arrival, I
found the Vardar bridge, quite unconcerned,
standing where it did, and I began to realise at
the very beginning that in these countries a
correspondent would do well to believe only what
his own eyes saw. Besides setting afloat this
most characteristic invention—I wonder what good
they thought it would do them?—the Greeks
attempted nothing else against the Turkish com-
munications till after the middle of April, when
with a small landing-party they tried to break the
line near Kavalla. This business they muffed as
badly as they muffed everything else.

Let us go back to the railway line. As it was
the only thing connected with the war that correspondents were allowed to look at, I spent such

hours as I could snatch from coffee and cigarettes in looking at it. It is a single-track line, not too well laid, and at the beginning of the mobilisation blocks were many. Trains stood still on sidings for thirty-six hours at a time. This was especially hard on the horses they were bringing up for the artillery and transport, many of which were so let down by it that they had to be left behind in Salonica to recruit. Nevertheless, so we were told, as many as 12,000 horses had passed through Salonica to the front by the end of March, which was enough to mount every trooper and horse every gun and leave thousands over for transport. There had passed along the line eighty-eight battalions of Redifs from Asia Minor, which, with troops of the line and Redifs from the European provinces, made well over 100 battalions—say, 65,000 to 75,000 infantry— between Salonica and the frontier. Add cavalry and artillery, and you get an army of close on 80,000 men, with not much short of 200 guns. Of course, the difficulty would be to feed everybody. But lamb was in season; contractors at Salonica were sending up biscuit and flour by the ton. The weather was bad up at the frontier, and that was the worst hardship; but the Albanians and Turks would at least rough it as well as the Greeks.

Thus we talked and reckoned up battalions and batteries, but what did it all come to? What had it all to do with Salonica? With the back-country it might have something to do; they had requisitioned all the horses and carts of the peasants for the transport. As I came down I was wondering why they could apparently grow nothing in Macedonia but two-year-olds, yearlings, and mares in foal. The rest were all gone, and the carts with them. The local waggons are not much to look at; the most British farmer's are Lord Mayor's coaches beside them. Wheels jolt and sway, and swing away from the axle and back again; but, after all, they are the only thing that could stand the roads. My first ride along the Sultan's highway was evidence enough of that. The pony scampered over slabs of rock, beds of streams, heaps of rubble, up and down 45° gradients, and round right-angled corners, with one breathless, business-like rush that made me pray for strength to fall off. Certainly roads are not the strong point of Turkey, and the Sultan may well congratulate himself on the construction of the more or less direct railway.

Such as they are, the carts had to creak over them, and the husbandman was left disconsolate. For that matter, the husbandman was not left, if he were a Mussulman; he was taken also. You

have to see a sight like the transport of these
enormous masses of Redifs to the front before
you quite realise what general conscription means
in war-time when the reserves are out.   The
Redifs were splendid fellows, but how many
neglected fields and untended sheep did they
represent?   They might be well trained, but
that was because they had left fields and sheep
untended now for three successive years.   Two
years ago they were called out to fight the rebels
in Macedonia; last year they were sent over sea
to fight the Druses.   This year they must turn
out again.   People talk of the sufferings of the
Armenians and the grievances of the Greeks, but
what about the Turk?   The Greek and Armenian
take Government contracts, and grow rich; the
Turk takes his rifle and his bandolier, and grows
poor.

But what had all that to do with Salonica?
Business was dull in a way.   Commercial travellers could get no orders for manufactured goods,
but there were plenty of orders for the army.
So Salonica sunned itself happily by the sea, and
enjoyed its three Sundays.   For Salonica has
come very nearly half-way to the far-off ideal
.of a week of Sundays.   There is Friday for the
Mussulman, Saturday for the Jew, Sunday for
the Christian.   Each religiously rests on his own

day, and abstains from his business; everybody
else has to abstain more or less because of him.
Three off days a-week is much, but not more
than Salonica can do with. It was quite happy.
The menace of war was very near in space, but
thousands of leagues away in interest. Behind
the wide white flanks of Olympus, which we could
see looming across the bay from the club window,
the great game might at each moment be beginning. Salonica did not know; Salonica did not
care. We were on the rim of war, but we could
not look over.

V.

A CORRESPONDENT'S TROUSSEAU.

ONE dragoman, one cavass, two saddle-horses, two pack-horses, saddle and bridle English style, saddle and bridle Turkish style, two pack-saddles, brushes and curry-comb, halters, hobbles, nose-bags, rope, two kit-bags, a chair, a table, a fez, a waterproof sheet, towels, knives, forks, spoons, a few yards of waterproof canvas, a bed, a pillow, a quilt, a cartridge-belt, water-bottle, bucket, quinine, hypermanganate of potassium, frying-pan, teapot, japanned dishes, japanned plates, japanned cups and mugs, two lanterns, a cheap watch, a thousand cigarettes, champagne, whisky, port, sauterne, punsch likor, native hams, native tongues, tea, sugar, cocoa, tinned beef, tinned salmon, tinned herrings, sardines, salt, biscuits, Worcester sauce, cheeses, Eno's fruit salt, corned beef, laundry soap, tinned peas, tinned beans, tinned oysters, tinned jam, tinned sausages, tinned egg-powder, tinned ginger-beer powder, tinned butter, and 180 lb. of oats.

The dashing war-correspondent was equipping himself for the front. It is easy to say you will be a war correspondent. It is rather less easy to get somebody to make you one. It is a shade less easy still, in Turkey at any rate, to get yourself accepted as one. But that was all over now; the Sultan, after due consideration, had satisfied himself of my good faith, and permission was on its way from Constantinople. I had triumphed. And then came the awful question: I am going into the wilderness — what shall I want there?

There surged torrentially into my mind all the things above-named: I could not possibly do without them. Afterwards I thought of about the same number of other things I could not possibly do without; but it was too late then, and I had to do without them. There came a time when I would cheerfully have swapped the ginger-beer powder for a thousand and first cigarette. The stuff was useless without a gallon of boiling water, a teaspoonful of good barm, and a cool place, none of which were to be found in Thessaly; so I had to turn it into insect-powder, for which purpose it was next to useless. But I thought I wanted it, and I thought I wanted all the other things. And there were only three days to get them in. Well, why not get them? You can get anything in three days, except the evacuation of Thessaly, and political trifles of that kind. I can only answer that you had better try it in Salonica.

One dragoman. With great prudence I had engaged a Jew provisionally the first day I arrived, foreseeing a heavy run on the commodity later. He said his name was Moritz, though those who had watched his career from childhood asserted that it was Levi. He treated me as his own for a few days, and I was rapidly acquiring his private method of speaking German. But when the glad news came that I was going up to Elassona, my Jew failed me. He could not get the necessary teskere, he pointed out. There were difficulties. Turkish procedure was notoriously slow, and he had a brother in Salonica, and he could not bear to leave him. I was glad enough to be rid of the tyrant, but where was I to find another master? The hour of departure was approaching; all the dragomans in Salonica must have been cornered long ago. But with the hour came the man.

A large, grey-suited man of about thirty came into a shop where I was wondering what I could do with egg-powder if I bought it. His projecting, fish-like eye rambled over me. I have seldom seen so large a face, and it shone with mingled sweat and enthusiasm.

"You want dragoman—interpret," he began, in a hurried and husky voice. He really said, "Yuwadramiterpa," but for convenience I quote the more regular form.

"Yes," I said. "What's your name?"

With an air of indescribable pride, he answered, "Charlie."

"What?"

"Charlie," he repeated, with an enormous smile —"Carlo Ardita. I bin go outside English ship *Ramillies, Trafalgar.* I bin go Gibraltar, Malta, Greekland, Africa, *partout.* I bin go two years round circus."

"What did you do aboard the ships?"

"Take letters."

"What did you do in the circus?"

"Stop outside."

It was enough. Charlie it was. I bought him on the spot. He afterwards produced testimonials from warrant officers of her Majesty's fleet which were unanimous in describing him as a good fellow. As I have tried to indicate, he had a constitutional inability to pronounce consonants. He was loose-jointed, loose-tongued, speaking all the known European languages with a snuffling accent and impartial inaccuracy; he was loose in his notions of time and compound arithmetic; for aught I knew, he might be loose in his morals too. But from his fascinating, if discursive, talk, I foresaw abundant entertainment in the slacker hours of the campaign, and I was weak enough to purchase him on that ground alone. The shining virtues which emerged later will be dealt with in their proper place.

There was no difficulty about the cavass. For two days a swollen torrent of black-browed, white ballet-skirted Albanians surged round the door of the first hotel in Salonica. All were men of unimpeached integrity, tried ferocity; all lovingly nursed revolvers in the leather mixture of belt and pocket which Albanians wear before them; all spoke fluently in every local language in which no civilised man could possibly examine them; all were content with four and a half Turkish pounds a-month. One recommended himself above the crowd by an air of pensive bloodthirstiness; he gave the impression of having a blood-feud on his mind, which he had let run too long. His age was about fifty, his temperament was morose, and his name was Aslan, which signifies " the lion." The lion's references were satisfactory, and I bought him up. It sounds ridiculous, but Aslan would have died to save my life in case of need. He gave his word to be faithful to death; he said, "*Bes a bes*," which appears to mean "word of honour," and having said that, it was far more desirable to die than to go back upon it. Only I had to treat him like a gentleman; if I had struck or insulted him he would have shot me like a dog. All the same, I believe Albania is the only place left in Europe where you can get a man to die for you at four pound ten (Turkish) per month.

Item : four horses—and here came the heart-breaking part of it. Buying a horse in England is a weighty and a wary business, but it can generally be done in an afternoon if you make up your mind to it. In Salonica it took three days.

There was no difficulty about the supply. I discovered a white-bearded, turbaned old sinner who kept a khan—a khan being in theory an inn, but in practice a large four-sided stable round a court, with some lofts over it in which the traveller sleeps. The old man produced horses on horses—hard-mouthed, sore-backed, scraggy little twelve-hand brutes, capable of everything except a walk, trot, canter, or gallop. Others also heard that an Ingles of boundless wealth was prepared to buy up all the weeds in Salonica : it was impossible to walk to the street corner without a score of grimy, befezzed, baggy-breeched horse-coupers dragging unwilling ponies behind me. I inspected and tried them at the rate of about two score a-day, and always found them wanting.

At last came the day when the purchase must be made if ever. I bade Charlie give it out that all the horses in Salonica were to be assembled, and went forth to buy. I don't know whether all the horses were there, but I am certain all the loafers were. With a serried host of men and horses and dogs at my heels, I sallied out and entered the nearest khan.

Solemnly the deal began. The first man, an enormous yellow-bearded Jew, wanted ten pounds. I wanted the horse, which I had tried; it was the leanest and meanest-looking I ever saw, but it could go and would go. But did I therefore suggest a price for it? Even innocent I was not so innocent of the East as that: I gave the dealer a look of scorn, and bade him take the beast away. In the same way I went through all the horses in the khan. The prices ranged from twice to four times the normal figure. I pretended not to want any of them, and the owners pretended to take them away. Of course they knew perfectly well I must have the horses, and I knew perfectly well that they had only dodged into the next khan round the corner. So after half an hour or so I followed them into the khan round the corner, and they pretended that they had never seen me before in their lives. I was looking at a miniature of a charger when an elderly Turkish gentleman came cantering down the street.

" Ahmed Effendi, Ahmed Effendi," cried a hundred voices.

Thereon Ahmed Effendi pulled up, dismounted, and offered to sell his horse for eighteen pounds. He took the saddle off, and pointed out that, though indisputably old, this was by far the best horse in Salonica. Its market price being five pounds, I did not buy it; but the sudden stress of competition enabled me to buy the other, worth six pounds, for eleven.

The moment of making the deal was an impressive one. Buyer and seller shook hands: it is not merely customary, but obligatory in law, for a Government official—a little Turk in a fur overcoat—stands by. The price you shake hands on you are compelled to stick to. The official then gives the buyer a certificate of ownership, and the buyer gives the official fourpence. But the real excitement comes when the handshaking begins before the price is quite fixed. Each shaker yells out his figure : " Ten, eleven; eleven, ten;" the bystanders crowd up and take sides, yelling "ten" or "eleven," according to their fancy. Then the official loses patience. He seizes the hands as they swing and pull and grip, in the fervent endeavour to shake out an extra pound. "Eleven," he bellows, in a voice of thunder, and eleven it has to be.

Ahmed Effendi mounted, and rode off without saying good-bye. On the top of that came back the yellow Jew with his horse. Its price was still ten pounds; but when I went to buy a pack-horse he began to think the demand was getting supplied. There was a heavy slump immediately, and I bought that horse for seven pounds and a half. And then, becoming reckless, I went into a third khan and bought the two first sound horses that came. The sellers were a little hurt; it seemed to them something of a slight that I should buy their horses within a quarter of an hour. But the manners of the Ingles are notoriously brusque — and after all, the double price was always a consideration.

The other two or three hundred articles indispensable to a war correspondent I bought in a morning. It was a heavy burden to own so many things—more than I ever had in my life. But they got less and less very rapidly as time went on. Some of them—such as the chair and the hypermanganate of potassium — I satisfied my conscience by buying, and then happily never saw again. · The eatable and drinkable things got eaten and drunk, and the rest followed me about in a steadily diminishing trail. From Charlie down to the Worcester sauce, everything got lost at one time or another—especially Charlie. Yet nearly everything turned up again, and I lived in a normal state of luxury, varied only by accidental privation, until the very end of the campaign. But did it ever occur to you that a war correspondent had to be a sort of travelling Gordon hotel, with a smack of portable Whiteley? It had never struck me before, and it rather weighed on my mind. I am not used to hotel-keeping nor to universal providing. And the point I could not get clear on was how I could ever tear myself from my caravan and find time to correspond.

VI.

OFF!

THAT was all right. The provisions were packed into boxes; the other things were stuffed into bags; the horses had been new-shod; Charlie had drawn two pounds in advance to buy a suit of velveteens and a pair of top-boots; Aslan had drawn half a pound, after the manner of Albanians, "to buy tobacco for the journey." And I had hired one-third of a special train to Karaveria: it was almost as cheap, with such a caravan, as the ordinary train, and it offered the great and, in war-time, unusual, advantage of being almost certain to get to its destination the day it started.

When I had come to the station before, I had not been allowed three yards inside the booking-office. I was then a putative spy. Now I had been considered and passed by Constantinople, and I was a great man and a friend. The gentle-

men who sit at little tables all about the little
booking-office—they appear to be a combination
of customs - officers and detectives — were now
cordial even to salaams. Instead of arguing on
the threshold, I now swaggered about the platform and the line and the station-master's office
as if I had bought them. There are not many
moneyed men in provincial Turkey, and such as
there are usually pretend not to be : three men
who could put down twenty-four pounds for a
special train, with the countenance of the Sultan
thrown in, are not a sight seen every day, and are
to be respected accordingly. To mark their sense
of this they even brought the train up punctually.
A host of porters sprang up from nowhere and
hurled in the baggage. The horses were on board
already. In the military horse-box, under their
noses, Aslan squatted on the floor; he smiled
affably as I passed him, and patted his revolver.
I got in with my co-proprietors, two other English
correspondents. The full official strength of the
Salonica - Monastir railway stood farewelling on
the platform, and through the falling night we
rumbled away to Karaveria.

We rumbled until we began to get sleepy—and
then suddenly the train stopped with a rattle and
a jerk, and somebody opened the door. We had
arrived—but what next? I had got a letter in

my pocket with a few lines of Turkish quiggles on it which I believed to be a direction to somebody it would be good to know. But outside the station it was inky dark, and where was somebody to be found? As a preliminary step we took an interpreter and groped our way out. A fire appeared about twenty yards off, throwing a fitful patch of light on a little shed and some soldiers. We made for it through the blackness, falling into a ditch by the way. There were two or three officers there. They made us welcome through the interpreter. We sat down in the flickering light round a table. A man issued from the hut with coffee; we drew out cigarettes, and another man brought a little cinder in a pair of tongs to light them with. We commenced, through the interpreter, a flickering conversation; but the Turks mainly confined themselves to looking steadily at us, and the conversation flickered out. We sat. More coffee and cigarettes were produced. But by now it began to occur to the mind that we were not making progress. We were getting no nearer the influential somebody, no nearer the night's lodging, no nearer the morrow's early start. I produced my letter: they looked at it for a little while without emotion, said a few words among themselves, and then handed it back. This was beginning to be stupid.

What were we waiting for? "He comes immediately," said the interpreter placidly. "Who comes immediately?" "A person." "What person?" "I do not know." Of course it would have been the grossest bad manners to suggest that the person should hurry himself a little. So we sat on and smoked and looked at the Turks, and the Turks looked at us.

At last a person came. An officer of about twenty-five, whose black silver-braided astrachan cap showed him to be of the cavalry. His air was authoritative; he accepted cigarettes with an air that suggested he had temporarily lent them to the owner, and was but taking back his own. Again I produced my letter; he looked at it and put it in his pocket. He sat down at the head of the table and opened a somewhat desultory conversation in French. He informed us that his name was Saad-ed-Din Bey, lieutenant of cavalry: I had taken him for a lieutenant-colonel at the least. He asked if we had not come from Salonica. We could not possibly have come from anywhere else; but when we answered "Yes," he assumed the look of a man of penetration. He volunteered the information that the Turkish headquarters were at Elassona, and that Edhem Pasha was in supreme command. So he prattled on for about half an hour. At

D

last we could stand it no longer, even from him, and suggested that we had to start very early next morning. "*Oui, monsieur*," he said, and rose to go. Somebody came up with a lantern, somebody else followed with half-a-dozen horses, and we started for the town. We appeared to be going over a ploughed field, though it afterwards came out that it was a road. Kicking into stones, stumbling over clods, bursting through thorns, plumping into ditches, jostling against horses, we slowly made our way through the night. We beguiled the way by asking Saad-ed-Din Bey questions about the Turkish army. He replied always with "*Oui*" or "*Non*," but always readily and courteously. A very affable, intelligent fellow, this Saad-ed-Din. And when he presently hinted that he would like us to suggest him to the Kaimakam as our escort to Elassona, we felt we had fallen on our feet indeed. If only the Kaimakam could spare him!

By now we were in the billowy streets of Karaveria. High courtyard walls, masses of pitch-black shadow, gurgling runnels—you could say no more about the place than that it seemed a very long way to the Kaimakam's. But presently our lieutenant stopped at a door in a dead wall, opened it, and plunged in. We plunged in

after him. The lantern fell blotchily on heaps
of stable-litter and dim horses half-awakened.
Thence we tramped up an open wooden stair,
very steep, along the wooden balcony of a
courtyard, along a passage, and then into a bare-
floored, bare-walled room with a divan. Here a
lamp was burning, and here we sat down to
await the Kaimakam. He appeared immediately
—a short man, blonde for a Turk—in an un-
buttoned uniform jacket and slippers. Cigarettes
accompanied him, and coffee followed. As he
was my first Kaimakam, I strove to make a
good impression upon him, but his demeanour,
I thought, was a little reserved. However, he
said Saad-ed-Din Bey should lead our escort, and
that was the main point gained. Therewith he
turned us over again to that saluting officer, and
we went forth to find the khan.

More dead walls and shadows and gurgling
streams, and presently we were standing in the
mud before the khan. It took a good deal of
kicking and rifle-butt to get the door open, for
by now it must have been nearly eleven. The
room we were to sleep in had a very clean
divan and a very clean floor, but there the
resources of the establishment left off. There
was nothing to eat, and nothing to drink, and
nothing to sleep on. There was no trace of

the men or the horses or the baggage, which
had been left to make their way from the station.
We wanted to get up at four next morning;
but it was plainly madness, not yet knowing
our men, to go to sleep without seeing what
had become of the rest of the caravan. It would
seem hopeless in England; in Turkey, as I came
to know—how well!—before I had done with it,
it was the normal course of events. In moments
like this the native plan is to sit down and wait:
the native will wait days on end, if need be,
quite unmoved. So we waited.

Presently, as I was expecting day to dawn
each moment, the street was suddenly filled with
men and horses. Charlie appeared at last!
"Got all the things, Charlie?" "No, sir," came
the cheerful reply. "What the——" But
Charlie hastened to explain that Karaveria only
ran to one cart, and it was quite impossible that
it should bring more than half at a time. So he
had brought half, and had left one man on the
other half—waiting. Now, when these things
had been unladen, he would go back and fetch
the others. There was no help for it. I perceived that being a war-correspondent was not
exactly the concentrated excitement I had
pictured it. We sat down to wait more.

The other half arrived: it was then about

half-past twelve, though I would have sworn it was six in the morning. All the things were at last stacked on a platform outside the door. The bags had to be opened to get out beds; the boxes had to be opened to get out food. Sleepily Charlie laid out the beds on the floor; sleepily we rummaged in the nearest box for a tin of salmon and a tin of biscuits. Charlie—the first budding of great qualities which came into full bloom later—produced, apparently from nowhere, a bottle of wine. All this time Saad-ed-Din Bey had been holding a kind of levée on our behalf outside the door. All the Turkish officers in Karaveria must have come in to be introduced; being introduced they showed no desire for profitless tittle-tattle, but merely sat smoking outside the room and looked in at us. When we got at food and drink we asked our Saad-ed-Din to do us the honour of joining us. But he declined politely; he had eaten already, and as for drink —— Of course, how could we have been so tactless as to suggest it? A fellow of a great deal of delicacy and principle, this Saad-ed-Din; certainly we were in luck. But it was past one by now; sleep was now or never. I inserted myself into my sleeping-bag and slept.

The next thing I knew was that somebody was moving in the street, and that it was certainly

getting light. The next was that Saad-ed-Din
Bey was sitting vaguely outside waiting for us:
O admirable Saad-ed-Din! It was already past
four, and we had to get up, wash, if possible,
breakfast, pack the goods into the boxes, pack
the beds into the bags, and saddle and load up
the horses. I got up, had a tentative wash in a
stable-bucket, and a tentative eat at a tin of
sardines; Charlie did the rest. The beds took
up all the floor, and as he heaved them up
beneath my feet, and pursued me from corner to
corner, it was with little enthusiasm that I
reflected that this sort of thing might happen
every morning for months. But the packing up-
stairs was as nothing to the loading-up below.
There were two of my men and three each of my
companions'; all had had urgent instructions to
hurry up. When I went down into the court
the thirteen horses of the party were standing
morosely about the yard, and the eight men were
holding eight of them. Some of the horses were
saddled and bridled; most were not. I only
knew one word suitable to the occasion—*Haide*,
which is in general use among all the Balkan
races, and may be translated " Hurry up." I
went from one man to another, and *haide'd*
each personally, with suitable oaths in English,
of which I thought he might grasp the general

tenor. Each man appeared to express his own personal anxiety to *haide*, but to deplore the slackness of each of the others. Each man on being *haide'd* hastily left the horse he was holding, and went and held another. Time was hurrying on; the sun would be up in a few minutes, and we were no nearer starting than we were last night. Saad-ed-Din Bey was looking on, and I thought I detected a look of amused contempt for the dilatory Occidental. The Kaimakam had come round to see us off, and I blushed that he should discover the Englishman stuck in this quagmire of helplessness. I recollected gloomily that it was the 1st of April.

Charlie found the way out. He came up to me as I was furtively trying to recover the esteem of the Kaimakam, hauling with him the ugliest and dirtiest man I ever saw. "M' S'evens," he began, with a voice half humble, half peremptory; this was his name for me.

"Well? Why the deuce don't you hurry up and start?"

"Yes, sir. Look 'ere. Other gentlemen got three servants; you got only two. Aslan 'e no good with the 'orse. You take this man for the 'orse."

"Who is he? Where does he come from?"

" Come from 'ere. Georghi — good man for the 'orse."

As I say, Georghi was the ugliest and dirtiest creature I ever set eyes on. He might have been thirty ; he might have been sixty ; he was past mark of mouth. He had rugged black hair and eyebrows and moustache, an enormous nose and deep - shining eyes, a greasy white cap, and a costume which left no impression on the eye but general squalor. He was a Greek, and he looked it : subject-race was written on him all over. But I liked his enterprise in offering to project himself into space—he didn't know where and he didn't know for how long— at five minutes' notice, and for four pounds a-month. I bought Georghi as groom, and a very good bargain he turned out. And then it struck me that his newly hired enthusiasm might be turned to good account. I showed him which was my baggage and which were my pack-horses and said " *Haide.*" To my delight, he worked. He got the boxes and the bags across the horses —they had got their wooden saddles on : they live in them — and had slung the ponderous things on with ropes in no time. And then he pushed them through the hotel door into the street and was ready to start. Hurrah ! And when the other men saw this they worked also.

They had hung back, not through idleness, but through etiquette. It is the proper thing in these parts of the world to wait before working. Not that you have any expectation that somebody else will come and do the work for you, but just for the sake of waiting. The Western mind can see no particular profit in wasting the hours between four and seven, and thereby finishing the day's march at eleven at night instead of eight. To the Eastern mind this is the only course a self-respecting man could take.

However, it was all ready at last—two hours looking at it and ten minutes doing it. The baggage was blocking the street in front of the khan; a dense crowd of Karaverians was blocking the baggage beyond. We said good-bye to the Kaimakam and settled into the saddle with joy. Past the vine-wreathed houses we emerged into a square by a mosque: in long lines across it were drawn up three companies of infantry, and as we passed they presented arms. It was beginning. At last I was off to the mountains, off probably to war. The air was eager; the fruit - trees were just stealing into blossom, and the road led upwards.

VII.

ON THE ROAD.

SOUTH-WESTWARD from Karaveria the road runs
over an enormous pass. It is not 5000 feet high,
but it must be some five-and-twenty miles across
from level to level, and it took a good five hours
to ride. This was the main route for infantry
and supplies to the front: the guns and heavy
waggons all went at this time to Sorovitch—I
should say nearly fifty miles further west along
the Monastir railway—whence a good carriage
road led through Kozani and Serfidje to Elassona.
The track we were on was not supposed to be a
driving road, although by the end of the campaign it had been patched up till it was quite
practicable alike for light carriages and strong-
built native carts. On the stretch between Karaveria and Serfidje, which we reckoned to cover
in eight or ten hours, there were said to be
three battalions on their way to the front. I

saw nothing of them; but as we scrambled up the loose stones into the mist, we met two or three files of ponies slipping down. They wore their pack-saddles empty, and were plainly going back for more. Half-way up we overtook a train of buffalo-carts resting on the road. Just a floor, mounted on a pair of solid wooden discs for wheels, guarded by two or three upright sticks and a cross-piece for sides—they must be still the model of the first cart man ever made. The buffaloes suit them—sleepy, heavy beasts, with necks pressed to the yoke, and noses almost on the ground, with wide horns and loose, grey, formless skins—oxen with an odd suggestion of elephants. Four or five boxes of cartridges, with a little green meat for the beasts, lay on the floor of each cart, like a very small bit of cheese on a very large slice of bread. But cartridges are heavy for their size, and the buffaloes were resting after the custom of the country.

Up and up we went, now leaving the main road, the ponies scrambling undauntedly up slopes that looked like walls and kicking down reckless torrents of stones. We went on for hours and hours, it seemed; but it was the first day, and nobody was going to admit that his horse had had enough of it. By this

time we were quite muffled in a clammy cloud:
the man riding in front looked like a ghost.
But as we, struggled to the top of the ascent
it cleared enough to give us a prospect of an
endless tangle of mountains. Shooting sheer up
from the level we could see below peak topping
peak, and white summits glistening in the sun.
This was my first and last sight of the snows
of Macedonia whose melting, we had been told
on the best authority in England, was to be
followed by such momentous events in the way
of Greek and Bulgarian and Servian and miscellaneous Macedonian risings all over the province. We turned our backs to the snow and
let the ponies go down the decline: they went
as if this was what they had been longing for
all the morning. Saad-ed-Din Bey and the
three zaptiehs — policemen, that is: ragged
ruffians riding in slippers with tags of rope for
stirrups — entered into the sport with a will:
a Turk is always ready for a bit of a race
when he is reasonably sure of his seat. Only
one man came off, and he didn't roll over the
precipice. Having come down the far side of
the pass in about a twentieth of the time it
took to come up, and finding a little village
with a little inn at the bottom, we voted unanimously for lunch.

The staple of the meal was hard-boiled eggs and sardines; its chief incident, I am sorry to say, the unmasking of the true character of Saad-ed-Din Bey. When we started he had been, as ever, intelligent and affable—nay, affectionate. "*Oui, mon cher;*" "*Non, mon cher,*" had been his discourse: it had been a little rapid perhaps, seeing that we had not yet known him twelve hours, and five of these passed in sleep; but you must make allowances for an impulsive child of nature. But as we rode I began to suspect his "*Oui*" and "*Non.*" "How many men are there to a battalion in your army?" "*Oui, mon cher,*" he would ingenuously reply. "No: I mean how many men are there — how many soldiers in one battalion?" "*Non, mon cher.*" Moreover, he pronounced each syllable with a kind of gentle staccato, as if he were teaching a child a lesson, which became irritating in the end. We had already despaired of his mind; at lunch, I am sorry to say, his manners and morals disappeared too. He manifested an intention—happily detected and frustrated in time — to take the one box of sardines for himself, and leave the three of us to divide the second. We had brought with us a couple of flasks of native wine and one of whisky, and of both unhallowed drinks Saad-ed-Din Bey drank largely. When there was no more left to eat and drink he developed a tendency towards sleep. We pointed out that he had undertaken to get us to Elassona in twenty-four hours; that it was our desire and our intention to get there. He gazed at us vaguely for a moment: "Impossible, my dear," he said thickly. "But you said yourself it could be done." "I thought so, my dear, but now— impossible." It had indeed for long been painfully apparent that Saad-ed-Din Bey had not the vaguest idea of the road, which he had professed to know like his pocket; by now he had given up the pretence of knowing it, and let the zaptiehs play guide. The zaptiehs said that we should only get to Serfidje by nightfall, whence it was a day's journey to Elassona. The only thing to do, after reflection, seemed to be to send on the best mounted zaptieh to Serfidje to order a carriage and four horses. It was no use to knock up our own beasts by a four-and-twenty-hours' day; we could leave them in Serfidje to come on with the baggage. And then we roused up Saad-ed-Din Bey and started off again. In the confusion of mounting he seized the opportunity of taking the horse of one of the dragomans—of course without asking leave of its owner—then started to ride races on it. Being asked not to, he resorted to the other kind of tactics, and desired to wait half an hour at each pool we came to. In a word, he became a complete and unrelieved nuisance. The only thing to be said for him was that he left off trying to talk French and conversed for the remainder of the journey with Charlie. We had had quite enough of the child of nature for one day.

The zaptiehs had taken a short cut, which, having afterwards travelled by the other way, I should reckon at from one-third to one-half as long again as the ordinary route. It led us over more mountains by a far worse path than the morning's — simply a track, a little hardened, where ponies had trod, winding in and out amidst a wilderness of loose grinding stones. Always up or down, not a foot of level, and the winding and the stones made it as impossible to go out of a wary walk down hill as up. A more heart-breaking, toe-breaking country to get over, on foot or on horseback, I had never seen, and the idea of supplying an army of a hundred thousand men by such a road seemed almost too ludicrous to be worth calling impossible. Yet here it was being done. Towards sunset, on an especially impossible part of the mountain, we overtook a battalion of infantry conveying ammunition and provisions. The line of ponies was miles long; it stretched down in and out of the rocks as far as I could see. Each carried its couple of boxes of cartridges or its couple of sacks of biscuit. Three or four were tied together, head to tail, and one soldier had charge of the lot. If the middle one had a difficulty with a stony bit of ground and hesitated, the beast before tugged at its head and the beast behind cannoned into its quarters. And then it stumbled and swayed and overbalanced: its legs were waving vaguely in the air, and the cartridge - boxes were bumping down the mountain, and miles of beasts in the rear were checking and bumping together and going over after the same manner. The pony had to be untied and picked up and its saddle refastened, and its load collected and reslung, and then the pony retied to its fellows. And then the baggage-train could move on again for a little—till the next beast went down.

This was my introduction to the Turkish soldier at work. The man was like the country —at first sight quite impossible. Ragged, dirty, casual, and slipshod, slouching along without an eye for his team—surely the phil-Hellenic prophets were right; these loafing ruffians could never stand up for a moment against a real army. The thing was absurd: why, they hadn't an untorn coat or a pair of boots to bless themselves with in the whole battalion! And yet—and yet we struggled on for an hour beside them, and we did not seem to be going ahead of them so fast. We were light riders, and they were heavy baggage, but somehow they seemed to stick to us. These Turkish soldiers appeared to have the qualities of their defects after all. They were dirty, but then they were not afraid to put their hands to what might soil them. They were ragged and bootless—but after all what could you do with boots over these stones? They seemed casual and careless, but then they were of an unending patience. Whether a horse went down for the first time or the twentieth, they helped it up and loaded it up again, without haste but without rest, and went imperturbably on. These were short, rather squat, bearded Reserves from Asia Minor: they were slow and heavy, and had lost the snap of youth. But if their legs were bandy and their shoulders bowed, they were inexhaustibly strong; they went on and on, and they looked as if they would go on for ever and ever. I began to perceive thus early what sort of tough stuff the Turkish soldier is.

So on and on, over the weary mountain, till at last, just as the sun was going down, we came out above a river-valley. At its far side, nestled

under another wall of mountain, just catching
the level rays of the evening light, was a little
white town. That was Serfidje—and it looked
about a day and a half's journey away. But
it was something even to have seen it. The
horses seemed to have seen it too, or else the cool
of the evening told them that the day's work
was coming to an end. They scrambled down
the remaining hour of mountain as nimbly as if
they had just come out of the stable. We clattered over a long wooden bridge across the Vis-
trica—the model of a broad, shallow, rock-strewn,
boiling mountain river. And then we trotted
briskly for a long, long hour on the level, and
entered the streets of Serfidje.

We were tired and hot and very dirty. But
Saad-ed-Din Bey considered it the right thing
to go straight to call on the Governor, and it
seemed a pity not to use the knowledge of Turkish etiquette which was the one qualification still
left to him. Into the Governor's house we
bundled — up his clean stairs and on to the
Turkey carpet of his drawing-room. There rose
up to meet us an elderly, bald, pointed-bearded
man in a frock-coat and white waistcoat — a
completely accoutred European gentleman down
to the slippers which all Turks wear indoors.
He received us as if we had been long-looked-

for friends. He sat us down on a broad cushioned
divan—the feel of that divan after twelve hours
of the Salonica saddle!—and a barefooted black
boy brought coffee and cigarettes and a nip of
brandy and tea. I began to put the Mutessarif
high among public benefactors, but after all this
was only the usual hospitality of the country:
the best the Turk has or can get is just good
enough for his guest. The Mutessarif introduced
us to his other guests, the commandant of the
garrison—grey-bearded and silent, with the demeanour of a high-priest, like all Turkish
grandees of the old school — and the Civil-
Inspector-General of the vilayet—a little, square,
black-bearded man, who looked like a Jew, and
was almost certainly a spy, but who spoke French
fluently enough to have a little to spare to help
out mine. We talked of the chances of war, of
the country, of the blockade of Crete: the
Mutessarif lent us the latest 'Independance
Belge.' He gave us a brief sketch of his life: he
had been before at Smyrna; one of his horses
was at Smyrna now, running in a race. That was
enough: we went instantly to inspect the four-
year-old and the two-year-old that he had at
present in his stables. And then we sat aghast,
for he began to talk of Archer and Ladas.
Archer and Ladas, I trouble you, in this little

hole, a day and a half's journey beyond the end
of the world at Salonica! To be sure he was of
the opinion that Ladas won the Derby with
Archer up, and we agreed with him that on that
occasion Archer rode an exceptionally fine race.
And I blush to say that we advised him to back
Velasquez, and offered to put him up for Goodwood, and asked him to stay over the Twelfth.
What could be too good for a man who talked
of Archer and Ladas in Serfidje?

Saad-ed-Din Bey, for a cavalry lieutenant, took
little interest in sport: he was trying to look as
if he thought best with his eyes shut. Even the
correspondent of a leading London newspaper
was leaning back on the divan with his head
on his hand murmuring inarticulate invitations
to shoot. We hinted that we had better go.
"Wait a little while," said the Mutessarif. And
in a little while came back the black boy and
salaamed. "Will you have a little dinner?"
asked the Mutessarif. Would we? We went
down to his dining-room and had a very big
dinner indeed. A noble soup that seemed to be
compounded of sour cream and tarragon, a ragout
of mutton, a joint of mutton, with a wondrous
salad of beetroot and cucumber, fish, a chicken,
sweets, and pilau of rice. The order of the dishes
was unorthodox, but the dishes were divine.

The wine, white and red, was the finest, and the Mutessarif gave us a gallon bottle to take away with us. Then up-stairs for coffee and a liqueur: by this time we could have worshipped the Mutessarif. But by this time we must go. Our host announced that he had requisitioned two carriages, and was sending an escort of twelve troopers. Saad-ed-Din Bey had left the table early, pretending that he didn't like wine: to do him justice, I think he did prefer whisky. He had sunk frankly on to a divan in the back-room, and his snores rolled rhythmically in upon us. We implored the Mutessarif to let him sleep on; he needed rest so badly. But he woke up by himself at the moment of starting, and we had to draw lots who should go in the carriage with him. We explained to the Mutessarif that it was an English form of gambling, and he was all eyes and ears in a second. "Who's won?" he cried joyously. "He's lost," said we, pointing to the groaning victim. Thereon our host preceded us down-stairs and shook hands most heartily at the carriage door. May Allah prosper the Mutessarif of Serfidje!

It seemed too uncomrade-like, on reflection, to leave a countryman all night in the arms of the unwashen Saad-ed-Din. So we three bundled ourselves into one carriage and put Charlie into the other.   Neither Charlie nor Saad-ed-Din Bey quite liked the arrangement at first, but their spirits rose visibly when they heard that the bottle of wine also was to travel in the second carriage.   The rest of the night was one of those dreams in which you are quite sure you are not asleep and are certainly not awake.   About six in the morning I realised that I was slipping down into the maze of legs and revolvers, and belts and flasks, and boots and spurs, which formed the floor of the carriage.   It was light, though the sun was not yet up.   We were going over a high mountain-ridge, and there was a further mountain-ridge a few miles in front.   The second ridge— I did not know it then—was the Col of Meluna. Two hours afterwards we were crossing a little river : soldiers were washing ragged linen in it. In front of us were two high hills, white with tents.   Bugles were ringing out from both hills and from the little village between.   We were at Elassona.

VIII.

ON THE FRONTIER.

In any other friendly country a three-days-un-shaved, two-days-unclothed, twelve-hours-un-washed, sweat-and-dust-caked correspondent would have sought out the military secretary, and asked when the Commander-in-Chief would allow him to pay his respects.

But as this was only backward, happy-go-lucky, generous, gentlemanly Turkey, we drove straight up to the headquarters gate, stumbled across the walled courtyard, over the mountainous cobbles which are the staple pavement of Turkey, and asked where was his Excellency. His Excellency Edhem Pasha, Commander-in-Chief of a hundred thousand odd soldiers, was squatting cross-legged on the drugget cushions of a little divan which ran along one side of a little room; besides this the room had a chair or two, a couple of smaller divans, a table, and a map. Littered

on the divan beside his Excellency were drifting
heaps of papers, with mysterious Turkish symbols
crawling over them, and an ash - tray or two.
From his broad forehead, his sharp, fine-cut nose,
his grey eyes — now motionlessly watchful, now
lively and humorous—his bushy, grizzling beard,
you might guess Edhem English, French, German,
Russian, Turk, or what you will. But you could
never guess him other than a man of quick intelligence and a gentleman.

They brought cigarettes and they brought
coffee. By now I was accustomed to that. You
can hardly spend half-a-crown in a shop—much
less pay a call—without them ; and I was learn-
ing not to settle myself in a seat till they were
delivered and satisfactorily arranged on the
neighbouring furniture or floor. Edhem Pasha
read my introduction, and called for an aide-
de-camp. A heavy man came in—very white-
skinned for a Turkish officer, though ruddy from
the sun—an open-faced, boyish Albanian of forty.
To him the Pasha confided me. He was to show
me the army, and I was to show him the telegrams I wrote about it. Never had a man such
luck as I had when I was delivered thus early
into the fostering hands of Kennan Bey. He
talked French with marvellous proficiency, considering that he had never been nearer Paris than

Belgrade; he laughed with a jolly explosion, like a child at a pantomime; he despised the Greeks; he was never tired of talking about Albanians; he had been wounded in action by Servians, Montenegrins, and Russians, though he said he never distinguished himself in battle; and he shouted "*A la bonne heure*" at every mention of war.

Kennan Bey took me round to present me to the authorities, and he presented me to the two-roomed house I was to share with my two companions of the road. In the afternoon—after we had refreshed ourselves with mutton, diffidently broiled by Charlie in a wash-hand basin, and eaten with pocket-knives and fingers—he appeared at the door with horses, and suggested a ride. So I climbed up into one of the Sultan's saddles, with stirrups that brought me in danger of knocking my chin against my knee, with balloon-like holsters fencing me in front and a mountainous cantle fencing me behind, and off we scrambled, and clattered through the rugged streets of Elassona.

We rode first to inspect the second brigade of the third or Memdhuk Pasha's division, which was camped on a hill, anticipating supper. All the men at that time were under canvas, and nearly all on high ground, for Elassona lies in a hole among hills, and when the Turks mobilised there on the similar occasion of 1886 twenty-five per cent of them went down with fever. As we rode up the hill we met Talat Pasha, the senior aide-de-camp of the Sultan present with the army; Kennan Bey said a few words to him in Turkish, and he galloped on ahead. Two minutes afterwards I saw white caps and dark uniforms swarming out of the tents; by the time we got to the top the brigade was under arms and in line. They had turned out the men for the inspection of a correspondent! And certainly they repaid inspection. Perhaps they did not form up quite so accurately as the Guards outside Wellington Barracks; perhaps they did not present arms with the same simultaneous click; perhaps they were a little out at elbow and knee. But they were hard, wiry men all. With a dash of black, rather than brown, tinging their yellow leather faces, with brows bold but puckered, and eyes fearless but expanding, they stared at the mysterious white face under a fez with something like the puzzled inquisitiveness of a spirited horse. They looked as if they were just going to shy. But there was no suspicion. I was with an Albanian like themselves, a man they knew and trusted. So they studied me carefully and strangely as they fell out, and two dusky-faced orderlies brought me their supper to taste. It was brown bread with a mess of lentils and haricot beans, rice cooked as they can only cook it in the East, and baked lamb. I could have eaten *okes* of it, and an *oke* is two pounds and three-quarters.

The next day we rode out to the frontier. Over a causeway of loose, tumbling stones, which ran up a bare-sided ravine, the native ponies picked their way without a stumble till we came out on a smooth space of lawn at the top. It was the Meluna Pass. The hills still rose bleak and barren on either side—on the left a sheer sugar-loaf, 2500 feet above sea-level, called Menekshe; on the right the slightly lower, slightly easier ascent of Parna Tepe—but in front lay the green plain of Thessaly. Two rough-stoned, red-tiled guardhouses faced each other not a hundred yards apart; between them was a yet rougher building, half hut, half cairn, which marked the frontier itself. With the Albanian sub-lieutenant in command of the dozen or fifteen men who occupied the post, we walked forward to meet the Greek lieutenant from the other side. The contrast was a strange one. There was the Greek, a dumpy young man, with forage-cap, waxed moustache, trim dark-blue tunic, sky-blue trousers, boots to the knee, and the strut of the Continental officer. And there was the Turk—old, lean, long-armed and long-legged, big-nosed and hollow-eyed, with a week's beard on his face, with fez and shabby dark-blue uniform torn at the knees, with sandals and dirty cloth gaiters wound round his legs. But the Turk strode over the rocks like a he-goat, and in this weather and this country I mentally put all my money at once on the Turk.

Then back over stony downs, with long-coated white and black ewes and lambs, over fields of young corn that would now be in ear in a matter of weeks, till we swung round to our left and began to climb again. Round a corner we came on tents, and presently I was saluting a sturdy, grey-bearded man in a blue pilot jacket and a fez down over his ears — Neshat Pasha, General of Division. Above his camp, between it and Meluna, rose the 2000 feet of Parna Mountain, a round mass of stones, thin grass, and juniper-bushes. Up, up, up on a new-cut soft-earth zigzag, till the ponies blew and the wind was edged with ice. Up, till we looked out over the checkered fallows and pastures of the little plain of Elassona, with its mountain ramparts speckled with white encampments on every side. Up, till the nearer hills sank, and the snowy head of Olympus gleamed majestically into view. Up, till at the very top we came to a battery of six Mantel field-guns, dragged up this back-breaking ascent in two hours by the untiring, invincible industry of the Turkish soldier.

The men were toiling at redoubts on the very crest of the hill. Down on the plain were some tiny black beetles, that seemed to be making a little toy rampart, as like as possible to the one I stood on. They were Greeks, but why they were erecting a redoubt in the middle of a ploughed field, just under the nose of a battery 2000 feet above them, I am not artilleryman enough to say. In company with an Albanian officer—nearly all the men used for mountain work seemed to be Albanians, and when you saw the way they skipped from stone to stone you were not surprised that it was so—I crept cautiously round a corner to see another Greek block-house. We had to stoop till we almost crawled for fear of being seen : all the officers on the frontier had the strictest orders to avoid anything that might provoke disputes, and for the most part they were almost absurdly careful to obey them. Here again were two hostile block-houses, this time within an easy revolver-shot one of the other. With two armies lined up like football teams, it was wonderful indeed that the kick-off had been delayed so long.

By now the sun was gone down, and the wind cut like a knife. Tramping down the mountain path, we came at every sheltered turn upon more tents—here a company, there a battalion, there two. Here was a patrol going out, their grey capotes ghost-like in the dusk; there the bakers were baking the evening bread in the ovens with which the commissariat had studded every mountain-side. Here were half-a-dozen ponies toiling upwards with what looked like a couple of carcasses apiece of black pigs; but the perpetual drip, drip over the ponies' flanks proclaimed them water-skins. Here was an encampment, its lines gemmed with fires: the tents, with their lights inside, gleamed more softly, like Chinese lanterns; in one of them somebody was playing a kind of bagpipe.

The stars were all out when we got down to the level. We rode home in single file and in dead silence. Albanian pickets do not hesitate to shoot if they hear a strange tongue, and a chance shot just now might mean, for aught we or Europe knew, the lives of a million of men. The stillness and the watching stars, the sleeping western mountains with the last pale streak of day sinking behind them — they seemed to give the lie to the guns and the forts and the long lines of wild-eyed riflemen. And then the hoarse challenge of the sentinels at the approaches to the village brought back the ominous truth again.

IX.

A DAY OF MY LIFE.

I WAKE up at half-past five, feeling very strong. I am lying in a bag on the bare floor of a bare little plastered room, with four windows filling up one side and a divan running below them. On either side snore two other correspondents. For a moment comes the shuddering suspicion that I am on a plank-bed in prison, for we have all had our hair cut with the horse-clippers.

"Charlie! Charlie! Where the devil are you?"

Enter Charlie in a velveteen-cord suit, knee-boots, and spurs : he bought them new in Salonica for this expedition. You wouldn't think it to look at them, but Charlie would contrive to be untidy in skin-tights.

"Any battle in the night, Charlie?"

"No, sir; no bin go fight. You wait other regiment go fight, you wait long time." "Other regiment" is Charlie's designation for the army of his Majesty the King of the Hellenes.

Thereon Charlie brings tea in blue-and-white japanned teacups, bought in Salonica. They are almost the only articles bought in Salonica that after a week are not yet worn out. You have to buy goods at a place like Salonica before you realise the full significance of that blessed phrase, "the export market." However, let us thank heaven for the cups and the tea—and then for the early cigarette. With that we get up: we all have to get up together, for the beds occupy more than half the room, and the three hobbling writing-tables the rest: the beds must be rolled up and taken away into the sun before any dressing can be thought of. Charlie rolls up the beds, we sitting the while in shaggy black goat-hair capotes on the divan. Beds gone, baths come. Baths are rare in Salonica, and in Elassona are quite unknown, so I have borrowed a sort of large wooden dish, like the things butchers carry meat in on their shoulders. They use such things here to wash clothes in, but propped up by a brick on each side they make very tolerable baths. It is said by people elsewhere that there is smallpox in Elassona. I have not seen or heard anything of it, but on an inspection of myself I note that I am pitted from forehead to

F

feet with little red-and-white blotches. It is not
smallpox, though, and I recommend Charlie to
try to recollect where he put the insect-powder.

I am mess-president this week, worse luck.
Until I had, first, to buy everything I should
want for a couple of months, and then to keep
house for three men for a week, I never fully
realised the importance of women and servants
in the social scheme. I am now able to appreciate
these most deserving classes of our population.
Breakfast, lunch, and dinner to order. I go out
down the stone steps; they vary in height anywhere from 4 inches to 3 feet, and the safest
way of getting down them is a bold jump. In
the outhouse which we have promoted to be a
kitchen is Andreas. Andreas is not my servant,
but the three tenants of this house have clubbed
dragomans on the principle of the division of
labour. Andreas is cook, Charlie butler, valet,
footman, and housemaid, while Dimitri, an elderly
Greek of clerical appearance and indolent disposition, exercises a general supervision over things
which do not concern him.

Andreas in the kitchen has got his coat off, and
his little charcoal fire burning. For himself he
is a little white and wispy-haired Levantine
German, of a meek expression, although he saw
Kassassin and Tel-el-Kebir.

"What flesh to-day, Andreas?"

"*Ach, Herr*, only sheep-flesh—always sheep-flesh."

"And what do you propose to give us for dinner?"

Thereon Andreas unfolds his simple *menu*—soup, mutton-ragout, mutton cutlets, roast mutton, and sweets. I contrive to mitigate the rigour of this diet by prefacing the whole with tinned oysters, and interpolating a curried fowl instead of one of the muttons; but with that we must be content. For breakfast, meanwhile, tinned haddock, tinned sausages, coffee, toast, tinned butter, lettuces, oranges, and tinned jam. For lunch pilau, which is certain to be excellent, cold tongue, and Dutch cheese, with native wine, earthy but excellent stuff, sold by weight at about a penny a pound. Who dares to talk of privations in the Turkish camp?

Before breakfast we must go and see the Kaimakam about the supply and the price of forage. Kaimakam I believe to be the Turkish for second-in-command; anyhow a lieutenant-colonel is so named, and so is the highest civil functionary in this village. I had long been familiar with the word, chiefly in connection with Joint Notes of the Powers providing for the appointment—or not—of Christian Kaimakams in

various parts.   But I never took any real interest
in the status and functions of a Kaimakam until
I knew one to speak to, and until my stable bill
depended on him.   After that I began to appreciate his power for good, and I am firmly opposed
to any project which would substitute a mere
Christian for my excellent friend the Kaimakam
of Elassona.   It is seven o'clock when we reach
his house, but he is already far into his morning's
business.   The Turks count their hours from each
day's sunset, giving night and day twelve hours
each from that moment.   It is thus possible, in
summer, to get up at ten o'clock at night in broad
daylight.   It follows also that any given Turkish
hour never happens at exactly the same time any
two days together, and that a Turkish watch,
being regulated only each week, is never exactly
right.   However, the arrangement seems to have
the merit of getting the Turk up by sunrise;
after that he can afford a little unpunctuality
through the day.

The Kaimakam is a little, black-bearded, liquid
black-eyed, black frock-coated Turk, with an expression mild almost to effeminacy.   As a man, I
own I was inclined to undervalue the Kaimakam
Bey, until one afternoon he provoked a race, and
rode away from my fastest pony with a boyish
laugh in his mouth, and his toes somewhere about

the level of his grey's ears. After that, he cheerfully trotted off up a half-perpendicular mountain
to try and smuggle over some extra-special Greek
wine for the use of the English strangers. Since
then I have loved and respected the Kaimakam.
As we enter he rises from before his desk on a
little dais, salaams, shakes hands, sets us down,
salaams again, and presents cigarettes. Presently
a servant comes in with the relentless cups of
coffee. From time to time an orderly comes in,
clicks his heels together, and presents some document to be dealt with: so far as I can make out, the
Kaimakam is at present performing the duties of
an extra-quartermaster- and commissary-general.
With the aid of Dimitri, the Kaimakam talking
little French, we unfold our case. The khan
where our horses are quartered is dark and dirty;
it contains soldiers who steal our oats and our
chopped straw; the owner, moreover, is a thief,
who charges exorbitant prices for food and litter.
At the beginning of our statement the Kaimakam
says two or three words in an undertone to a subordinate, who goes quickly out of the room. At
the end of it, the subordinate returns and says
a few words in an undertone to the Kaimakam.
It is all over; the new stable has been found,
and the price of fodder fixed. Salaam, O just
Kaimakam, protector of the stranger!

Then breakfast, looking out over the municipal garden—where they seem to grow mainly onions and coffee-tables—on to the fifty yards of pebbles, with five feet of stream running through it which is the river Xerias in embryo: the other end of it is in Greece. Greek women are washing clothes there in the sunshine, and not one of the untaught Asiatic Reservists dreams for a moment of offering them an incivility. Greek tradesmen make their profit out of the troops; the Greek Consul flies the Greek flag, manufactures stories of outrages, and circulates predictions of coming Greek attacks. But the rudest Anatolian or Circassian never lifts a finger against the Greek; and I believe I can say with perfect truth that fifty thousand of Tommy Atkins would have done more outrage on a Saturday night than these Turks have done all the time they have been here.

Then the unpleasantest part of the day—writing. Writing is a duty, no doubt, and therefore a pleasure, of course. But when the sun is shining through budding poplars, and long files of gun-horses are being led down to water, and bugles are singing from every hill till the blood leaps up and down in tune with them—why, then even writing letters for an influential London newspaper seems for the moment less of a privilege than it really is. So tell Georghi to bring my pony round—the one I didn't ride yesterday. Here is the orderly saying that Kennan Bey presents much salaam—"good compliments" is Charlie's rendering—and is ready to take us to see what is going on. Gobble up your lunch, if you can eat any after that breakfast. Let us get into the sun and the air of the hills. The air is always with us if we like to go up to it: Elassona itself lies in a hole. We canter through the lines, we race along the dusty unmetalled roads, we switchback precariously over the rocky hilltracks, till we come to the encampment chosen for the day's inspection. For let it be said that the Turk treats the British correspondent like an inspecting general; the commander-in-chief waits for him when he rides out to the frontier. Having made up his mind to take a correspondent with his army, he treats him as a guest and as a friend. To-day it is the cavalry—four regiments—quartered at Ormanli, five miles in rear of Elassona. It is no use keeping them on the frontier, where they could not move among the mountains, and the horses would have nothing to eat and only take cold. Kennan Bey presents us to Colonel Yakoub Bey, a grizzled Circassian, and makes a bet that two regiments will parade within ten minutes of the bugle-call. They do it too—

in eleven, which after all is the same thing in
Turkey.

On coming back I desire to cash a cheque.
Charlie and I walk through the market-place—
the size of a good-sized London back-garden.
Dirty pedlars implore us to try musty corn, but
we pass on over a dunghill to the unpainted
wooden bank.   An empty packing-case decorates
the threshold, whereto you climb up a wooden
ladder.   The banker's clerk—he is really a sub-
agent of the tobacco monopoly—wears a rusty
overcoat and a partly buttoned pair of trousers,
a pink shirt and a fez, a pair of spectacles and a
week's beard.   He regards me with suspicion, and
my cheque with positive aversion.   But presently
he makes some spidery marks on my letter of
credit, counts out twenty dirty Turkish pounds,
wipes his pen on his finger, wipes his finger on
his seal, licks the paper, and makes the imprint.
Great is the credit system.

Then dinner; take care not to put your chair-
leg through the hole in the floor.   Then one pipe,
for English tobacco must be husbanded.   Then
bed at nine.   As Charlie sprawls massively over
the floor, laying out the beds, we read out from a
grammar Turkish proverbs for him to translate.
Perhaps his happiest effort is what the book gives
as "If we die, we die": "he no live, dead him

got," is Charlie's construe. But you get tired even of laughing, so I crawl inside my bag on the floor. I wonder if Charlie remembered the insect-powder; but sleep is too urgent to trouble about that. It is time to dream I am directing the battery on Parna-tepe, and that Charlie will get in front of the guns to lay out my bed. But if this is roughing it, where is luxury to be found?

X.

THE ARMY.

A CUP of tea, a five-mile canter on a willing pony through budding mulberry-trees, sprouting vines, green corn, and blood-red anemones; a breakfast of porridge and treacle, tinned haddock, ham and eggs, jam and cocoa—it was magnificent, but it was not war. War was what we were there for; it was war that had flushed Elassona with men and spangled every purple hill with white tents. Rumours of war there were in plenty—stories of bandits trooping across the frontier with the King of Greece's commission left behind, to be called for, in a convenient guardhouse—bandits in hundreds, bandits with cannon, bandits fighting for eight-and-forty hours at a stretch, bandits to east and west, — everywhere bandits except where you could get at them.

But still it was not war. And though I was living from day to day in the midst of 50,000 soldiers, though I was under military law and technically a first-class camp-follower, though I slept nightly with saddle-bags packed with two days' provisions, and a servant listening for the ever-expected orderly from headquarters—up to the very moment of action I could hardly have told you whether I regarded the army of the Sultan as a reality, or only as the most elaborate, most extensive, most expensive box of toy soldiers my eyes ever saw. An empire under arms—even half an empire or a tenth of an empire under arms—must surely have something strange and new to hit the eye and leave its mark on the heart. Few people have seen it. For myself, I had never seen anything in the least like it. Yet I seemed to ride daily through this great concentration with nothing but the half-dazed yet unsurprised acceptance with which we pass through the most fantastic of our dreams.

The first impression of the Turkish army was one of melancholy. The men were so old. The Boers at Krugersdorp said it went against the grain to have to shoot such young men. But surely the spectacle of these middle-aged privates was far more pathetic. As I rode down the long, dark-coated, dusty-gaitered, loose-sandalled lines, nearly every man must be the father of a family.

Brown-bearded, solidly set, almost stiffening into
elderliness, steady-eyed, but sober-eyed and
grave, with faces speaking of the toils and dim
perplexities of half a lifetime—who were these
to be called away from their sheep-pens and
opium-gardens to meet bullets and shell? It
seems right and natural somehow that war should
be for the young. In our own army it is different.
A man chooses to be a soldier; it is his trade, and
he must live by it; if he ties himself up with
wife and children he does it at his own risk and
at theirs. But these men had come from the hills
of Macedonia, from the Marmora, from distant
Angora and Trebizond, because they must. It was
not their chosen life, yet they had no other. From
twenty to thirty-four—in war-time even until
forty—one month, two months, six months, eight
months, almost every year they must turn out on
to bleak mountains to defend their race and their
faith against disaffection at home and menace
abroad. This year it was Greece; last year it
had been the Druses in Syria; the year before
Greek and Bulgarian bands in Macedonia. What
life was this? The rim of hills round Elassona
held in the first weeks of April perhaps the
greatest tragedy in the world.

Greek against Turk was no business of mine.
But when I saw those patient, weary, steadfast

soldiers standing to their arms in sheets of rain, patrolling mountain-tops in stabbing winds, humped on pack-saddles, marching by cartridge-boxes twelve hours a-day — why, then I, too, became a Turk, soaked to the marrow with Turkish bitterness against the Greek. The quarrel was none of these men's seeking, and though they were ready and anxious to fight, they had none of the exaltation that effervesces out of mastik and Panhellenism. They were eager to fight only because they wanted to get it over once and for all—to get back to their homes with the promise of a few years in peace. They were called out by the menace of Greece; they stayed out to await attack, to do their duty, and to say nothing. The attack did not come, and their mucky little homes were going to rack and ruin the while. Little wonder that with the long days they grew impatient to go down into the green plain, with Larissa a dim blotch at its far end—to crumple up the Greeks and crush them under foot. Down at Larissa there must be hay for horses and fresh vegetables for men. In God's name, let us put an end to this weariness of waiting, and go down to Larissa.

There was not a doubt in anybody's mind that we could walk into Larissa whenever we pleased.

There were those, indeed, who expected to be viewing the Acropolis within forty-eight hours of the declaration of war; for though the Turkish War Office maps of the country looked the best extant—at any rate to eyes that could not read Turkish—the Turkish officer is occasionally hazy in his geography. Better informed or more cautious spirits did not expect being further than Larissa at the end of the time quoted — allowing time for a decisive action and a circuitous march, crossing the Xerias and Salamvria, so as to take Larissa on its unfortified southern side.

Whether this was Edhem Pasha's plan of campaign during the first half of April I am not able to say: that was one of the things he did not reveal to correspondents. At least one staff-officer, however, confided to me—not for publication and in the strictest confidence—that it was so; but then half-a-dozen others similarly confided half-a-dozen other schemes, each incompatible with this and with each of the others. All a correspondent could be reasonably sure of was the amount and distribution of Edhem's force, as to which all accounts did roughly tally, and which was as follows. The army along the frontier consisted of seven infantry divisions — of which one afterwards turned out to be only a brigade—with artillery, a cavalry division with horse-artillery, and eleven batteries of reserve artillery. At Serfidje there was an infantry division in reserve—which also at this time was only a brigade. The several divisions had best be designated by the names of their generals, which was the way the Turks always spoke of them. I believe they had numbers, but as no two authorities ever gave a division the same number, these were only a fruitful source of confusion. It was both humorous and pathetic to see the various military attachés, as they arrived one after another on the scene of action, eagerly copy down the numbers into their note-books—and then later try to come to an understanding among themselves as to the handling of a corps which one conceived to be at one end of the line and another fifty miles away at the other.

The seven divisions were posted to cover the line of frontier from Grevena on the west to Katarina on the Gulf of Salonica. Beginning in the west, on the Turkish extreme right, Hakki Pasha's division occupied the country between Grevena and Diskata: for practical purposes he may be said to have been at Diskata, as there were no operations of any moment westward of this point. Hairi Pasha was at Domenik, Neshat Pasha at Skompa, Memdhuk Pasha and Haidar Pasha at

Elassona, Hamdi Pasha at Koskey — the Greek
Karya, by which name the place has usually been
called—and Hassan Pasha, who had only a brigade, at Platamona, though his headquarters in
the early part of April were northward of this,
by the coast, at Katarina. The cavalry division
was at Ormanli, some five miles north of Elassona, and the artillery reserve at headquarters
at Elassona. Measuring off a zigzag line on
the map to pass through the various divisional
headquarters named, the distance from the extreme right to the extreme left comes out roughly
at 160 kilometers, or 100 miles.

The normal strength of a division was two
infantry brigades of eight battalions apiece.
The nominal strength of a battalion was 1000
men ; moderate Turkish accounts put the normal
strength at 750; for my own part, judging from
all the battalions I saw during the campaign, I
should doubt whether their average effective was
much more than 600. Each division had four
batteries of six guns apiece. Six divisions and
a brigade thus works out at 62,400 men with 156
guns. The artillery reserve counted sixty-six
guns more. The cavalry division was supposed
to number four regiments of 1000 sabres apiece ;
I afterwards heard of, but did not see, a fifth
regiment. In reality it was of nothing like this

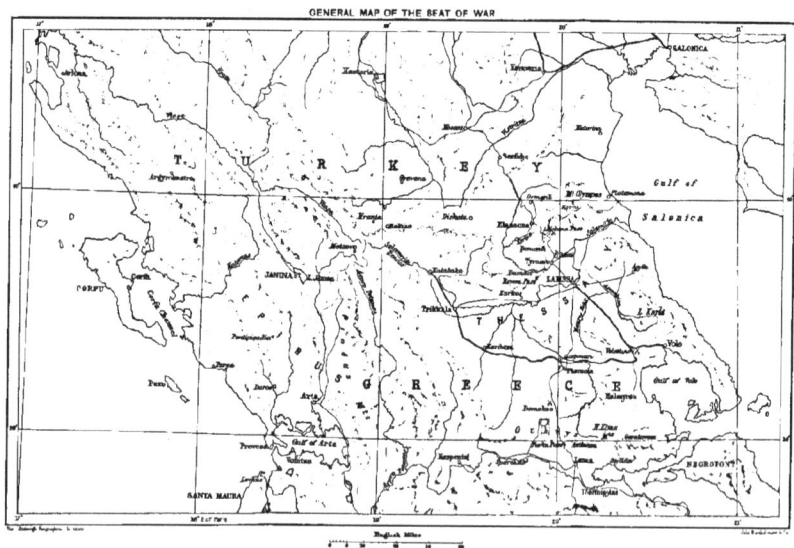

English Miles

strength. When I saw two regiments paraded at Ormanli, I was told that about half the men were away on patrol, or escort, or orderly duty ; and it is certain that, considering the weakness of this arm, the Turks were most generous in telling off troopers to attend on almost anybody who asked for them. One reason, perhaps, was that the troopers knew their way about the country, which many officers never did up to the very end. The cavalry as I saw it—at Ormanli ; on the way to the front when an attack was expected on April 6th, and when it was presumably up to its full strength ; and subsequently during the whole campaign—ran to one or two short of forty horses to the squadron. Giving it twenty-five squadrons of forty horses, the total effective force of the cavalry comes to 1000,[1] and it was certainly not more ; the horse-artillery gives another eighteen guns. The reserve brigade at Serfidje adds another 4800 men. The grand total of the army of Thessaly, therefore, works out at 67,200 infantry (4800 in reserve, a day's march back), 1000 cavalry, and 240 guns.

[1] General von der Goltz ('Militär Wochenblatt,' 2nd June 1897) personally had better information than I could get, and he puts the strength of the cavalry at 25 squadrons of 40 to 50 horses apiece. I do not think I ever saw a squadron in the field with so many as 50 horses, but then probably no squadron ever put its full strength into the field.

The positions of the several divisions corresponded roughly to the several breaks in the mountain-chain which formed the frontier line. Hakki Pasha was posted so as to meet any attack by the mountain paths from Kalabaka and Trikkala, though these did not lend themselves to the passage of large bodies of troops. Hairi Pasha at Domenik covered the defiles of Damasi (the Turkish Tchaihissar) and Kalamaki, through which the rivers Xerias and Salamvria pass respectively through the mountains into the plain of Thessaly. Neshat Pasha covered a practicable route between Skompa and the Greek post of Kurtsiovali (spelt Gritzovali by writers from the Greek side). Memdhuk and Haidar covered the Meluna Pass, Hamdi Pasha the gap of Davia and the pass from Nezeros, and Hassan Pasha the line of march along the coast. The explanation of this extended front is to be found in the Sultan's order to Edhem Pasha to prevent the violation of Turkish territory at any point. The dispositions taken were doubtless admirably adapted to this end; no band of irregulars could get very far into Macedonia without running up against Turkish troops. Only when it came to the question of a counter-attack in force the strategical position was plainly a weak one. A hundred miles is a prodigiously long front for

70,000 men, and to concentrate a powerful force at any point must take a long time. The strongest point of the line was Elassona, where 28,800 infantry, 1000 cavalry, and 156 guns could be concentrated in some five hours; in a day the reserve brigade from Serfidje would add 4800 infantry more.

Now when a Greek war was threatened in 1886 —according to General von der Goltz,[1] who presumably drew up the plan of campaign himself— the intention was to make the main attack by the defiles of Damasi and Kalamaki, so as to take the Greeks on their left flank and Larissa in rear. The advantages of this scheme were many and obvious. It would not be necessary, as in the case of a front attack over the Meluna, to cross the Xerias and Salamvria in the face of the enemy. Larissa was fortified on the north of the Salamvria, and not on the south. And the cavalry could work round the rear of the Greek army and cut its retreat either south to Pharsala or south-east to Velestino and Volo: the army, in short, if defeated, must be annihilated. Whether Edhem Pasha—to be perhaps more accurate, his instructors at the Yildiz Kiosk—entertained this plan during the early part of April I cannot say.

[1] 'Militär Wochenblatt,' May 27 and June 2, 1897—a strategical exposition which it would be impertinence in a civilian to praise.

He must have known of it. The weakness of his cavalry, as General von der Goltz has himself tolerantly pointed out, may have determined him against it. It was, indeed, possibly significant of an intention to act on Von der Goltz's plan that on the afternoon of 5th April, the day before the Greek National Fête, he sent a regiment of cavalry to Hairi Pasha at Domenik, and also began to move a brigade of Memdhuk Pasha's division, with guns, from Elassona in that direction. But nothing happened on the 6th, and otherwise Edhem's dispositions appeared from the first rather to point to the frontal attack, which was simpler, though it promised much less decisive advantages.

That we could possibly be beaten in a decisive action—whether on front or flank—nobody imagined for one moment. I did not know myself the strength of the Greek force opposite us; I did not even know our Commander-in-Chief's estimate of it, though, from the conversations I had with him, I gathered that he did not rate it very high. Seeing that the wildest accounts of the Greek army put it at 100,000, that its paper total was some 70,000, and that it was distributed along the whole frontier from sea to sea—an even longer line than ours, so as to cover Epiras, which on the Turkish side was practi-

cally an independent command—it was impossible
to imagine that Edhem Pasha would possibly
have to meet more than 40,000 men at the
very outside. And Edhem, including Hairi's
division of 9600 infantry and 24 guns, in ad-
dition to the force he could concentrate before
the Meluna, could direct over 40,000 men upon
Larissa at a day's notice. In numbers, therefore, he could hardly help having an equality
or a superiority at the decisive point.

When we pass from quantity to quality, the
case became clearer still. I had not seen the
Greek army. It might be very fine, but it had
not yet proved itself. In the Turkish army I
had been looking for faults nearly all day for
eight days, and of essential weaknesses as yet I
could find none. The Turkish army had been
represented by correspondents who saw it as
specks along a sky-line, as undisciplined, as prone
to disorder and outrage, as eaten up by disease,
as lacking horses, transport, clothes, everything.
Every statement was most untrue. I am not
here to write a history of modern Turkey or
discuss the wrongs of Armenian usurers and
Anarchists. I only say what I saw. I heard a
rumour — possibly emanating from the Greek
Consulate at Elassona — about the desecration
of Greek churches by Albanians. I saw many

Greek churches in the villages round Elassona,
but none desecrated. Troops were camped ten
paces from the Greek monastery, whose little
brown bit of Byzantine overhangs Elassona, but
the monastery had not crumbled away any faster
for that. The Greeks in the town pursued their
normal course of swindling the stranger four
days in the week and observing feast-days the
other three. Nobody interfered with them. You
never saw a drunken soldier: the Turkish troops
drink nothing but water and coffee; stewed
grapes twice a-week furnish their nearest
approach to a carouse. You never saw a
street brawl. Black-browed Albanians, swarthy
Asiatics, refined-looking Constantinopolitans, flat-
nosed yellow Circassians, Syrians, Arabs, negroes
— here were all the races of the hither East
mixing in camp and coffee-house in discipline
and good-humoured comradeship without flaw.

Smart, it must be owned, the army of Elassona
was not. I saw a battery starting for the
frontier one day: the gun-carriages and the
horses were piled up with ragged bundles,
beside which a bank-holiday excursionist's baggage is a model of trimness. When a battalion
lined up on parade you might see one man in
a blue-faced uniform and another in a green.
Their sandals looked like old list-slippers, their

gaiters like badly-wound hospital bandages; they were tied up with loose ends of string. In the marching regiments, and especially those of the Reserve, the officers were sometimes out at elbow and at knee. The men moved a little slovenly at their drill, and their double hinted at rheumatism; what wonder in a peasant of five-and-thirty?

But all these were small matters. The uniforms might be curious, but they were warm; the men want no better protection. The sandals and gaiters might not fit like ammunition boots and putties, but neither did they gall the foot and cause men to fall out on the march. The officers might be a little dishevelled, but every one was dead keen and—at any rate among the Albanians, of whom I had seen most up to now—utterly a stranger to fear; they knew their men, and their men trusted them. The elder were tried in war. The younger were well trained in the military college at Constantinople; many of these spoke French fluently, though they were never nearer Paris than the Bulgarian frontier. There was indeed the other side of the medal: the elder officers were not trained and the younger were not tried; but at any rate they were likely to be as good as the Greeks. As for stiffness at the double, a man has a right to be a little stiff when he can march twelve hours a-day, knapsack on back, as many days as his officers like to keep him at it. Smart the army assuredly was not; useful, workmanlike, untiring, fearless, it most assuredly was.

For disease, it was said there had been small-pox, and that some ten men died of it. The very Greeks now admitted, with regret, that it had disappeared. There was a good deal of pulmonary sickness and some dysentery; two or three men died daily in the outlying camps; but what was that in 40,000? Here and there on the broken hill-paths you met a man, painfully humped on a wooden pack-saddle, clinging to the pommel, his heels stuck through stirrups of string. A comrade led his beast carefully; you needed only to look at the rider's paste-white, drum-drawn skin to know he was on his way to hospital. No doubt there was sickness. But seeing that half the hospital at Elassona was still used as a barrack, while best part of the very complete, even luxurious, English-made hospital stores were still unpacked on the 17th of April, it may be said with confidence that sickness was surprisingly small. The troops were nearly all camped on hills, and if the wind was asthma and bronchitis at night, it was quinine and iron in the morning.

. Lastly, transport. Edhem Pasha told me without reserve that there were only provisions for fifteen days, and he spoke of it as a defect to be remedied immediately. Depots were being rapidly established at Serfidje and at Elassona. Who, if anybody, was responsible for the transport and commissariat service as a whole, I inquired again and again from the headquarters staff, and I could find nobody who knew. It seemed to work itself. Of course it was utterly un-organised, and yet it was wonderfully efficient. There was naturally no Army Service Corps in the army—there were not even any Engineers that I ever saw — and infantry battalions had to do the work. Each battalion so detached was of course so much off the fighting strength of the army; and it is here worth while to remark, in the case of a war wherein, on a superficial view, the Greek command of the sea appeared to bring no advantage with it, that the impossibility of sea-transport cost the Turkish army thousands of ineffective infantry and thousands of pounds. As for the pack-ponies, somebody seems to have discovered that biscuit or fodder was wanted, and somebody sent off the beasts and the men. Each battalion of Reserves from Asia Minor was supposed to have brought 200 baggage-animals with it —

and curiously enough it generally had. The
beasts and the men went somewhere and got
what was wanted and brought it in : they took
their time about it, but they always brought it
in. The truth was that, for transport purposes,
each battalion was an independent unit as in Germany; thus the Turks accomplished piecemeal
what they would never have done in combination. The transport, in short, was as eloquent
a testimony as any observer could have asked
both to the weakness and to the strength of
the Turkish army—to the faults of its organisa-
tion and the rough common-sense and unwearied
industry that correct them.

XI.

AMONG THE GREEKS.

CERTAINLY the Greek village was clean, well-liking, and prosperous. I had ridden through a Turkish village the day before—at any rate, it was partly Turkish—and I had not got the stench of it out of my throat yet. It was a jumble of huts, partly unmortared stone, partly mud-bricks dried in the sun and washed by the rain into mud again. The tiles of the country are half cylinders: they lay one course concave side up, the next convex side up. This makes a pretty roof, and an effective, till the wind blows; then, as the tiles are not fastened in any way to the rafters, they begin to crack and carry away. The dirty little houses had dirty little courts before them, enclosed in high stone or mud walls. Here and there squatted a soldier; here and there a beggar; here and there a black blot which, on a nearer view, became a Turkish woman in domino. The road that ran through this village was an open sewer; the horses plashed along it hock-deep in filth. In the middle of it dogs were gnawing at a dead donkey, one half bones and the other half putrefaction. Now and again we had to scramble over heaps of dung as high as a man. And on the top of these played children—pretty, brown-skinned, limpid-eyed girls, with pigtails down their backs, and trousers down to their bare feet. They were fat and ruddy enough, the children; but the stink of that village was an abiding horror.

The Greek village was very different. It lies snugly in a corner, under bare hills; but on what short grass there is live little flocks of sheep and goats, and a few cows. On the two level sides it is deeply fringed with mulberry orchards and vineyards; the mulberries were rushing out into leaf till all the village was fragrant of young green. The road to this village is broad and level, and is blocked by only one bank and two or three ditches in a couple of miles or so. The streets in the village itself are many of them but six feet wide, it is true, but they are decently clean and decently paved. Many of the windows are blind, being boarded up for want of glass; but the houses are all stably built, the courtyards are evenly paved; there are wells in the courtyards, mulberry trees again, and sometimes little flower-gardens. Some of the richer houses are even stuccoed. There is a main street with cafés, a wooden bridge over a dry river-bed, and seven churches. In this village there is no permanent inhabitant who is not Greek.

And that was the only thing against it. But for its Greek inhabitants, that village would be a little paradise. You will call me prejudiced for saying that—perhaps even anti-Christian; listen while I tell you about it.

I rode over on a Sunday afternoon to buy some photographs. The photographer was a leading citizen of this village, " although," said my guide —himself a Greek—" there are others also who are very rich." The photographer was a tall, thin man, with a hooked nose, bright eyes, high forehead, and a general expression of predatory intelligence. There was a restless deference about all his movements which was not the self-contained politeness of the Turk. The Turk is always polite, but you can see that he always holds himself your equal, not to say your superior; the Greek is always obviously, even jerkily, anxious to please and to conciliate. In this Greek village the people squatting on the roadside got up as the Frank rode past and touched their dirty leather skull-caps; the Turk never, unless the Frank was with an officer or somebody he knew. When the Frank alighted, crowds of Greek children sprang up from nowhere to hold his horse, not entirely out of disinterested hospitality; the Turkish infant is rather disposed to heave half a brick at the infidel, till he has convinced himself that the infidel is a friend; then he regards him with solemn, not impertinent, curiosity. He will even unbend so far as to accept of backsheesh if it is offered, but he will not go out of his way to seek it.

The purchase of photographs took some little time, although there were only two possible things to purchase. But in Turkey it would be grossly rude to buy even a view of Elassona and a portrait of Edhem in less than half an hour or so. That done, I was carried off by the Greek dragoman to see the notables of the village. Up bare stairs, into a bare room, and there was a doctor—lean, pale, stooping, a weak beard appearing patchily on his pinched face. He wore a fez and an ill-fitting grey overcoat, though the sun glared out of a cloudless sky. There, too, was his wife — a double-pigtailed, aproned, untidy caricature of a German shopkeeper's wife. His drawing-room was uncarpeted and bare-walled; but there was a vague hint of the Western hire-system about his furniture. Presently came in a slipshod child, also double-pigtailed, with a tray of little glasses of sweet brandy. Other eminent citizens dropped in, and began to converse in whispers of broken French. All were thin, even cadaverous; all were pale and unshaven; all talked in half-voices; all wore overcoats and insinuating smiles.

One especially—an advocate in a sloppy, snuffy, brown overcoat, a smile more humbly conciliatory, a voice more meekly hushed than all the others— was evidently the spokesman. With sighs and deprecatory smiles, he began to hint of the sufferings of the Greeks. He said nothing definite; he hardly said anything aloud, but there was a world of suggestion in the way he left his sentences unfinished. I asked him about his practice.

"Ah, here we have Turkish law; I might almost say that we have no law at——" and then he checked, with a resigned smile. I suggested that as he admitted he had left Athens to spend two years in Constantinople to qualify for the Turkish courts, there was presumably some sort of law and possibly even a little money in it.

"Well, yes,"—and again that smile of resigna-tion,—"a very little, perhaps; but then you see they have taken away my house and quartered a general in it."

"Did you expect generals to take houses with them to the front?"

"Well, well; no doubt they are right; one must have patience."

"But they pay you for it, I suppose?"

"Well, well; perhaps they may — a little — a very little; one must be patient. Only I saw, the other day, a Turkish soldier selling eggs."

"You mean he had stolen them?"

"Oh no; I do not say that. Still"—smile— "I saw him selling eggs. Four eggs. Who knows? Well, the Turks are here in great numbers; what can we do?"

He left these remarks to soak in, and took me round to another leading inhabitant. This one was like the first, except that his slipshod little girl gave mastik instead of cognac—mastik being a poor relation of absinthe. Each leading inhabitant took his nip. This drawing-room was more elaborate than the last; the walls were partly adorned with a paper suggesting Gossage's navy-blue soap; the furniture breathed stronger hints of the hire - system; there were a few tawdry ornaments, which might have been bought at the sale of a Bloomsbury lodging-house. The brown reach-me-down began to improve the occasion again.

"A Turkish soldier died this morning."

"Really."

"Yes," and the smile crawled over his face; "he died this morning. Many have died now."

"How many? Is it true that there is smallpox here?"

"Well, no; not exactly smallpox. Still many have died—perhaps ten or twelve."

I thought I would go back to Elassona, and I told him so. But no, that could not be. He begged me, as a friend—my flesh crept—to come and see his own house. His own house was the most comfortable I had seen. He had a large garden, rugs on the floor and the divan, and some sticky-looking pictures of saints, which he called antiquities; his tipple was sweeter and oilier than any of the others.

"But I thought the Pasha had taken your house."

"Well, yes; he has. I have a much better house than this, and the Pasha has taken my best house. Still, it is but a little while; I can shift here."

Then suddenly his whisper became more confidential, his smile more greasily fawning than ever.

H

" I saw a man to-day who overheard one Turkish officer talking to another."

" Well ? "

" He said he wished he had lived in the days of Sultan Selim."

" Well ? "

" Do you not know what Sultan Selim said ? He said, 'If you wish to live happily in this country, you must first of all kill all the Christians.'"

" And did the Turkish officer kill all the Christians ? "

" Not all."

" Any ? "

" Well, no ; not yet. But who knows ? "

With that he called my attention to a bedraggled Greek who was muttering thickly in a corner.

" He crossed last night from Greece ; he says they are all mad there—mad for war."

Madness I know little about, but I am a fair judge of intoxication, and certainly this man had all the symptoms of a *bona-fide* traveller. Therewith the little man launched out into stories of half-a-dozen Greek bands who had crossed the frontier in the night and were fighting the Turks at that moment. Some of them, it appeared, had got several days' march into the interior during

the ten hours of darkness; others were exchanging
murderous volleys with the oppressor on hills so
near that you could almost have heard a donkey
bray upon them. I since convinced myself that
every single tale was false.

I departed. As he stood by my stirrup, the
brown overcoat made one more attempt.

"They say that our children can learn in the
public schools. That is so in theory; but in
practice——"

I had had enough of it. I wanted to gallop in
the evening air. I wanted to get the taste of
the mastik out of my mouth—and the taste of
the Greeks too. I preferred the smell of the
Turkish village. I was almost half converted to
the abominable theories of Sultan Selim.

XII.

THE RAID.

IT was on the morning of the 9th of April that we first heard of the raid on Baltino. It was the custom of the correspondents in Elassona to stroll round the headquarters some time after breakfast —not with any lively expectation of getting news, but with the desire of satisfying their consciences that there was no news to get. The positions had all been inspected; the promise of war seemed to be fading further away with each day; the routine of asking for news and being told there was none seemed all the duty left. But on this 9th of April, as I stood in the little wooden hall of headquarters, I discerned the familiar portly legs of Kennan Bey coming down the steep stairs in unwonted excitement. Next minute his ruddy face appeared, and he almost rushed into my arms. "News, my dear friend, news!" he shouted. "A thousand Greek brigands have crossed the frontier near Krania. They are fighting now, my friend—in a great forest — shooting since daybreak — pst, pst!" Kennan Bey's style was nothing if not picturesque.

"Then we shall have war after all ?"

"Hush! Listen, my dear friend. The brigands at present conceal themselves in the forest. We wait to know for sure whether there are Greek regulars among them. As soon as we learn that there are—ha, ha, my dear friend! Larissa in six hours! Athens in fifty - eight hours! *Du bon vin! Des jolies femmes!* Ha, ha! *A la bonne heure! A la bonne heure!*"

It was something to telegraph at any rate— but it was not much more. For Krania—this particular Krania ; the woods are full of Kranias on the Turko-Greek frontier — is a good forty miles' journey from Elassona as the crow flies, and I knew by weary experience that the crow flies a good deal straighter, as well as faster, than horses could go in this country. It meant at least two good days' journey there and two back : allowing a day there, that meant five days away from Elassona; and in the meantime it was obvious, even without Kennan Bey's rapid imagination, that most important events might happen at headquarters. So I stayed where I was.

What happened, therefore, I only know by hearsay, and by now I had learned that hearsay in this country was worth very, very little more than nothing. Sure enough, when I went to see Kennan Bey later in the day, the brigands had grown to 2000; next morning they were 3000 with guns. I greatly doubt whether Edhem Pasha had received more than one message meantime from the scene of the fighting. It was going on in a country whose wildness I could well imagine from the specimens I had seen; the nearest telegraph station was presumably Metzvo, some ten miles away; as the direct wire from Grevena was said to be cut by the Greeks, all news had to fetch an enormous circuit by Monastir, and I knew enough of the Turkish telegraph to know what that meant. Was Kennan Bey, therefore, a liar? Heaven forbid! He merely said what he firmly believed to be true. His oriental imagination had run away with him: 3000 men with guns were certainly more picturesque than 1000 men without. For the Levantine mind — Turk or Greek, Armenian or Jew — is the slave of the picturesque. It has no comprehension of the Western desire for hard, literal fact. Why take pains to be accurate when it is so much easier and more amusing to be picturesque? Kennan Bey was simply Tartarin de Tarascon in aiguillettes and a fez. And so was everybody else from Edhem Pasha on his divan to Georghi sleeping under the horses' bellies in the stable. They do not wish—as a rule—to deceive; they cannot help it; they are deceived and deceive themselves.

So much in self-defence for the many confessions of ignorance I have already made and shall have to make. I bound myself by a vow long before the war began to state nothing on any authority unless I had either seen it myself or had heard it from a European who had seen it; and though the resolution cost me some excellent stories, on the whole I do not regret it. To return to our brigands. Seyfoullah Pasha, Sub-Chief of the General Staff—Seyfoullah Bey he was then; an officer becomes a Pasha only when he becomes a general—was sent off at once to Krania to see if he could recognise among them any officers of the Greek regular army. Seyfoullah had been Military Attaché in Athens and Turkish Consul at Larissa; he knew most of the officers of the Greek army to speak to, most of the rest by sight, and all the others by reputation; an ardent sportsman, always riding, shooting, or

walking, he also knew all Thessaly and all the
road to Athens like his pocket, as the Greeks
found out to their sorrow. It was the first
prominent service of this most brilliant officer,
and on his report, as we supposed, hung the
chances of peace and war. During the next days
life was all expectancy. We heard that the
invaders had had temporary successes, as was
natural with a band of their force acting against
isolated frontier-posts; they had burned four
block-houses and surrounded two others; they
had taken eight prisoners. But fourteen battalions
were closing in on them from Hakki's division at
Grevena and from the Epirus army at Metzvo
and Janina; their disposal and capture was only
a question of time. The enemy were being held
at bay in the forest, and only creeping out by
night. And then, on the night of the 10th, came
the news that they had been repulsed. Two days
later they had got unrepulsed somehow and were
besieging Baltino, a village close to the frontier.
But they had lost fifty-two killed as against the
Turks' two. They were certainly a little puzzling,
these official reports. Meanwhile it was stated
for certain that Seyfoullah had distinctly recognised two Greek officers, whom he had known in
Athens; also that two of the killed wore Greek
uniforms. That was all we wanted—but still war

did not come. Then we heard, on the 14th, that the invaders had been finally driven back into Greece; then that rifles and sword-bayonets had been picked up which bore the Greek government stamp—but still war did not come. Finally, one night as we were at dinner, there clanked in an aide-de-camp of his Majesty the Sultan, and behind him an orderly with a Gras rifle and a couple of Greek bayonets. There they were on the table, and we could see for ourselves if it was not true that the Greek Government had been cognisant of the whole thing all through. Certainly it was true, said we, with conviction, as indeed there is little enough room for doubt that it was. But still no declaration of war.

"But never mind, my dear friend," cried Kennan Bey. "Prisoners are coming — fifty prisoners, my friend: what fun!" Next day when I saw him I asked when the fifty prisoners would arrive. "Fifty prisoners? No, no, my friend, you have been misinformed. Nine prisoners. Ha, ha! Fifty would be too much to expect." Next day I asked after the nine. "Nine? Ah yes, the nine. But they couldn't march—ha, ha, ha!— these poor Greeks—but they are bringing one. *Un gros gaillard—gros comme ça!*"

The whole population of Elassona had been in

the streets for days, firmly convinced that prisoners were coming in every moment. Nothing would persuade, for example, the Levantine imagination of Charlie that prisoners were not coming in whenever he saw a crowd in the streets. "The soldiers say so," he cried, with a superior smile; "of course they know, the soldiers." But at last one afternoon the prisoner arrived.

I was coming in from an attempt to teach my horse to jump—the only recreation left, now that war seemed to have blown over for good. In the blackening dusk I saw a dim knot of men under the portico of the Kaimakam's house; the prison is in the Kaimakam's back-garden. Inside a ring of braided and buttoned Turkish officers, of breeched and gaitered English correspondents, stood a man, talking fast and loudly. I was excited, for I had never seen a brigand before: I went up to the ring and looked at him. And this was a brigand! The *gros gaillard* was a squat, little man, well under five feet, slouching, dirty, unshaven, with a greasy, red skull-cap and an ill-fitting cord suit. As he gabbled on, now crossing his arms, now waving them like windmill-sails round his head, he looked for all the world like an unemployed orator on Tower-hill. Defiantly, and even proudly, he told his story to the interpreter. He came from Corfu, and he belonged to a battalion of the Reserve. He went first to Larissa, then to Trikkala, then to Kala-baka. His captain and his lieutenant ordered him to make war, and the whole battalion—so I gathered—went forward together. With others they were a thousand strong. The officers put off their uniforms and put on kilts. Everybody knew they were going to make war—at Trikkala, at Kalabaka, everywhere. They all cried, "*Zeto ho polemos*"—and as he said the words, the grubby little prisoner flourished his arms, and stood up his whole four feet six. They went over the frontier at sunrise; he did not know whether the Greek officers stationed at the block-houses saw them, though he admitted that a thousand men cannot hide behind a juniper-bush. They came to the Turkish blockhouses; some of the garrisons retired, and they burnt their block-houses. One they besieged, and when the Turks had fought many hours and shot away all their ammunition, they surrendered—eight men to a thousand. The eight were taken back to Kala-baka. After that they went on four hours' march into Turkey. Then they met the Turks again, and they were defeated. They had an army doctor with them and he was shot, but they saved the colours. Then he got cut off from his comrades with twenty-five others. Twenty-four were shot, and so he surrendered. And there he was—till an orderly took him away to the prison again. And this absurd little brigand was the first I saw, and the last I heard of the raid on Baltino.

XIII.

A BIRD'S-EYE BATTLE.

"One band Greeks come inside last night," remarked Charlie, as his large red face met my awakening eyes. "Where?" "Karya; bin shoot all night; bin shooting always."

I thought it was only another Baltino affair —Greek Reservists disguised as brigands, two days' shooting, and the matter handed over to be settled between Constantinople and Athens. However, it was certainly worth going to headquarters about: Charlie might have stumbled on to the truth for once. And at headquarters, sure enough, I found my friend Kennan Bey unwontedly grave. It was serious this time. The Greeks had attacked in force at seven on the evening of the 16th; hard fighting had been going on all night. Kennan himself had just been ordered to Karya with reinforcements. "You had better be off at once, my friend."

Karya is not far from Elassona—perhaps fifteen miles or so. I would go and spend the night. So I had them pack up my bed and a box of food and load them on a pack-saddle. I mounted my larger and more brazen-mouthed pony, mounted Charlie on the one which trotted like the gas in a seltzer syphon—it suited his style of riding, with a pillow on the saddle, better than it did mine—and off we went to Karya.

The road to Karya—which the Turks call Koskeuy—is like the road to everywhere else in this country. Now up, now down, here a precipice on the right, there a torrent on the left; stones everywhere, prickles everywhere, baggage-animals everywhere. We met the usual maddening files of donkeys, quite hidden under stacks of brushwood for fuel: this is the worst kind of baggage-beast. You know there must be a donkey somewhere in the middle of the moving mass, but you can't get at him with the longest whip to drive him off the path; you have to hitch yourself over the edge of the precipice and let Birnam Wood go by. All this was usual. But as we struggled on the Karya road there came a new experience. "Pop, pop; pop, pop, pop; pop, pop, pop, pop, pop; pop." It was not very different from the sound of shooting many

pheasants, but I knew they were shooting men.
My heart began to try to beat in time with the
pops. When four or five came together I wondered how many were down that time; I hurried
lest both sides should be killed out before I got
there. So I turned a corner and came on the
village of Karya — small and ramshackle and
dirty — wedged into a recess under hills like
cataracts suddenly turned to stone, above these
the solemn whiteness of Olympus. Olympus
is the back-scene of Karya; its foreground was
the fight.

There was a broad valley, perhaps a mile to a
couple of miles across; at the other side of it
grey-green hills, part stones, part young grass,
part wood. The hills rose to various summits—
four or five in all, though these were hardly
individual enough to make the whole thing more
than a crested ridge: you might as well call it
one hill as five. I suppose they were 3000 feet
or 4000 feet high, and quite steep. Along them
ran the frontier; you could recognise it by the
little dabs of white which stood for blockhouses.
Across the valley came the pops — sometimes
rare and distinct, sometimes a rapid popple when
all the separate reports ran into each other. It
sounded like a machine that was now going
round slowly, now quickly. Every now and then

the pops were varied by a boom—a gun. Here
and there a tiny patch of dirty smoke curled
languidly off the broad hillside. That was the
battle. Through a glass I watched it for a long
time from Hamdi Pasha's headquarters, and I
made out some black dots on a tongue of the
ridge about one-third of the way up. That was
a battery of artillery. At the very top was a
line rather like the leg of a beetle under a
microscope : that was a battalion of infantry.
Pop, popple, boom, little black dots, and little
black streaks : that was all.

No ; there was a little more of it. On the
other side of the trickling burn in which Karya
does not wash was the hospital, and they were
bringing in wounded. I went over and entered
in. Of course it reeked of iodoform : hospitals do.
But though iodoform is not a smell that allows
rivals to live with it, there was distinctly another
smell. Blood. And there was another sound
besides the sort of rustle which rises out of the
swift half-stealthy movements of a hospital staff.
Groans, wails, sentences cried out aloud, in
strange, thick gutturals—a volume of sound like
a man's voice, and a fretful, passionate intonation
like a child's.

There came to meet me at the door a very
young surgeon, an Albanian, as fair as a fair

Englishman, with a skin like strawberries and cream, hair like vine tendrils, eyes as simple as a baby's, and as compassionate as a good woman's —the most beautiful man I ever saw. He wore a blue overall, his sleeves were tucked above the elbow, and to the elbow and above it his arms were clotted with blood. Yet the young man looked to me then like an angel. The wounded turned on their beds and looked at me with eyes that felt as if they would bore through me. One man howled aloud like a beast, and tore off the bandage from his wound. A white-bearded captain shot through the thigh showed his bullet-rent with a smile of humorous patience. But beast or humorous gentleman, the beautiful young Albanian looked at all with the same clear pitiful eyes, tormented them with the same quick, unsparing, merciful hand.

It was pleasanter to go out into the sun and listen to the battle. It still popped on—now fast, now slow, as if the gods were opening much champagne for a picnic on Olympus. I went no nearer it, for I saw a little shiver of excitement run round a group of aides-de-camp, and hastened to ask about it. It had come. This last Greek outrage was too much, I heard ; war was declared, and the Marshal Pasha would advance in force to-morrow all along the line. I jumped on my

I

pony, turned round the tired pack-horse, not yet unladen of his baggage, and started full scramble back to headquarters. The fight I left to crackle out if it liked.

It was going on all right. During the night the Greeks had pushed right down to the base of the frontier hills; but Hamdi now had nine battalions of his division engaged, and the Greeks were back again on the sky-line. But the whole thing was a joke compared with what was to happen at Elassona to-morrow. I must be with the Marshal. A war-correspondent's place in general actions is not before the firing line, but behind the general staff, and I hastened to put myself in that romantic position with as little delay as might be.

But there was no doubt about it. War, long promised, long delayed—war, which, in my letter posted the night before, I had solemnly declared not to be coming—war was on us at last. As I rode along the valley path, the sound of rifle-fire kept pace as it ran like a train of gunpowder along the sheer heights above. A third of the way back I met Kennan Bey's four battalions— the men, loaded up with biscuits and water and ammunition, toiling painfully through the scrub, their eyes glued to the blackening hills before them. For the second half of the journey the road climbs; by this time the sun had gone down, and under the shadow of the mountain-side even the white baggage-horse was no more than a patch of ghostly grey. But at the top we came out into the moonlight—full moon as bright as a London winter sun—and there was no doubt about it. On the heights blazed signal-fires, and the plain replied to them. On the horizon, near Meluna, blazed a blockhouse — whose, it was impossible to say. And the ripple of musketry all round the hill-fenced plain of Elassona was deepened more and more often by the voice of cannon. As we rode into Elassona the lines of tents lacked the soft glimmer of other nights; they were all dark and cold and empty; the men had gone up to the fighting front. It was war all along the line, and it was war in force. To - morrow we should fight over fifty miles of frontier, with over 50,000 men.

XIV.

THE BATTLE OF THE MELUNA.

TO-MORROW came. I woke in my boots, and I was out before daybreak. Not for one moment in the night—so I was told—had the rifles and artillery kept silence. Now the sun came out clear in the blue sky; Olympus had even taken off his cloud-cap for the great day. As the sun stood up over Mount Menekshe I saw along the foot of the Meluna Pass what looked like a thick streak of white cloud : it was the banked smoke of the night's fighting. The still air let it rest where it lay. There was not a breath of wind; but for the firing there would not have been a sound; the whole plain glowed in the flooding sunshine. I remembered that it was Easter Sunday.

But I forgot it again in a moment. I rode off to find the Marshal and his staff, childishly happy; was I not going to see the biggest fight since Plevna ? The Marshal was just moving down to the front from the little hill where was the camp of the Second Brigade of Memdhuk Pasha's division. With him were the long lines of red fezzes and white, blue uniforms and dancing rifles, of four Albanian battalions—the reserve, the best men in the army, perhaps almost the best soldiers in the world. They roared with a deep bass of delight, and a little ferocity, as they swung down the little hill, across the fallows and the fields of young corn. Some way behind a black centipede wound over the plain — the cavalry coming up from their quarters, five miles in rear. With the Marshal went the Staff—bearded veterans of the Servian, Montenegrin, and Russian wars, and spruce young aides-de-camp from the Yildiz. We marched towards the line of smoke at the foot of the hills. We marched till we drew up on the road to the Col of Meluna. There we halted in face of the row of low but steep and bare hills. Three blockhouses, their chimneys perked impudently into the sky-line, marked equal intervals of perhaps half a mile along the summit ; Menekshe and Parna Tepe towering on either hand marked the limits of the field of the main fight. On either side of us stood fields of the same green barley, but in them three batteries of six guns apiece thrust out their grimly impertinent nozzles, sniffing at the wreaths of smoke on the

hills.   A fourth battery was driving up ; the
horses swung round and the guns were unlimbered in line with the others.   The teams to
work them squatted round in the attitude of
humble adoration proper to the gunner in presence of his gun ; the red fezzes only appeared like
poppies above the green.   Here all dismounted
and set themselves to watch the battle of
Meluna.

And the battle ?   It was the battle of Karya
over again on a larger scale.   The Greeks had
again been first.   Attacking in force at dusk on
Saturday evening, they had swarmed up the low
hills which flank the Pass and occupied the line
of the frontier ; they had surrounded the Turkish
blockhouse at the head of the Pass itself ; they
had come down the Turkish side almost on to the
plain.   It is nearly five miles from Elassona to the
head of the Pass, and it was two in the morning
—so they told me—before the Turks came into
action in force.   With four battalions they drove
the Greeks back up the hills, and rescued Sub-
Lieutenant Yunus and his beleaguered outpost
from the blockhouse.   They said the fighting had
been tremendous, but from what I saw this day I
question it.   The shooting off of rifles was tremendous, no doubt ; but if the fighting had been very
fierce, how could Yunus and his score of men

have been left alive after an attack of eight hours ?

The position now, at seven in the morning, was exactly the same as I had left it at Karya at seven the last evening. The Greeks had been driven back to the crest, where they held the line of the three blockhouses. The road up the Pass makes a bend to the left, about a mile in front of where we sat, round a low hill : on this hill a battery of mountain-guns was in action against the left-hand blockhouse. Infantry were crawling slowly down below the guns, across the road, and then up to the attack of the hill. Infantry were crawling up the hill right in front of us to attack the central blockhouse. Infantry were crawling up over the skirts of Parna Tepe to attack the right-hand blockhouse. At the bottom of the hills they were black blotches on the grey steeps ; towards the top they spread out into lines of dots, as the men deployed, lay down and opened fire. They fired no volleys. They simply crept, crept upwards : now a dot was a fixed point for a quarter of an hour : the man had found good cover. Then it began to travel upwards again—always nearer to the goal—the black chimney against the blue. It was slow ; but the attack was developing.

Bang ! An ear - cracking explosion not ten

yards behind me, and the horses were dancing like mad. The artillery was beginning. They had sent a couple of guns forward before this to the turn of the road, but they had come trailing back again : the elevation was too great just under the hills. Now they were opening from where they stood—three thousand nine hundred metres from the blockhouses. I looked at my watch : it was only eight o'clock, but the battle seemed to have been going on half a lifetime. Ali Riza Pasha, the smart and jovial General responsible for the artillery, leapt on to the roadside and prepared to enjoy himself. " Mehemet Ali Effendi," he sang out ; the tall black-browed officer in command of the battery replied ; there came an unintelligible order, and then Mehemet Ali was bending tenderly over the gun. Then the word of command—"Hey-y-y—hutt !"—it sounded, with a furious accent on the " hutt." A gunner flung his weight on to the lanyard—bang, the fizz of a rocket, a scream as the shell passed between the echoing heights on either side ; all eyes strained on the blockhouse ; then a crack, a flash, and a belch of dirty smoke as the shell burst every time in the right spot—two miles and a half away. At the bang the gun had jumped back as if it had put all its strength into the shot and wanted to watch what it had done ;

its men rushed round it and caressed it as if it were a baby, and they were afraid it might have hurt itself. Shell after shell seemed to pitch on to the very foot of the left-hand blockhouse : at each good shot there was a burst of little exclamations : grey-bearded generals clapped their hands. Edhem himself—seated cross-legged on the ground, gazing impassively in front of him, as if this were somebody else's battle and he was an intelligent critic—Edhem himself looked up and laughed. It was curiously like Gentlemen v. Players.

The fields behind us were red and white with fezzes, where the reserves squatted in long lines in the furrows, and blinked lazily at the grey puffs on the hills. At ten o'clock, " Memdhuk Pasha ! " suddenly cried Edhem. Up bustled short, round, white-bearded Memdhuk Pasha— " a man of little instruction," as a superior young aide-de-camp had informed me, " but popular with the soldiers, because he always fights when he can get at the enemy." A few words to Memdhuk Pasha and he was bustling away rearward. And presently the long lines of fezzes rose up into men and went forward towards the Pass. Slowly, but with an adamant resolution in the set of the men's bodies, they spread out over the fields and rolled forward. Now we should see! At the very base of the heights, in green meadows, they massed again—and halted. It must be to get their breath for the assault. But eleven o'clock came, and twelve o'clock came, and one o'clock came — and still they halted under the shelter of the hills. And it occurred to me as a self‑evident truth, which common‑sense should have impressed before, that a battle which takes half an hour to read about takes a good deal longer to happen.

But what was happening? Was anything going to happen at all? The guns were still banging away: they must be killing the killed ten times over, and the very horses no longer condescended to shy at them. Up on the heights the black lines of our infantry seemed to be going up a kind of treadmill—ever advancing, never arriving. But at last, towards one in the day, there was a stir round the middle block‑house, which lay opener than the other two. Surely our men were getting forward this time. They were now on the level: they must surely be on either side of the blockhouse by now; surely, surely they must be past it. Yes, they were. An orderly came galloping furiously along the road and passed a dirty scrap of paper to the Marshal: the Greeks had fallen back. The centre of their defence was ours.

The ambulances were coming up by now—by rights they ought to have been up hours before. Half-a-dozen wounded, heads or hands or legs roughly bound up with red-stained bandages, were already sitting by the roadside near us, looking neither at the battle nor the Marshal. Most of them shut their eyes or stared at the ground; they gave the impression of being quite dazed and very sick. The ambulances rumbled past us in a cloud of dust, and bumped along the road till they got to the foot of the ascent, where the reserves were lying. Presently they came rumbling back again—not very full, only with two or three men apiece, making perhaps a dozen all told. Some looked full of fight yet—Memdhuk Pasha hauled one man out and sent him up into the fighting line again; others were lying all of a heap, heads only held up a little by comrades hardly better off than themselves, just as they had been dumped in. First and last I do not think the ambulances took in more than twenty to thirty wounded by nightfall. But that was not all: those who were hit up on the hills, and could not get down, had to lie where they were till nightfall.

It was now two in the afternoon. The sun was pitiless: if you sat down, the road was almost like a baker's oven. The plain and the hills swam in

the glare, and the black infantry on the face of
the slopes looked as if they were blinking at us.
The guns beside us were now lobbing shrapnel
over the ridge to break the steadiness of the
Greek supports below. But their fire was slack-
ening, till only two guns were left in action, and
they but slackly served. The fusillade above us
had died out almost entirely. What wonder?
The men had some of them been in action over
twenty hours now, without any more food and
drink than the dry biscuit they carried with them
and the water in their canteens, and without a
wink of sleep. And from now on, if I may say
so, the battle of Meluna became a bore. Charlie
gave his Excellency Field-Marshal Edhem Pasha
my horse-rug to sit down on. Villagers lined the
roadside as if a battle were a Jubilee procession.
Some grey-bearded sons of the Prophet went so
far as to put up sunshades. The fighting became
Oriental or Balkanic—no attempt to gain ground
and break the enemy, but a dogged firing from
behind cover till a man dropped. It became a
kind of picnic battle—a thing you might invite
a few friends to, and take them in to Elassona
and give them afternoon tea when they got tired
of it.

And so it went on, or stood still, till seven in
the evening. By this time it was beginning to

get dark, but it was also beginning to get cool. Now, if ever, was the moment which was to turn the action from a profitless twenty-six hours' fusilade to a decisive advantage. It was too dark to see the hill-tops plainly, but it was possible to hear the bugles singing out the advance. The Turks charged with fixed bayonets. The Greeks stood their ground till the assailants were some thirty yards away—and then gave back. They had had enough : the Turks had outstayed them. The battle of the Meluna was over. Everybody was dog-tired, famishing for sleep. But the Turks had won the gate of Thessaly.

XV.

THE MORROW OF THE BATTLE.

In the battle of the Meluna, according to the official information, the Turks lost thirty men killed and two hundred and seventy wounded. The loss of the Greeks we did not know—so far as I am aware nobody knows it yet—but it was probably not much heavier. There were engaged on the Turkish side the divisions of Memdhuk and Haidar Pashas, though five battalions of the latter never actually went into action. Besides these, Neshat Pasha's division was engaged all day to the south, on Edhem's right—the Pass of Meluna looks roughly south-east—in what may perhaps be called strategically, though, owing to the broken ground, not tactically, the same battle. The Turkish force engaged was thus very little, if any, short of 30,000 men, with four field-batteries as well as mountain-guns. What the Greek strength was I do not know—again nobody seems to know, and there were no European correspondents present with them—but it was probably not much inferior to the Turkish. The conclusion is that 60,000 men, in twenty-six hours' continuous fighting, only lost sixty killed and something under six hundred wounded. At Gravelotte the Germans lost over 19,000 men out of 230,000—more than 8 in 100. At Leipzig—which, to be sure, took four days to fight—the Allies lost over 45,000 out of 300,000—15 to the 100. At Meluna the loss can hardly have been more than 1 to the 1000. The battle deserves to be immortal merely for its bloodlessness; never was a decisive advantage more cheaply gained.

On the morning of April 19th, I went up at sunrise to the ground over which the battle had been fought and perceived the truth. The truth was that the forces were very much spread out; they fired no volleys; each man built him a little heap of stones, lay down behind it, and fired when the spirit moved him. That is the way they naturally fight in this part of the world— because they enjoy it. This kind of battle takes a long time. It is the traditional hill-fighting of all the Balkan peninsula—the method of the irregular bands in Macedonia, of the private feuds of Albania, of faction-fighters and brigands everywhere. It bespeaks want of energy rather than want of courage : an English correspondent told me he had seen a company of Turks fight so until the last man was killed.   None the less the three blockhouses might be the centre of furious firing to-day if it had not been for the Turkish artillery. At a distance of very nearly 4000 yards their batteries planted round after round within ten yards of the blockhouses.   If there was one man who enjoyed the battle and had reason to be proud of it, it was Ali Riza Pasha.   The Turkish artillery, when it is limbered up, gives the general impression that somebody is taking dirty old clothes to the wash.   The harness is patchy, the traces are rope ; one horse or another has generally got his leg over the traces ; the guns seldom go quicker than a walk.   But plainly the Turkish artillery could shoot.

When I got to the sward on the head of the Meluna the first person I saw — and I have seldom been so surprised to see any one still alive — was my friend Yunus Effendi.   I have described him already — the elderly, tatterdemalion, dare-devil, Albanian sub-lieutenant who commanded at the blockhouse.   Everybody knew Yunus, and despite his undeniable ferocity everybody liked him.   The top of the Meluna was a favourite picnicking ground for correspondents on both sides before the war began ; the officers

of the General Staff were constantly up there,
so that Yunus numbered among his friends all
the Europeans and all the high officers, as well
as the Greek officers at the blockhouse opposite.
He had a performing ram, which he had trained
to go to sleep at the word of command, and
which never failed to please. Yunus descried us
in the distance, and came waving his arms to
greet us. He was in boisterous spirits. He had
killed Greeks and Greeks and Greeks! When
the fighting began he had seized a rifle, and
commenced operations by picking off his friend
in command of the Greek blockhouse. After
that he had killed two more officers, including
a major, and had sent his sword down to Edhem
as a guarantee of good faith. There seemed at
last a reasonable probability that Yunus would
be promoted.

We got up on to the rough stone breastwork,
which the Turks had already run up on the
Greek side of the captured Greek blockhouse,
and looked over down into the plain. The
enemy were firing desultorily from the foothills
on the right, which still remained to them, but I
did not see anybody hit. They fired a shell or
two from some guns they had mounted during
the night, but these did no damage either. All
along the line of the fight there were built little

K

shelters of loose stones, anything from eighteen inches to four feet high—some big enough for one man only, some for two or three or four. Behind these the cartridge-cases lay in piles— some Turkish Martini, some Greek Gras, sometimes both mixed when a position had changed hands. Between these little breastworks there was hardly an empty case to be seen; hardly anybody had fought except under cover. You could understand then that the fight had looked and sounded as if two army corps were annihilating each other, and that really there were less than a hundred men killed.

The Greek blockhouses were half smashed. The furniture was gone—carried off, or looted, or burned. Two especially were nothing but heaps of rubble and skeletons of charred beams. The ground round them was cut up till it looked like a badly ploughed field. The floors were littered with every kind of paper, official and unofficial. I picked up a Greek prayer-book with a ragged bullet-hole right through the middle of it; curiously, there was no blood on it, and I wondered whether its owner could have propped it up in a loophole as a sacred shield. At one blockhouse were three Greek bodies; the Turks had buried their dead already. Later on I came on a dozen more. Stripped to shirt and drawers;

heads caked with blood; brown faces contrasting with white arms and chests; flesh puffed and swollen; skin yellow like wax; flies feasting on the half-decomposed faces; hands clenched, looking curiously small and smooth, like hands at Mme. Tussaud's; wounds dry, but dirty and gaping; one man's face torn and bashed into a mass of squashy red,—that is enough, once and for all, to say of the dead.

I had now come to the extreme right of our battlefield of the previous day, tending southwards along the frontier, on the Greek side of Parna Tepe, so as to reach the sphere of influence of Neshat Pasha. All along the line the soldiers were sitting about smoking, making coffee, singing, and laughing. They had had a night's sleep, and were ready for as much more fight as the officers liked to put them to. Some were hard at work taking the stones from the little shelters, and building ramparts on the Greek side of the blockhouses. Imagine a vastly superior army on vastly superior ground entrenching itself on the morrow of a victory, and you will get some idea why it is that a Turkish campaign takes time.

After a little while the casual shooting began to crystallise about the lower hills of the Greeks. A battalion came slouching past me—a long line of shuffling sandals, rifles held anyhow, fezzes worn anyhow, but scorched faces that bespoke the spirit of a soldier better than all the buttons and pipeclay in the world. I joined myself to this battalion as it began to spread itself into the order of attack. As a matter of fact, it never attacked. The battalion just in front of it had split up into two long irregular lines of men, shambling carelessly across a stony dip, and climbing up a hill that looked like a petrified waterfall with the petrifaction all broken loose.

At the top they began firing down on the Greeks, without haste and without rest, quietly going each man about his business. The Greeks replied, but the Turks remained quite unperturbed, strolling up and down into favourable positions, now firing five rounds in five minutes, now putting in a hot crackle like a bonfire of dry wood. Then at last the bugler put his bugle to his lips and his face to the sky, like a duck drinking. Then rang out the advance, and the Turks went forward with a swinging trot. And then, before I had quite made out what it was all about, that little fight was over. The Greeks had scuttled into the plain. I only saw two dead, but probably there were more. There were also eleven prisoners—young men, beautifully attired in neat blue and black uniforms, excellent boots, smart

forage-caps, and stylish blue-grey overcoats. One
was an Italian, who could speak neither to his
comrades nor to his captors. "*Io Italiano; par-
late Italiano?*" was all he had to say. The
dishevelled Turks stared, round-eyed, with half-
curious, half-scornful wonder at their dandy
prisoners. But Captain Mehemet Bey, strolling
casually about to look for dead, summed the
matter up. "*Soldatt Grek*," he epigrammatically
remarked, "*costume bienn, cœur mauvais; soldatt
Turk, costume mauvais, cœur bienn.*"

I rode fourteen weary hours over the hills that
day, desiring to find my old acquaintance Neshat
Pasha, and hear what he had done the day before.
I came on him about five in the evening, walking
up and down the parapet of a captured redoubt—
looking with his glass and his pilot-jacket like a
master-mariner on his bridge. His knowledge of
French is limited to the word "mademoiselle," so
that I was not able to gather very clearly at first
hand what he had done the day before. He had
had to hold his men hard all day, I gathered, to
prevent them from going forward too fast and
being outflanked. In the afternoon he had
assaulted the Greek positions on Papa Livad,
the mountain on his right front, and taken them
without serious loss. The Greeks had evacuated
the little village of Kurtsiovali—their end of the

Pass of which Skompa, Neshat's original headquarters, is the Turkish. The village was entirely
commanded all round by heights now in the hands
of the Turks; nevertheless the Crown Prince was
severely blamed in Athens for ordering, or per-
mitting, its evacuation—which gives a good idea
of the capacity of Athens for military criticism.
Neshat had lost one of his Brigadiers — Hafiz
Pasha, a grave long-bearded veteran of eighty
who had been through the Crimean and the
Russo-Turkish wars. He led his brigade into
action — so the Turks told us — on horseback:
when his aides-de-camp urged him to dismount
he answered, "My children, I never dismounted
for the Russians; shall I now dismount for the
Greeks?" A moment later he was hit in the left
arm, but still refused to dismount; next moment
his right hand also was shattered. Even then
he refused to retire, and a third bullet hit him
in the throat and finished the brave old man.

Neshat had got up some mountain guns, and
was under the impression that he was about to
bombard and capture Tyrnavo. But between
Neshat and Tyrnavo rose the lofty mountain of
Kritiri, still in Greek hands, of which more later.

XVI.

ON THE COL OF MELUNA.

THE week which followed the battle of the Meluna was in many respects the most farcical of a farcical campaign. On Monday, Tuesday, Wednesday, and Thursday, there was next to nothing done at all. In the battle of Meluna the Turks had given twenty-six hours to an issue which a European army would have decided one way or the other in four or five. They now devoted the best part of a week to reconnaissances and combinations which a European general would probably have got through within a day. For correspondents the week was a long but slightly tiresome picnic. We got up religiously at four every morning, for it was the one element of excitement that we never knew from day to day that the grand advance would not take place. We rode up to the Col and sat down; about an hour afterwards would arrive the Marshal with his staff. They also sat down,

and looked at Thessaly. There was usually something going on in the plain of a nature which at
last threw light on Mr Gladstone's once puzzling
distinction between military operations and war.
Then came lunch—"*le plus interestant portion
de la jour*," as an English correspondent idio-
matically described it. Then we looked at Thessaly during the afternoon—there were sentinels
at the head of the descent to prevent us from
going down into it—and rode home to dinner.
Andreas was in the kitchen, as usual, with his
coat off: "*Was für Schlacht heute?*" he would
cheerfully ask.

From my own point of view the week was
chiefly remarkable for the development of Charlie
and of the censorship. I had been inclined at
first to look with some little suspicion on Charlie.
He was entirely without honour in his own country, his reputation in Salonica being more than
shady. But very quickly Charlie developed into
an ideal correspondent's servant. His command
of English was small, and hardly improved in
quantity during the campaign, while it steadily
declined in quality. It was embarrassing, when
giving lunch to a German officer who knew English a great deal better than Charlie ever will,
to have him stroll up and ask, "'Oo's this feller?"
But it was rather lucky that it was no worse.

Yet although Charlie always professed his incompetence to do anything that was suggested to him — the word "possible" never exists in a dragoman's vocabulary — he not only could do, but in the end would do, any mortal thing required of him, from looting a reel of cotton to interviewing the Commander-in-Chief, the great Mushir Pasha himself. Neither work nor play came amiss to him; he was never at a loss in the most unexpected turn of circumstances. Although a Jew, he had no objection to going under a mild fire. Best of all, he entirely grasped the importance of getting news quickly on the wire. It was his great delight during this week to keep a horse saddled in a quiet corner where he thought no other correspondent would notice it; then when there was a message to send, to lead it unobtrusively down the hill, gallop at top speed to Elassona, take the dispatch to the office, and then get a fresh horse from the stable and repeat the process. I should think he must be almost the only one of the Sultan's subjects who appreciates the value of time.

The other main development of the first half of the week was the censorship. You must know that at Turkish headquarters there were four— afterwards more—aides-de-camp of the Sultan. Nominally they were a kind of extra aides-de-

camp to Edhem; really they were spies with
the power of telegraphing cipher reports of what
went on behind Edhem's back to the Yildiz. One
of these—Nedjib Bey, an exceedingly able and
promising young man if only anybody could have
trusted him—was understood to be more or less
responsible for seeing that the European correspondents committed no indiscretion. If there
was an official censor, it was he. If he was not
straight, and was alternately rude and fawning,
he was at all events intelligent. Other officers,
however, were quite ready to censor telegrams,
and nobody seemed to object to their assuming
the authority to do so: Seyfoullah, for example,
was an excellent censor, not afraid to let you
criticise, and with the additional advantage of
being always present when there was anything
to telegraph about. Before the war the censorship worked well enough. But when we all got
up to the Col of Meluna we were suddenly told
one morning that there was a new censor
appointed — Enver Bey; all telegrams must be
seen by Enver Bey. Enver, otherwise a very
capable officer, professed his inability to read our
telegrams, though he understood French well
enough and they were all in capital letters.
Next day we were told that no telegrams could
be allowed at all—not even a telegram to say

that no telegrams could be allowed—until after a decisive action had been fought. There was no reason to expect that a decisive action would ever be fought at the rate things were going on, but as it was the same for everybody, nobody objected.

But later in the day it was discovered that it was not the same for everybody; that one correspondent had taken telegrams to Enver—who apparently knew nothing of the new rule; what should the censor know about the censorship regulations?—and had got them through. On that we went in wrath to the Marshal Pasha. The Marshal—exceedingly bored—ordered that in future Mustapha Natik Bey — Grumbkow Pasha's aide-de-camp, who had little else to do—should be censor, and he alone. I took a telegram to Mustapha Natik which contained, as everybody's despatches did, the word "stop," meaning that was the end of a sentence. The device is usually adopted in telegraphing long reports to newspapers for clearness' sake; in view of the Turkish telegraph service it was as necessary as it was inadequate. The censor had just passed two telegrams which bristled with the word. He looked at me sternly. "Stop," he cried, in a voice of thunder: "*qu'est ce que veut dire 'stop'?*" I translated it into French and German, both of which he spoke fluently. "*Point*," he roared, with rising horror! "*Punkt! Nein, nein; das geht nicht; ça ne convient pas; croisez ça, je vous en prie.*" I explained in sandwiches of French and German that it was a punctuation mark—that it was to facilitate deciphering. But no! That "stop" was evidently a code word of the profoundest and most damnable significance. Out it had to go.

Meanwhile the war was pretty well standing still. The operations of the days from Monday to Thursday were most puzzling to an ignorant mind; it was some consolation to find that they were equally incomprehensible to German experts of the highest standing. I am not sure that I can give a coherent account of them even now; but I will try. First, as to the proceedings of the main army, which I saw. A little before nine on Tuesday morning, April 20th, the cavalry went down into the plain to reconnoitre. Why this was not done on Monday I cannot say, since the Greeks were driven off all the foot-hills at about ten in the morning. I believe that Grumbkow Pasha—a colonel in the Kaiser's army, but serving as Inspector-General of Artillery in the Turkish service—advised Edhem to send down a battery of horse-artillery with the cavalry, but the cautious Marshal declined, and the cavalry

at first went down unsupported. From where
we sat, as in an amphitheatre seat at the
opera, we could see every movement. The
plain is patchwork of green corn and brown
fallow, with a blue stream cutting it down
the middle, and a yellow one—the Xerias—
cutting it parallel with the horizon. Two roads
diverge in the shape of a V from the village of
Ligaria at the bottom of the Pass and run along
under the opening hills — on the left to the
village of Karatsali, on the right to Tyrnavo.
On the left half of the blue stream are woods,
full of cover; beyond them the villages of Deliler
and Mussalar. On the right, perhaps half of
the way between the Pass and the Xerias, is a
little round hill—a molehill it looks away down
in the plain; behind it the long line of Larissa,
white houses set in green trees, twinkles hazily
half-way across; the mountains of Othrys close
the plain at the further end.

The cavalry wound down the long zigzags of
the Pass, where the Greeks had most considerately mended the road unto Thessaly. One
squadron grey horses and the next browns, dark
uniforms, black sheepskin caps, swarthy Circassian faces, they got smaller and smaller, disappeared behind hills, reappeared lower down,
and finally began to crawl over the chequer-board

of young corn and fallow. Along the road, among the deserted Greek tents, under the hills, out on to the plain, by the wavy blue line of the river, now a black serpent, now straightening into a column, now spreading into two or three lines, in the openest order, they advanced into Thessaly.

Then suddenly from beside the little hill came a white puff, and then a yellowish-grey one— the shell bursting in a fallow a quarter of a mile ahead of the cavalry. The Greeks were there, with guns. The cavalry drew back under cover by the river-side. By this time, though, Albanian infantry had gone down with hoarse cheers and growling national songs. Guns had gone down, too, after all Edhem's caution, and presently a battery crawled up by the cavalry, and opened. Then came puffs of Greek smoke to the right, then more to the left, till four of their batteries were in action. Clouds of rapid dust revealed skirmishing cavalry; clouds of slower dust, supporting infantry. There was a pretty exchange of shells, but I don't think many people were hurt. It was only a reconnaissance, and it showed that the Greeks meant to defend the line of the Xerias.

Next day came the invasion of Thessaly. Down, down they wound, along the zigzags of Meluna—horse and foot and guns in a stream that looked as if it would last for ever and choke up the whole plain. The top of the Col, where there is a little lawn between the blockhouses, was the starting-point. The lawn was blocked with battalions of infantry. Some had piled arms, propping up four, one against the other, as if they were going to roast meat under them. Others nursed their rifles lovingly. Some stood, others squatted on the grass; the lawn and the lower slopes were dark blue and red with them. In the interstices of these stood the artillery horses—six in a team, grey and bay and chestnut, with the peculiar look of patience in their eyes and the set of their heads that only a horse can really assume. They were waiting for their guns, and their guns blocked the whole road on the horrible, as yet but half-mended, Turkish ascent of the pass; ropes trailed out before them, waiting for infantry to pull them up. No six horses and no twelve could ever have got them up those hopeless, rolling, scrunching screes.

Down, down, the army of Turkey began to wind—sometimes slowly, sometimes bent-backed at the double, according as the distances between battalions opened or closed. If you are to get fifteen or twenty thousand men down a pass in a morning, you cannot afford to waste a single yard of ground. Even the dozen pack-horses which

carry the frugal baggage of each battalion—the
rest of the regulation 200 were probably fetching
ammunition, of which a prodigious amount had
been blazed away—seemed almost space wasted.
On one spiral or another the head of the gigantic
column appeared, winding, winding endlessly.
Then the head was lost, and nothing left but the
tailless body. Presently the head crawled out
again at the very bottom. A dark mass began to
form, to enlarge, till it spread all over the rich,
moist-looking green below. Still the black descending line was unbroken, only now it was
dappled grey chargers going down, and then guns
were harnessed and began to follow them. A
gun is a meek-looking creature enough when it
is limbered up, and the descending batteries
looked curiously graceful by the side of the unlimbered, short, peppery little devils protecting
their position from above. Gun after gun, battery after battery—then more cavalry, then more
infantry—men and men, horses and horses, guns
and guns—a world of living energy and mechani-
cal force poured itself slowly, but very remorse-
lessly, down into Greece.

The black lines shown up by the very, very
faint red thread of the fezzes began to divide and
crawl over the plain. Columns began to work
away to left and right. Slowly, slowly — how

agonisingly slowly — they crept over the plain towards the line where we knew that there were Greeks. Would they be fired on now—or in five minutes—or in ten—or in half an hour? Then the perpendicular lines shifted slowly into horizontal lines; they were forming up into skirmishers and supports and all the order of battle. On, on, on— were the Greeks blind? No; a puff of smoke and a puff of dust, what seemed half an hour after —but well ahead of the dimmest dots. And after that, nothing. Only the lines of little black dots moved on, and on, and on. So slow, so steady, so relentless. At last they stayed, and there was a system of black Turkish dots stretched fanwise over the Grecian plain. Black, and waiting grimly, inexorably. The head of the force from Elassona was presumably on a level with Neshat and Hairi on the right. It was all ready now. Would it be for to-morrow?

L

XVII.

THE BATTLE OF MATI.

IT was not for to-morrow. On the morning of the morrow—Thursday, April 22nd—occurred a mysterious manœuvre, which so far as I know remains yet unexplained. At eight in the morning began the usual artillery duel with the usual futility. This was the third day of desultory shooting, and both sides profess not to have lost a single man by it. Almost the whole force of the Turkish infantry was massed on the plain, working along to the left. They occupied the village of Karatsali, which was found empty. At the same time there appeared to be a forward movement on the right also, and the cavalry was screening everything in front. Then, as I sat on a low hill on the Turkish right some way into the plain, I saw the columns marching back from Karatsali. There was with me a well-known German military writer, Major Falkner von Sollenburg, and I asked him if he knew what it meant. He thought they had got mixed some-how, as there was hardly space to move all the troops. But still they came back. And when they began to pile arms about Ligaria whence they started, Major von Sollenburg grimly re-marked that he did not know what it meant.

When we saw the leftward movement we natur-ally concluded that the intention was to join hands with Hamdi Pasha, advancing from Karya, and envelop the Greek right, which rested on the villages of Deliler and Mussalar. Hamdi had had very hard—at any rate very lengthy—fighting since we left him on the afternoon be-fore Meluna. He was said to have lost heavily, but in the absence of any statistics at the Turk-ish headquarters it is impossible to say how much. However he had now at last cleared his front and was advancing upon the right of the Greeks. Major von Sollenburg told me—though he can only have had it from Turkish sources: there was no European with Hamdi — that on this Thursday morning the left of the Elassona force was actually in touch with the division from Karya. If this is true, the loss of the day is even more wonderful than ever.

However, the strategy of both sides was now apparent. The Greeks had made their main

attack on the Meluna, but their flank attacks on
Hamdi at Karya and Hairi at Damasi had also
been strong. It is probable that the incursions at
Karya had been intended to draw a large part of
Edhem's force thither to the left wing, and leave
him weak in front at Meluna. That failed. But
both this attack and that on our right wing by
the Reveni Pass was so far successful that they
delayed Edhem's advance four days. The Marshal
seems not to have entertained at this stage the
plan mentioned above, and originally outlined by
General von der Goltz. This plan, it will be
remembered, was to attack Larissa in rear from
beyond the Salamvria and thus cut the Greek
retreat: if that had been done, Hairi's division
would have been the force to do it. Whether this
general was really held in check by the Greeks
for five days I cannot tell. He struck me from
all I heard and saw of his conduct in the field
as a sluggish and incapable commander. I met
him at the very end of the war, and he produced
a pocket-book, whence he triumphantly stated that
he had only lost ten men killed and thirty - six
wounded during the whole week. This is very
likely true; as by his subsequent action—or inac-
tion—at both Pharsala and Domoko Hairi gave
the impression that he thought it the function of
a general to lose battles, if necessary, but on no

account to lose men. But if Edhem had really meant to make his main attack on the Greek left flank, he could have gone to Damasi and exercised the same personal supervision over Hairi as he did over Memdhuk at Meluna. Moreover, he could have reinforced him by Hakki Pasha's division from Diskata; whereas he preferred in fact to bring Hakki round behind the right to the centre. The plan was now plain. The Greeks would be simultaneously attacked in the centre by three divisions and a brigade from Elassona, on the right—our left—by Hamdi, and on their left by Hairi. Hairi was only ready by Thursday night, which perhaps explains why the manœuvre of Thursday morning was not finished, though it hardly explains why it was begun. As for the general scheme of this frontal attack, there may very likely have been good reasons for it which I did not know. But there was one great reason against it: it left the Greeks an open line of retreat—as we were soon to find out.

Another conceivable reason for Edhem's delay might be suggested in the continued Greek possession of Kritiri. Kritiri, at least, I believe to be its Greek name; the Turks called it Losphaki; in any case it is a very high mountain with a blockhouse on the top, and it commands

Tyrnavo.[1] The mountain is high and steep, and horribly stony. It was approachable only in front by a stony ravine, and was defended by tier on tier of escarpment and stone wall; to take it by assault was almost impossible. From this position—the last high one in their possession—the Greeks on Tuesday and again on Wednesday morning delivered a furious attack on the division of Neshat Pasha. The firing was the heaviest of the war so far. The Turks brought several guns into action, and shelled the enemy intermittently for a couple of hours or so. Some of the shrapnel burst two hundred yards in mid-air—little round white clouds they looked like, suddenly springing into sight out of nothing, and then expanding, thinning, and floating away into nothing again. But others burst dead on the ridge of the mountain, and may have done some damage. Anyhow, the artillery served its real purpose—less to kill than to flurry and frighten; a hot infantry fire also was poured in from the defence. The attack on the Turkish position was repulsed, and the firing weakened from banging

---

[1] Mr Wilfrid Pollock, in his entertaining book, 'War and a Wheel,' says that Kritiri was the name of the little hill to the left of which the Greeks had their batteries. I think, however, he must have been misinformed. At any rate, in the Austrian General Staff map Kritiri is a mountain of the frontier range. Possibly the Greek officers knew little more of the topography than did the Turkish.

volleys to crackles, and from crackles to rare pops, and then went out altogether. Neshat lost but a few men—among them was his second brigadier, Djelal Pasha. But the Greeks still held Kritiri; Kritiri, therefore, had to be out-flanked. It is true that, as it was never assaulted and was never intended to be assaulted, Edhem might as well have outflanked it on Wednesday as on Friday. But probably he did not wish to advance his centre into the plain between the Greeks on the high ground about Nezeros and those on Kritiri. That would explain the delay in attacking until Thursday, Edhem wishing first to have Hamdi clear his left flank; but it would not explain the delay in attacking until Friday afternoon.

On Friday afternoon, April 23rd, however, was fought the so-called battle of Mati—the deciding action of the first stage of the war. Until we saw the English newspapers none of us with the Turks had ever heard the name of Mati, or knew that there had been a battle at all. Mati, it appears, is the name of a spring and chapel near the little hill on the Greek left centre. The battle consisted of the usual artillery practice and the capture of Deliler and Mussalar. The position was exactly what it had been all the week. The Turkish centre—consisting of Memdhuk's division, the reserve brigade, under Mehemet Pasha, which had been moved up to Elassona from Serfidje before the opening of the war, and Hakki Pasha's division in support—was crowded into the narrow end of the V-shaped plain below. The left centre rested on the village of Karatsali, secured by the hills above; the extreme left was Hamdi's division, which, however, we could not see from the Col. The right was Neshat and Hairi, but they took no part in this day's engagement. The Turkish front looked south-east. The Greek right faced our left in the village of Deliler—a long, straggling group of stone and mud cottages, nominally two villages, really one. A quarter of a mile to its right rear is the village of Mussalar, also occupied; about half a mile to the right rear again the junction of the Xerias and Salamvria. Thence their batteries stretched across the plain to the little round hill, and thence on again to Tyrnavo on their left. Above Tyrnavo they still held the formidable Kritiri. The Turks had of course the advantage of numbers—35,000 men, or 55,000 counting Neshat and Hairi; the whole Greek force, according to Reuter's correspondent, was thirteen battalions of 1000 infantry apiece, five squadrons and 36 guns. Their right wing, which was the only force seriously engaged, had 8000 infantry. On the other hand, the Turkish

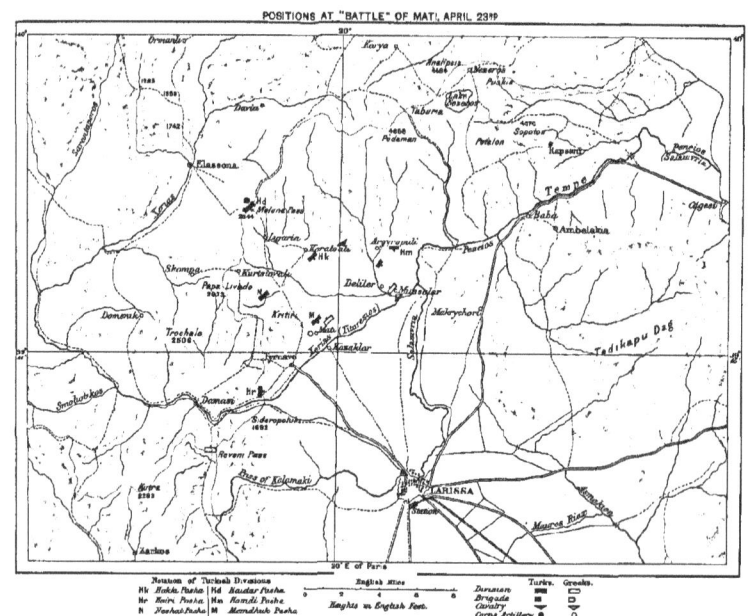

POSITIONS AT "BATTLE" OF MATI, APRIL 23ᴿᴰ

position on the left centre was too cramped to enable it to display its full strength; moreover, the Greeks, having been allowed for days to entrench themselves, had the odds of position. Between the armies the fields of barley were already waist high and in ear, but in the dry fallows every shell and bullet, hoof or foot, kicked up clouds of dust. There was good cover, however, in the grateful patches of thick wood. All that you saw from the Col of Meluna. No troops could cross the brown without showing dust storms on it; none could cross the green without showing black lines for infantry, black and brown and white lines for cavalry, black blots with smaller black satellites grouped round them for guns. Except in the woods you could see every move on a chessboard a hundred square miles in size, with 70,000 men for pieces, and the fate of two nations for the stake.

It was the finest place to see a battle one could imagine. Only—there was no battle to see.

It began with the artillery, and with the artillery, as it turned out, it practically ended. It began in the centre with a smart cannonade from either side. Both shot wild at first: the Turkish shrapnel burst in little white balloons the height of Nelson's column above the Greek batteries; the salvoes from the Greek batteries raised six separate whirls of earthy cloud, now in the plough before the Turks, now in the plough behind them, but on them never. But presently the Turks began to drop shells right round the little black swarming ant-hills that stood for Greek guns; the Greeks went on banging away, now short, now over, impartially, the whole afternoon.

Meanwhile—it was now about one o'clock—the main attack was developing two miles to the left. Here the Turkish artillery seemed to be putting in splendid work. A vast ploughed field, perhaps a mile across, lies before the village of Deliler. At its right hand top corner is a big square, many-windowed, grey-brown house on a little knoll; it may be a convent, it may be a private house, but it looks like a furniture re-pository. To the right the knoll slopes down among trees to a little minaret; this point was the fulcrum of the defence. Ali Riza Pasha, enjoying himself thoroughly, as always when his darling guns were in action, moved three batteries nearly up to the edge of the ploughed field, well under the fire of the Greek skirmishers, and plugged round after round plump on to the knoll. It may not have cost the Greeks much blood, but artillery aims mainly at the nerves. By now a battalion of infantry was stealing round on the

right of the knoll—the Greek left. Covered by
trees the black dots strolled leisurely forward.
From above they did not seem to move; they
looked like pieces on a board worked automa-
tically by some great player behind. They
established themselves under cover of an open
wood on our right of the minaret, and the curling
blue smoke showed they were making good use
of the position. The Greeks knew it too; they
were firing hard at Riza's three batteries from
their right of Mati hill, but the range was too
great to touch him. They advanced a battery on
their right and tried from there. They shot miserably as ever, and Riza took no notice. They
advanced half the battery nearer still; Riza still
took no notice.

And now was come the moment for the main
attack in front of the house and knoll and
minaret—two battalions of infantry across the
great fallow. Little dots of skirmishers, little
clumps of main body, black lumps of supports
began to dapple the brown. Slowly, slowly they
moved—but they moved. The field began to be
full of them. It began to be so full that the
men seemed to be standing still and the field
to be drawn slowly back through them, like the
great brown roll of a musical box through the
black teeth. The Greeks kept up their fire

briskly, yet there were but few Turkish dots left to be drawn back with the brown field. Now the foremost assailants were nearly at the green margin beyond; now they were on the very edge; now they were over and scampering up the slope. The fight was over, too. Some little black dots and streaks, some wisps of blue smoke, some puffs of bursting shell—that was the battle of Mati, the fight that won Larissa.

The Greek position was now broken up—by three battalions and three batteries, with the loss of ten men killed and thirty-eight wounded. About four o'clock the artillery opened on their left, under Kritiri, and a feint was made of an infantry advance. But meanwhile their right was turned. Our left advanced; it occupied Mussalar, and reached the junction of the rivers. The cavalry began to rush round their rear. At dusk the Greek army began to realise what was happening—and it was all over.

For next morning, when I came up to the top of the Pass, the Greeks were gone. Gone from the line of entrenched batteries, gone from the little round hill, gone from Tyrnavo, gone from impregnable Kritiri—clean gone and not to be found anywhere. The plain was wrapped in blue smoke from burning Deliler and Mussalar, and behind the smoke had vanished the Greek army.

XVIII.

THE OCCUPATION OF LARISSA.

THE Marshal sat in his captured tent on the lowest spur of the frontier mountains. Below gushed a spring of living water out of the rock; soldiers filled their cans from it and drank greedily; just below, where the spring widened to a pool, horses splashed knee-deep and drank greedily also. Beside the pool was a huge tree, such a tree as is not found on the bare Turkish side. Under its grateful shade, kicked at by horses and bitten at by unnumbered flies, sat the correspondent of the 'Daily Mail' writing—need you ask?—a telegram.

To him entered an aide-de-camp of his Majesty the Sultan, radiant in blue and scarlet and gold. His Excellency informs you that Larissa is taken. Larissa taken! Why, it was for to-morrow that we still expected that long promised, long delayed great battle along the Salamvria before Larissa.

Larissa taken! When and how and by whom, and above all why? Only half an hour before the Marshal had said "*C'est fini*," but this was finishing with a vengeance. Larissa taken early this morning, almost without a shot fired! Well, let us at least go and see.

I started off to ride straight across country, intending to swim the rivers, but at all costs to get into Larissa with all speed. There proved to be no water in the first river, and over the second the Greeks in their panic had not even broken the bridge, though they had left a case of dynamite on the further side of it. I saw it two mornings after still there; the Turks, with their magnificent carelessness, had never thought of clearing it away, and there it may be still.

The plan of going across country did not succeed. I fell in with some Turks, and joined myself with them, and as the Turk has no great love for going across country, and hardly ever knows his way anywhere, we decided to take the main road from Tyrnavo. So to Tyrnavo we rode, under Kritiri, the inaccessible. Tyrnavo was empty and quite silent. A few fowls in the courtyards, a few dogs in the streets. But all the houses empty, doors and windows wide open, broken tables blocking the gates, pillows, shirts, and petticoats littering the streets—the village was as cold and dead as if the last day were come. Having decided to retreat, the Greeks had not done things by halves.

Clattering over the long wooden bridge across the broad, dry, stony bed of the Xerias, I came out on to the main road to Larissa. Two inches thick with white dust, it was yet the broadest and best-metalled road I have seen in this part of the world. On the right was a vast cavalry barrack. "That was built by us," said a Turkish officer. Never could there be seen more hopeless, handless, headless confusion. Saddles and harness were strewn in heaps; regimental papers flew before the wind in clouds. There was a knapsack, here a cap, there an artillery ammunition-waggon hanging over the ditch, with the wheels broken and the traces cut; there—shame! —a little pile of cartridges. A soldier may throw away much, and there is still hope for him; once he begins to throw away cartridges, there is none. And there by the roadside were a couple of dead Greeks — their swollen heads black with flies: they had been killed by their comrades in the stampede.

Over the scattered, smashed, dishevelled, disgraceful relics of Greece marched the conquering Turk. Already a huge army was pouring in from every opening into the plain — horse and foot and the perpetual patient baggage-trains. The Turkish transport might be rough, but it was very ready. But the conquering Turk displayed no exultation. Here, between the rich corn-fields of the plain of Thessaly, he marched as always — strongly, sloppily, composedly: what news to such as he that the Greeks were afraid of him, and that he was going in to take their city? The Turk had been there before, and no Greek ever drove him out of it. "We built that," said my little lieutenant.

And it was still so when the faint blotch on the skyline hardened into the lattice-work of white houses and dark green cypress-trees that I had often seen from the mountains as Larissa. As the dominant impression of the town was the sweet smell of laburnums in the public places, of roses and sweet peas in the gardens, so the impression of the occupation of the town was fragrant and kindly. The entry of the Turkish troops into Larissa was the sweetest and most lovable thing I had seen during this week of war. I am afraid that Canon McColl will not believe me, but I am speaking the truth. That the Turkish army entering a town taken from the enemy should be a pleasant sight, should be almost a kind of Sunday-school treat, will be surprising information to many English-

men.   But I have eyes in my head, and I
saw it.

The little lieutenant I had ridden in with had
two uncles in the town—the most substantial
Mussulman citizens of the place; the elder was
one of the deputies for Larissa in the Assembly
at Athens.   To his house we rode.   Hassan
Avni Bey had been there before—he had property in Thessaly himself—and from the moment the town had come in sight his face had
been relaxed into an irrepressible boyish smile.
As we turned a corner and reached his uncle's
gate he jumped down from his horse and rushed
inside.   Some of his uncle's grooms were in the
flowery garden; they shook his hand and laughed
aloud with joy.   We went into the house; the
steward caught him in his arms and kissed him.
His uncle came rushing into the hall and hugged
him and kissed him till the little lieutenant's
body was like a pricked balloon; then his uncle
took to kissing me.   He took us into his room
and sat us down.   And then came a babble of
inquiry, of congratulation, of irresponsible, half-
childish happiness.   Out of it all I tried to ex-
tract the story of the flight and of the capture.
But my host knew little enough.   He had not
left the house for twelve days—he had not dared.
The Mussulmans of Larissa had been assaulted

M

in the street; their fezzes had been torn off and themselves half-killed. He put it all down, good man, to the Ethnika Etairia. He did not think his Greek fellow-townsmen would have done him any harm—and they would have been devils indeed if they did, since half-a-dozen of them, who could not get away, were taking refuge in his back-kitchen at that very moment. Presently there was brought in a sick Greek officer, who had been deserted by his comrades and by the Greek doctors. Hassan Bey took him in on parole, and the best his estate could provide was not too good for the Greek prisoner.

He told me that the Greeks had fled in panic from Tyrnavo on Friday night; I had seen the signs of that for myself. The Crown Prince had come in on Friday evening, and was off again for Pharsala by two in the morning. Troops had come bolting and screaming into Larissa all night; in the morning they too were off for Pharsala. All Saturday the population fled wildly southwards. The Greek authorities had let the two hundred convicts out of jail and armed them; and they had been smashing and stealing and shooting all Saturday night. On Sunday morning came the Turks. That was all he knew. The Turks had come, and that was all he wanted to know.

The rest I heard from Seyfoullah. At eleven on Saturday night a squadron of Turkish cavalry stole up to the entrenchments and found them empty. But they lit on four Greeks, and from these prisoners learned the truth. The town was garrisoned by pickpockets and wife-beaters; the Greek army had vanished. At daybreak Seyfoullah and Grumbkow advanced with two squadrons of cavalry and a horse battery. The pickpockets opened fire, but a shell or two sickened them. One squadron dismounted and stood to their carbines; the other defiled over a little wooden accommodation bridge into the town. The big stone and iron bridge over the Salamvria—here fast and deep, and as broad as the Thames at Oxford—the pickpockets were going to dynamite. But four horsemen dashed across—and it was over. The Greeks had taken all the engines and rolling-stock of the railway to Volo; short of that they had deserted everything. Town and fortifications, guns and ammunition, clothing and provisions, and fodder—the Greeks had taken to their heels and left it all. They had lost everything — including honour. They had not been beaten; they had scuttled for their lives after two days of desultory shell-fire that, on their own showing, had killed nobody. It was not the retreat that damned them; for

that the Crown Prince has been most unjustly
blamed, since with the position at Mati turned
there was no natural line of defence left north
of Pharsala. What whelmed Prince and people
in equal damnation was the shameful manner of
their flight—a flight in which officers ran bellowing with terror and left their men behind,
a flight headed by the Commander-in-Chief, the
King's son. He will make a fit king for Greece.
A brave race may swagger; an unwarlike one
may placidly confess to cowardice. But for a
race of swaggerers and cowards at the same
time it is difficult to see a place in the future
of Europe.

But never mind the Greeks. We went out
into the streets again to see the troops marching
in. The veiled Mussulman women had come out,
now that the soldiers were abroad in the town;
they were walking up and down under their para-
sols. Children—Turk and Jew and Greek alike—
were playing in the streets. Dogs were basking
in the sun. Hens were pecking with a hen's pre-
sumption up and down the main thoroughfares
with no fear of the looter before their eyes.
The shops were mostly close-shuttered. Up
and down with wondering eyes—they had hardly
seen Salonica coming through, and to many
Larissa was the first town of their lives—strolled

half-barbarous Anatolians. And with it all no outrage. I will not say that there was no single case of disorder; a few men were arrested for looting. They were condemned to be shot, but I am happy to say they were let off next morning with a thrashing. But I patrolled the city for hours, and I do say that the order, the discipline, and the good - humour of the Turks could have been exceeded by no nation in the world; more, I do not believe that any nation could have equalled it. In no other country I ever heard of are soldiers so well disciplined, so simply, unquestioningly, even childishly obedient to their officers. The officers had forbidden pillage and violence, and the soldiers obeyed. I have seen more rioting at a supper bar in the National Liberal Club than I saw on the first day of the occupation of Larissa.

Why? Partly, no doubt, it was due to the admirable arrangements made by the officers. I saw Hakki Pasha, who had entered the town with his Division—a Turk of the old type, short, stout, grey - bearded, grave, yet with a jolly twinkle somewhere under the surface of his eyes. When I congratulated him he was almost embarrassed, and said it was an accident. So, in truth, it was. But the discipline he established was not an accident, and any general in the world,

might be proud of it to his death. Sentinels
stood at every corner, mounted patrols paced
down every street. The bank and all the other
principal buildings had sentries of their own,
and it was pleasant to see how hard Albanians
scorned the Greek sentry-boxes and sat down
contentedly on the stones. There was only one
possible objection to the arrangements made—
they were not necessary.

Partly, too, the good order may have been due
to the fact that the Turks entered Larissa in cold
blood; also that the Greek population had for the
most part bolted, and that the Greek criminals
released from jail had skimmed the cream of the
loot. But to the Turk, you must remember, it is
almost less irritating to have to fight for a place
than to be cheated of his battle and come in
without firing a shot. Yet, when all is said and
done, the great fact remains that Larissa was
only half a hostile city. The thousands of Jews
remained — these dauntless soldiers of current
coin—the Jews remained, and did good business
in Greek notes, taken from the dead, at 30 per
cent of their face value. Many Greeks remained
also, and each hour of the occupation brought
more into the streets.

But Larissa was not a hostile town. The Turk
was returning to his own. On the dusty road in

I passed many families on horseback, in carts, on foot, hastening home again now that the day of persecution was over. I met more than one Turkish soldier who had been born in Larissa and lived there all his life. The persecutions of their Greek neighbours had driven such to Salonica; thence to volunteer for the front was an easy step. Now they were coming home to their homes and their children. As the troops marched in, the Mussulman population came trooping into the streets to salute their deliverers. For a fortnight many had not left their houses because of the Ethnike Etairia; the night before they had been promiscuously fired at, after the evacuation, by Greek irregulars: I kicked up dozens of regulation Gras cartridge-cases in the street. They streamed out to meet their brothers and their sons, to welcome the exiles and the volunteers to their birthplace. They laughed and cried and hugged each other in the street. The stranger did not escape: even I, because I came with the army and wore a fez, was laughed at and kissed and saluted till my arm was stiff with salaaming, and my stomach sugared with cups of coffee. The Greeks were quite forgotten, and all Larissa shone with one expansive, grave, courteous, friendly, very happy, Turkish smile. The Turk was come to his own again.

But always no outrages—let us end with that. If you have never ridden into a conquered city, where the conquered are in terror of you, where all their stuff lies masterless before you, when you have many short, cold, hard nights and many long, dry, sweat - and - dusty, not quite undangerous days to avenge—if you have never felt it you do not know what temptation is. It is the richest moment of your life. But it is full of temptation. It was not my conquered city, and it was not my enemy, but if it had been I know quite well I should have behaved a hundred times less considerately than the Turks.

XIX.

CAPUA.

In Larissa I set up housekeeping with the same two companions as at Elassona: no man could have asked for better. Hassan Bey gave us dinner that Sunday night, for our men and beasts and goods were all scattered over the thirty miles of up and down between us and Elassona. After dinner—I have described a Turkish gentleman's dinner already; the order of the dishes is confusing, but the dishes themselves are beyond the dreams of gluttony—his steward took us to sleep in a house over the way. I don't know whose house it was, and we never paid a piastre of rent for it; but Hassan Bey had been civil governor for nearly twelve hours, and it was doubtless quite regular. We went up half-a-dozen steps into a bare-boarded hall with bare rooms opening on either side; the house seemed empty. Then into an inner room and—could it be? In the name of the Prophet, beds! Clean deal trestles and planks, clean mattresses, clean sheets and pillows! We slept that night.

Housekeeping in Larissa was a perplexing business the first day or two for men who tried to be honest. Nothing belonged to anybody. Our baggage arrived the next morning. All we knew about the rights of property at present was that the house we were in seemed to be ours, and that our horses and provisions and clothes certainly were, so we crammed the latter into the former. For two days that house was a combination of a casual ward, a left-luggage office, and a circus. You could not walk from one room to another without tumbling over rifles and bayonets—for rifles and bayonets had slumped heavily with the capture of Larissa, and now ran 3s. 4d. and 10d. respectively—bits, bags, saddles, dirty shirts, and cooking-pans. In the little courtyard—about the size of an average suburban drawing-room — stood thirteen horses; the less trustworthy tethered to trees and the railings of the steps, the more pious left to stand by themselves. We had found a derelict puppy in Elassona, and it had been carefully brought on in a nose-bag to the new base; within two days it had attracted four other dogs worse than itself; they refused to be cast out, and as the parents and guardians of the poor little devils were quaking at Volo or Pharsala or Athens, we had to give them food and shelter.

Most embarrassing of all, Charlie had come in not a quarter of an hour after his arrival in Larissa with a more than usually complacent grin on his face and under his arm a peacock. I began to explain to him the wickedness of looting, but he cut me short. "I bin find 'im," he said with indignation, "and I bin fetch 'im to Mushir Pasha." I gathered he had wished to present him to his Excellency the Commander-in-Chief as a small testimonial of esteem. "But Mushir Pasha he say, 'What I bin do with 'im? You fetch 'im for yourself.'" And then almost timidly, "You want 'im, M'S'eevens?" It was a stringent rule in our household (*a*) that no looting was allowed; (*b*) that if any looting did accidentally take place, the master of the looter had the first call on the loot. I said I didn't want him. I have a rough general notion how to provide for hens, geese, ducks, or turkeys, but I am quite ignorant of the very elements of peacock-culture. However, the other men thought it would make for the decoration of the house, so Charlie was allowed to put it down and leave it. Thereon, with an expression of wounded dignity I have never seen equalled, it got under my bed and refused to be addressed.

It sat there four hours with an occasional grunt
of indignation, till at last it condescended to be
persuaded to go out into the yard. And there it
stayed five days, very angry with the horses, who
regarded it with unaffected terror, and all shied,
as at the word of command, whenever the peacock
wagged its tail. At the end of that time we
went forth to war again, and when we returned I was thankful to find that somebody had
re-looted it.

As for the men, the first day of their arrival
the nine of them slept in the hall, which was
carpeted with snoring bodies. After that the
dragomans put down our beds on the floor of one
room, the cavasses slept on the provision-boxes in
the hall—always one across the door of our room.
And when Hassan Bey gave us a deserted stable
the grooms slept, after their manner, under the
horses' bellies. Looking back, I am not quite sure
I was a good master to Georghi, my groom; about
Charlie and Aslan my conscience is quite clear.
Georghi was a most deserving and hard-working
man; being a Greek, he had to do all the little
jobs of hewing wood and drawing water which no
self-respecting Turk could put his hand to. In
theory he got a few extra pence daily for this
service, deducted from the wages of his fellows;
in practice it was commuted for a handsome

backsheesh at the end of the campaign. I do not think that Georghi took his clothes off once during the two months he was in my employ; certainly he never slept in, or even on, a bed. For him the only variation on the stable was the grass and the sky, which I should have preferred, but he did not. On one occasion also, I am ashamed to say, I hit him for kicking a horse; after all, the horses were always kicking him. Yet he was always cheerful, always very careful of his beasts, and latterly turned out a very handy needlewoman. I console my conscience with the reflection that at the end of the campaign he was much richer and not appreciably dirtier than before.

Larissa was our base during the remainder of the campaign. A day or two after the occupation they brought over the little Salonica-Jewish operator who could read French capitals; and where the correspondent's telegraph operator is, there must his base be. After the taking of Volo it was possible to telegraph thence also, but Larissa was still nearer the scene of the main action. So that if any of us sent in one of his men from time to time with a telegram, the messenger used to bring back his saddle-bags stuffed with wine, sardines, corned-beef, tea, and especially bread. You never know how useful humble bread is—even black bread—until you are called on to go without it. And it was curious that all the things a man rightly despises in England —tea and jam, for example—became the richest delights of life in Greece. Even champagne —by restricting its use to the night of a victory, we just made it last out the war—champagne, most despicable and pernicious drink in our hours of ease, was bubbling exhilaration after a sixteen hours' day on that dusty, dusty plain of Thessaly. As for more solid food, the staple was still "*Fleisch mit Bohnen, frische Bohnen, meine Herrn,*" as Andreas would alluringly remark from day to day : that is to say, leather mutton and a wooden kind of broad-bean ; but the time came when we should have been glad enough to get it. Our stuff in tins was beginning to run out by now, though tinned oysters never failed ; still even tinned oysters pall in time. But taking it altogether, I recall with pride that our mess all through the campaign was the envy of the Europeans and the hardly disguised objective of any Turk who wanted a good dinner ; it was the best table in Larissa after the Marshal's. And if anybody thinks us sybarites, let him who was not welcome to his share, and uncommonly glad to get it, throw the first stone at us.

I stayed in Capua from Sunday April 25th until the small hours of April 30th—and what about the war all this time? Again, I am afraid, we enter on a period during which I know little of the war—except that there was no war to know about. Information as to its progress came mainly from Kennan Bey, who turned up at our house, with loud cries of *Mashallah* (Thank God) and *A la bonne heure*, the second morning at nine o'clock, and stayed to lunch. The more I look back on the Turco-Grecian war the fainter become the lines of men and the crash of guns, and the clearer Kennan's round and ruddy face and his jovial voice. But as a source of information Kennan was not, on the whole, trustworthy. It was aptly remarked at the time that he would have made a magnificent journalist. You remember about the *gros gaillard*, that inimitable touch? Kennan had a firm grasp on the principle that picturesqueness of description is attained by the use of particular rather than general terms. He was just as good on the morning of the Greek flight. "*Mais, mon cher ami*," he began in a hushed voice, as if he hardly liked to say it, "*ils sont lâches, ces Grecs—lâches, mon ami.*" Then, his pictorial enthusiasm rising,—"*des fusils, des cartouches, des canons, du maïs, du cognac—ils semblant vivre de cognac, ces Grecs—les bas de leurs femmes—ils ont tout laissé.*" "Their wives' stockings": what could be better put? There

was also a good deal of the melodramatic about
him. The first time he dined with us he said he
was an Albanian, and then in a hushed whisper:
"We Albanians carry two weapons: this," tap-
ping his regulation Smith - Wesson, "for our
enemies, and this"—he hauled out a deringer
from under his trousers and his voice rang—"for
our friends." One day in Meluna he planted
himself within easy ear-shot of us as an Albanian
battalion went by, and began an audible soliloquy
about his countrymen: "*Aslan, aslan—les lions,
les lions*," he almost sobbed. He was at the top
of his histrionic form one day when I offered him
a drink of wine in the presence of half-a-dozen
officers, all of whom had taken it gladly. He
waved his hand with a gesture of renunciation.
"*Non, non, mon ami*," he said with the manner
of a St Antony; "*c'est défendu par notre
religion.*" And then his jollity got the better of
him; "*Moi, je bois secrètement*," he roared in a
voice of thunder. Only once did I ever know him
weaken. He was accustomed to represent that
he was always on most important missions, riding
all night with two hours' sleep in the twenty-four.
One morning, when he was playing his very best,
I was so indiscreet as to ask him where he had
been. "*Elassona peut - être?*" I suggested—
sixty miles there and back. "*Oui, oui*," he re-

sponded wearily, "*Elassona—peut-être.*" "*Peut-être*" was not worthy of Kennan Bey.

A cautious correspondent was not likely to telegraph home too much of Kennan's information, and though he and others announced the fall of Volo daily, I waited for official information. The general scheme of operations was a slow, a very slow, parallel advance by the Turkish troops all along the line. The truth was that everybody was taking it easy, partly to enable provisions and ammunition to come up to Larissa, and partly because it is the Turkish tradition to take things easy in the hour of victory. However, Hairi Pasha on the extreme right had occupied Zarkos without opposition apparently on the 27th, and Trikkala apparently after an insignificant skirmish on the 28th. In the centre Memdhuk and Neshat's divisions were strolling towards Pharsala. On the left Hakki's division was supporting the cavalry under Suleyman Pasha, which seemed to be alternately taking Volo and being repulsed at Velestino, eight miles on the hither side of it. Hamdi was at Larissa, Haidar at the Meluna; Hassan of Katerina seemed to have strayed into the sea and been swallowed up. The only thing certain was that the advance was being made very slowly, but that in a day or two the heads of our

N

columns must run up against the Greeks. The
difficulty was to know whether it would be at
Velestino or at Pharsala. It looked fairly plain,
however, that the main attack would be made
at Pharsala, which was known to be the Crown
Prince's headquarters, and on which three divisions were converging. Now when that attack
was made Edhem would be there, and Edhem
was sitting in the Crown Prince's deserted quarters at Larissa without any immediate sign of
getting up. Reasoning thus, I started out at
dawn on April 30th for Velestino.

XX.

DEFEAT AND WATER.

In the first battle of Velestino we were beaten by the Greeks. It might be called a repulse or a postponed attack, if you like : one correspondent, with the censorship in his eye, had the happy inspiration of calling it a concentration in rear. The phrase was polite and perfectly correct, but beaten is the plain English of it. Frankly, it was a defeat—the only one of the war. The action was not ordered by Edhem Pasha ; had he been present he would unquestionably have forbidden it. The Greeks under Colonel Smolenski numbered, according to correspondents with him, 12,000 men, with four batteries, in an exceedingly strong defensive position. The Turkish force engaged consisted of one brigade of Hakki's division under Naim Pasha, and the Cavalry division under Suleyman Pasha—roughly, 6000 men with four batteries.

To attempt to take such a position with half the defending force was plain madness. The only possible excuse for it was that the Greeks, after their flight from Larissa, were supposed to be so demoralised that the mere sight of a Turkish soldier was expected to start them on the run again. But at Velestino the Greeks were commanded by their best leader. Smolenski's task was a very easy one, but he showed it to be possible that, given a capable command, the Greeks might make soldiers yet.

It was unquestionably foolhardy to tackle Velestino with so inadequate a force. Yet it might be said for Naim and Suleyman — or, more accurately perhaps, for Colonel Mahmud Bey, a son of Ghazi Mukhtar, who was the real inspirer of the attack—that to tackle Velestino somehow or another was emphatically the right thing to do. It was the most vital strategic point at that time in Greek hands. They were now defending the line of the Volo-Pharsala railway; their main force was at Pharsala on their left wing; Velestino was the centre, and Volo the right wing. Velestino was the junction of the Volo-Larissa and Volo-Pharsala-Trikkala railways. If Velestino were taken the Greek line would be cut in half; Smolenski then must either retire to Volo into a corner or fall back southward to Halmyro, leaving Volo isolated, and the Crown Prince at Pharsala with his right flank uncovered.

Thus, no doubt, reasoned Mahmud. But Edhem's strategy remained the sounder. The enemy's connecting line, it must be remembered, was the railway, and his base was, as always, the sea. From these facts two deductions followed. First, it was manifestly perilous to attack one point singly, for at whatever point was attacked the Greeks could concentrate a superior force by means of the railway, and the attacking force ran a danger of being destroyed. The right course was to attack Pharsala and Velestino simultaneously, so that neither position could call up aid from the other. This was what Edhem subsequently did with success; but on April 30th, as Mahmud should have known, there were no Turkish troops near enough to Pharsala to make themselves felt. Secondly, the Greek base being the sea, there was no point in breaking the centre. If it fell back on Halmyro the left would simultaneously fall back on Domoko — as it happened a much stronger position—and would continue to draw its supplies, through Stylida and Lamia, from the sea. If Smolenski went to Volo he could transport his army by sea to Stylida, and fall

into line as the right wing of the force at
Domoko. The only justification of Mahmud's
plan would be the probability of a much more
rapid and energetic pursuit than, knowing his
countrymen, he had a right to count on.
Edhem's plan was to make a feint on Velestino, while attacking the Greek left at Pharsala, and endeavouring to envelop and destroy
it. This last he failed to do, but that was
the fault, not of the plan, but of its execution. Europeans would naturally sympathise
with Mahmud's wish to be at the enemy and
keep him on the run; for all that, the first
battle of Velestino, though a pretty fight, was
an inexcusable blunder.

It is some forty miles from Larissa to Velestino, and by the time we got to the Turkish
headquarters, at about 10 o'clock, the action was
in full swing. The position was rather like an
inverted Meluna. There was the same V-shaped
plain running up to the base of the heights—
only this time the Greeks had the heights, and
the Turks were in the plain. In the centre,
as at Meluna, the heights sank to a long Col;
to right and left swept forward bare and pre-
cipitous grey mountains. Those on the right
were spurs of the Kara Dagh — a triangular
mass of mountains which projects into the plain

of Thessaly, with the valley of the Pharsala-
Velestino railway as its base; on our left front
was Pilaf Tepe, a spur of Pelion, and on our left
flank the steel-blue sheet of Lake Karla. We
could just see Velestino—white minarets sparkling
among green poplars—below the right-hand corner
of the Col: more was hidden by a thick wood
straight in front of our centre; it looked a few
hundred yards deep, but it was really a matter
of miles. The railway junction was masked by
this wood; the Pharsala branch swept round
southward over the Col, the Volo branch disappeared behind Pilaf Tepe.

From the hills, when I rode up, sounded the
usual spluttering fire. I passed through the
little village of Rizomylo, where stood the am-
munition-horses and a weak reserve of a battalion:
in the shade, at the foot of the belfry-tower, sat
three Greek prisoners. I was told I should find
the Pasha in front of the village to the left. I
did—and when I found him even I was tactician
enough to stand aghast. The Turkish army had
no centre! In the wood before us, they said, the
Greeks had made earthworks. One company of
our skirmishers was just inside the fringe of the
trees: now and again the crack of a rifle floated
back to us on the still air. A couple of hundred
yards in front of the wood a couple of companies

had thrown up a light shelter-trench; on their right, in a corn-field, was a fourth company. Half a mile of plough and dried grass behind them, and there stood Naim and Suleyman, a battery unlimbered on their right, with its horses a quarter of a mile behind; on their left, a little forward, the motionless line of a couple of squadrons of cavalry: the rest of the cavalry was on the right with Mahmud. Besides this, nothing!

Naim had stripped his centre bare to feed the wings, and all the fighting was on the hills. He was making the desperate effort to turn both flanks of the enemy with half the enemy's force. The heaviest fighting was on the left. We could see our men toiling up the grey flanks of Pilaf Tepe; we could hear their irregular, intermittent, individual fusilade, and the volleys with which the Greeks answered them. The enemy had mountain-guns up there too. On the right—far, far away up the heights on the right—there were also guns on both sides, hammering slowly and methodically away at each other. There were Greek entrenchments here also on the lower slopes, and Greek infantry, too, up on the crest: every now and then a movement from the Turkish infantry on the skirts of the hills awoke a growling volley. But there seemed little doing.

Our men appear to struggle forward, but to get no forwarder. Plainly the enemy was holding them; it seemed a moment to send in the reserves. Only where were the reserves to send?

It was a day of foolhardy desperation. For about mid-day, feeling no doubt that unless some added pressure drove back the Greek left it was hopeless to lie firing all day in the cruel sun, Mahmud charged with cavalry against the Greek entrenchments on their left centre. I did not see it, for it was away on the right: there were trees between, and the ground dipped before rising to the Kara Dagh. But Mahmud told me the story of it himself riding into Volo, and he seemed in no way ashamed of it. There was not space, he said, to deploy with some 300 troopers. He charged in column, up-hill, against earthworks filled with infantry and artillery. There were two earthworks, one a little in front of and above the other: he had directed his men at that. But the horses swerved from the ascent, and carried them against the second, so that they got the fire on flank and front. The horses began to drop: he bade the men dismount and charge on foot. But the fire was too hot: they got close up to the entrenchment, and he was exchanging revolver-shots with an officer in the earthwork, when a trooper beside him shot the

Greek dead. But it was no use; the fire was too hot, and they went back again. It was as desperate a piece of heroism as Balaclava, and as wickedly useless. The cavalry were lucky to get off with the loss of thirty odd; but the killed and disabled horses were far more. And that is what comes of giving colonelcies to men of thirty, and allowing them to command brigades.

This battle of Velestino will be remembered chiefly for Mahmud's charge. But in my mind it will stick for ever as the battle of thirst. Never have I seen such thirst. Men, horses, asses, the heavens above and the earth beneath, all were parched and caked and burned and split with a raging thirst. Not a breath of air came over the hills, where the Greek smoke hung heavily. As the sun climbed up the hard blue sky to mid-day it became more than could be borne—even by the Turk, the sturdiest bearer of things unbearable in the whole world. The horses seemed dazed and stupid in the pitiless glare; the troopers lay down, each behind his horse, in the little patches of shadow, and went to sleep with their dry mouths open. In the little trenches they had thrown up the infantry had less even than the poor protection of a horse. As I rode along that line my eyes met eyes of wild, wondering distress, mixed with the beginnings of despair. Up on the hills there may have been a whiff of breeze now and again, but the rocks and loose stones were fiery furnaces by noon.

"Send water," cried the querulous bugles from the heated slopes all the afternoon. They sent water, as much as they could. The centre of our position was the village Rizomylo; from its little belfry I watched the fight when the sun began to sear that part of my head left defenceless by the fez. In the village was a well, and on its loose stone wall stood men dipping and hoisting like madmen: the amount of water they turned up in the hour might mean victory or defeat, — must needs mean many men's lives. Out of the buckets they tipped into skins—two slung over a pack-saddle. Then off went the dirty, tan-faced philanthropist, tugging at his horse's unbridled head, tramping all over the field, all up the hills, dealing out precious, precious water. Men tipped the cans till the sun heliographed on their shiny bottoms: they did not drink—they poured the water down; you could fancy you heard it hiss.

But then more sun, more heat, more maddening thirst! Water would not quench it. The dripping trail of the water-skins over the baked fields faded away as if the earth were made of

blotting - paper.   And opposite the very wells
flamed redly a solitary house, which had caught
fire in the attack.   The heat of it was nothing to
the skin, but the dry glare of it under the dry
glaring sun was red - hot torment to the eye.
It quite burnt up all the refreshment of the
well.

About three o'clock, when the last drop of
moisture had been squeezed out of men's bodies,
the Greeks began to pour their men over the
hills behind Velestino in swarms.   Four trains
had come in since the first shot; hour by hour
we were more hopelessly outnumbered.   Some in
column, some in line, they swarmed blackly down
the slopes; their fire swelled from a swift succession of cracks into the gr-r-r-r-r of an angry
beast.   The Turks held their position, though
they answered the fire but sparsely, being short
of ammunition—and there was none nearer than
Larissa.   The Greeks had plenty—another gift
of the railway.   The musketry on the left had
almost crackled out now, but the Greek cannon
boomed ominously faster.   On the right the
Greeks now swayed forward, now drew back;
our men now swayed back, now dashed smartly
forward.   But on the whole they were shifting
down and inwards, outflanked and driven back
on the centre.   If the Greeks had but come out

of the wood in front they must have crumpled up the weak centre like paper and the brigade would have been lost.

So as the shadows began to stretch across the plain our general realised that he had some 6000 men spread over a front of six miles or so, and began to draw them in. The Greeks opened briskly with their guns, but they did not succeed in flurrying the operation. Slowly, reluctantly, but always with the calm bearing of conscious superiority, the Turks retreated to Gherli, seven miles in rear. The Greeks stuck to their heights and made no attempt to follow. Strategically they were victorious. We tried to take the village and the railway junction, and failed. But spiritually I never saw anything less like a beaten army than the Turks. Some of them insisted on singing, despite all their officers could do : it was just what they wanted, said they, that the Greeks should know where they were and come down to follow them. And there they were at half-past five next morning, marching out to their positions before the village, composed, alert, and trim, though not to the point of affectation : one man in three attired in part of the uniform of some Greek regiment, and all quite ready to go and look for the rest of the suit.

As dusk fell most of the correspondents present

started to ride to Larissa with their despatches.
But thirty-five miles at night and thirty-five
miles back next morning after that parching day
was too much to ask even of a Salonica pony;
besides, if there were fighting next morning it
would probably begin at sunrise. So my two
messmates and I decided to make a night of it
at Gherli. We rode off the field with our friend,
Hussein Avni Bey, and it so happened that his
family owned Gherli : he called out a gross old
Greek with unearthly red rims round his eyes,
and told him to put us in the best house and give
us of Gherli's best. So we were left in the bare
upper rooms of the best house in Gherli with two
Albanian cavasses but no interpreter. Luckily,
both Aslan and Hassan spoke Greek, so the only
thing to do was to communicate with them. I
gave a very fair imitation, as I flatter myself, of
a cock, and thereafter tucked like a hen to indicate
eggs. Enormous grins spread over the faces of
the Albanians—they were the only people in the
army besides ourselves who enjoyed playing the
fool — and they disappeared. Then returning,
" Too, ta-too, ta-tooo — no ; tuck, tuck, tuck,
tuck, tegg—yes." So we ordered tuck, tuck, tuck,
tuck, tegg, and be quick about it, and banked up
our belts and saddles and bridles on the divan,
and began to smoke.

The eggs were just about due when Hassan
appeared on the stairs—which ran straight into
the rooms, of course, after the manner of a loft—
and, with much gesticulation, uttered the word
Mulazim. It means "lieutenant," and for a
moment we had the horrible suspicion that he
meant a lieutenant had come and taken the eggs.
But there was the clank of spurs and a sabre on
the stairs; evidently a lieutenant was coming up.
And then uprose the face—of Saad-ed-Din Bey,
by all that's wonderful! "*Bon soir, mon cher*,"
he prattled, just as if we had never been parted.
He was looking for quarters for Suleyman Pasha,
whose aide-de-camp he now was. He had evidently not washed since we left him at Elassona
when first we saw the Marshal; he was yellow
with dust, and had a bullet-hole through his sleeve;
his face was heavy with sleep. And yet somehow
he was not the old Saad-ed-Din. War had taken
hold of the stupid, sponging, unmannerly cub,
and made a man of him. He refused wine and
tobacco, he refused food, he refused conversation.
His General had sent him to find a house, and he
went away to find it.

The eggs were satisfactory in quality, though
disappointing in number. There was some white
wine, made chiefly of resin, to cool the feverish
blood of a Thessalian summer: nearly all Greek

wine is thus resinated, and the only person I ever knew who could drink it is myself. The red-eyed Greek showed a disposition to visit us at bed-time, but we got the cavasses to clear him away. And then Aslan appeared at the top of the stairs, spread out his—or rather my—sheepskin at the top, pulled out his long-barrelled revolver with a mixture of a smile and a scowl, and went to sleep upon the stairs. He was a born brigand, Aslan, if ever I saw one, but as true as a bull-dog. And so we curled up in our coats and went to sleep on the crawling divan, and woke up in time for the fight at dawn.

But, of course, there was no fight. And we had started to ride back, when, at ten in the morning, we met reinforcements coming in. At their head Hakki Pasha — short, stout, grey, cut to what seems the regulation pattern of a Turkish General of Division. Then battalion after battalion till there was a brigade, with guns crawling smoothly and relentlessly through the dust. Then my eye lit on Yunus Effendi—his keen eye measuring the distance to the Greek hills, striding out elastically as though five-and-twenty miles of marching were a before-breakfast appetiser. Yunus appeared to belong to no special battalion or division that he knew of.

He attached himself to any corps that seemed likely to see fighting, and it was all one to him whether he had an independent command or fell into the line with his captured Gras rifle.

But Yunus saw no fighting that day. Reuter's Agency and I decided to put in another night at Gherli on the chance. Nothing happened. Reuter had the happy gift of laying in reserves of sleep during odd moments, and snored steadily with face under a handkerchief. And I spent the day looking out of window, with the tail of my eye on the guns : as long as they didn't harness them there could be nothing much doing. But the great joy of the window was that it commanded a view of three wells. I watched them, hour by hour, trying to wash yesterday out of my eyes. Every now and then I took a swallow of resin-and-water myself to make quite sure it was real. From the two smaller wells they were ladling out water in empty petroleum cases. The biggest was of the primitive lever kind. The cross-bar balances on a tree ; the bucket hangs from one end of the cross-bar, and there is a weight on the other. When the weight is slacked off by the hand the bucket goes down and fills ; when the weight is released the bucket bounds up. Round the well's mouth was a stone

o

platform—dripping wet. The stones were all wet, and the ground round was wet with damp, cool, blessed mud. The soldier on the platform hauled up bucket by bucket, and sluiced it with a splash into the trough for the horses.

Swish, swish! Gulp, gulp, gulp! Ah-h-h!

XXI.

IN A CONQUERED CITY.

THE action at Velestino was incidental music between the first act of the war and the second. It was no part of Edhem's scheme, and except in the way of reconnaissance had no influence on it. The Greeks generously put down our loss at 550, but it was certainly less. Even in the way of reviving the self-confidence of the Greeks it was wholly unimportant, as they retreated just as consistently, though perhaps not quite so unsteadily, after it as before. The second act of the war, which now began, was punctuated by an even longer wait than Edhem had yet indulged us with. Nevertheless this second half, the operations on the southern border of Thessaly, was a great deal more interesting than the first. It gave us two real battles —battles with some combination in them, such as there was not at Meluna, and battles with some fight in them, such as there was not at Mati.

We rode back to Larissa, finding that there was no present intention of doing anything at Velestino, on the morning of May 2nd. Aslan was left at Gherli with a horse on vedette duty; the moment they took out the guns he was to ride top speed into Larissa and let me know.

At headquarters they told you it was the necessary interval of calm between the first and second phases of the war. The troops had to be re-victualled over a hundred miles of road from their base. They had to be concentrated for attack on the Greek line along the railway in front of Mount Othrys. It was a strong position, and must be attacked with deliberation. Had they only had the fight in them on that last day of April, the strategical importance of a railway might have been illustrated by the utter destruction of a whole brigade. However, they did not attack, and now we were going to attack them.

Only when? To-morrow, of course; is not this the land of to-morrow? But on the impatient Western man to-morrow palls when he gets too many of it running. You would never believe that war could be dull, — but it can. More, dulness is the worst hardship of it. It was so here, at any rate. Food was not plentiful, but day by day you saw more little shopkeepers peeping out timidly over their counters through half-opened shutters, more hawkers on the pavement, dozing under carcasses of lambs, or over heaps of onions, lettuce, and peas. Sleep, too, was fairly abundant when once you had schooled yourself to disregard solemn prophecies of great things for to-morrow : you might go to bed in your pyjamas, get up after sunrise, even take a bath. Fatigue, the worst strain of this straddling campaign, disappeared when you rode only to keep your horses in condition. But the hardship of boredom remained.

You got sick of the sun beating mercilessly down on the emptiness of Larissa. You got sick of the sun, seriously angry with the flies, the fleas, moths, bugs, beetles, and mosquitoes. When you were on the move they were a joke ; when you were idle they magnified themselves into a plague. You got sick of the orderly soldiers tramping, round-eyed but contented, up and down the parched streets, till you could almost pray for a mutiny or a massacre. I suppose it was the revulsion from excitement that made all tame ; else why should not an Englishman be able to spend a placid week in one of the first cities of Greece — even a city without inhabitants ? No doubt the excitement of war may be exaggerated — especially in an Eastern campaign, where leisurely, all-day fights tend to degenerate into pleasure - parties. But you do not realise the full value of the excitement of battle till you get a spell of war without it.

Yet, after all, I think that what really bored, what really killed energy and intelligence—killed everything except time—was the dead emptiness of the place. Larissa was a dead city—a city with the skeleton of houses, without the flesh and blood of men and business. It was the curse of this campaign that it was not really war, but a political demonstration. It began as the servant of diplomacy, instead of its master, as war should be; so it went on. Everybody had his eye on the Concert of Europe and the terms of peace. And it was a move in the game that the Greek inhabitants of Larissa should bolt out of it as the Turks approached. It always looks well to be afraid of massacre. As a matter of fact, the move failed utterly: not only was nobody massacred, but hardly anybody was even robbed. Yet Larissa remained dead.

It was not dead now exactly for want of people. There were very many Mussulmans in Larissa, who all remained. Most of the Jews remained, and those who fled mostly came back within a couple of days. Even of the poorer Greeks many returned, not being able to afford the luxury of fictitious martyrdom. I rode out to the battle of Velestino in company with a young Greek, who was going to Volo to fetch home his mother; only as he could not ride head down through the battle he had to return disconsolate. Even on the second day of the occupation I found a typical Greek patriot. My guide — a Jew — unearthed him from a blank-looking house with a high wall and a locked gate. He unlocked the gate and leaned in the gateway to talk,—a young man with hair like a new clothes-brush, and a beard like an old tooth-brush, dressed in a shirt, trousers, and slippers, smiling a smile of mingled self-gratulation and nervousness. He had been to a village two hours to the south, but hearing that the Turks did nothing to anybody he had come back again. He swore he had not been a soldier, but from his age I inferred that he had; I drew the same conclusion from his condemnation of the Greek officers.

"They are no use except to drink mastik and talk big words in the cafés," he said; "but the soldiers are brave."

About the officers he may have been right. But considering how the roads out of Larissa were littered with arms, ammunition, and accoutrements—considering also himself—I rather doubted him about the soldiers. After all there is no getting away from that panic, and if anybody still says the Greeks fought well after the first day, let him try to imagine the Turks smitten with the like terror.

But even the fight at Velestino and Greek deserters did not suffice to make Larissa exciting. For the rest there was nothing to do but look at the soldiers. The uniforms which the Greeks left about had come in very handy for the Turks. Not the very least in the world did they care whose uniform it was, or whether it fitted, or how it looked; so long as it held together and they could get it on it did well enough. One dark-green uniform appeared to be especially popular; I don't know in the least what it was, and no more did the present owners of it, but infantry, cavalry, and artillery now wore it quite impartially.

For a few days Larissa accordingly turned dark green, but later on dark blue and white became the prevailing colours. Huge swarms of Albanian irregulars arrived, and, much as I admired the Albanians, I must own that they were very irregular indeed. More than half of them must have been boys of seventeen or eighteen, smooth-faced, clean-limbed, tireless, agile, and enjoying themselves like a school cricket team going out to play a match. Their dark-blue jackets were mostly new, their white national fezzes—varying in shape from a skull-cap to a Pierrot's hat—unearthly clean. But the older men were irregular indeed. Many were masses of rags, for the Greek uniforms were all snapped up before they arrived. One man wore his bayonet dangling between his legs in front, another sticking horizontally out behind; many carried it always fixed, ready for any sport that might turn up. One day I was riding out as a party of them marched in. They had come through many hours of scorching sun, and they were laden with rifles and cartridges and knap-sacks and overcoats. But they saw some soldiers chasing that unclean and accursed animal, a pig. The double call of religion and sport was too strong. Off they dashed after it in heavy marching order; some headed it off in front, others set off to run it down from behind. Most tried to pig-stick it with bayonets; but many, whether in front or behind, fired frequent snap-shots with the gayest disregard of their comrades on the other side. By some wonder they hit neither the pig, each other, nor me. But it was decidedly more dangerous than the battles of Meluna and Velestino put together.

Still, you can get tired even of Albanian

irregulars. It even became pathetic to see them prowling disconsolately up and down the lines of closed shutters, or poking wistful heads into the dark shops, where they had again begun a tentative trade in bread and milk and tobacco. The Albanians did not come for pay, which they never expected to get; much less out of loyalty to the Sultan, which they never profess. They came for loot, and to loot they were not allowed. Seyfoullah Pasha had been appointed Governor: night and day he was about the streets, on foot or on horseback, but always alert, always athletic, often with a stick, and always with a fist. " It is the only way," he remarked, with a genial brandish. It was; and the malefactor respected him for it. Seyfoullah organised a mixed gendarmery of Mussulmans, Christians, and Jews to help keep order. The day it began operations I saw a hubbub at the street corner and Seyfoullah with his sword drawn. I rushed out and found that a Christian guardian of law had been detected by the Governor himself in the attempt to take up a fellow-Christian's bed and walk. It was not the best testimonial to the mixed gendarmery system, but Seyfoullah was most soundly thrashing the mixed gendarme. Yet even among the police and the irregulars malefactors were almost lamentably rare.

After all, a city wants citizens to make it live. A city peopled only by soldiers and those who cater for them is not a city. It is the shell of civilisation, with primitive barbarism inside it. Armies and war are the negation of all the complexities of civilisation — of complex commerce, of complex enjoyments, of complex annoyances, of complex social relations. You buy your food; you enjoy it; you are tired or wounded; you obey your officer. War is all simple, and a city is not the place for it. It is a country sport, and in town it is out of place and tiresome.

On May 4th, thank heaven, a thunderstorm came on; that at least was a change from the sun. And to-morrow we were going out into the country again to attack Pharsala. No more empty streets and blind, deaf houses. But when would to-morrow come?

Of course the unexpected always happens; to-morrow came to-morrow. At five o'clock on the morning of Wednesday, May 5th, our sentinels, whom we always kept all night at the head-quarters gate, rushed in to say that the Mushir Pasha was starting for Pharsala.

XXII.

THE BATTLE OF PHARSALA.

IT may as well be owned at this point that the war, as a war, had not hitherto been a success. In the general view war is neither a science nor an art, nor yet a resource of diplomacy, so much as a contrivance for killing men on the largest scale that men have yet devised. Looked at in this light, the war failed for two reasons: first, the reluctance of the Greeks, who would not stand up to be killed; and, secondly, the evil fate, whether it were bad luck or bad management, which beset the designs of the Turks to kill them. Again and again the plans of Edhem Pasha, which anybody must admit to be conceived in the best spirit of generalship, just failed of full execution. Again and again he was just on the point of annihilating the Greeks —when the Greeks had run away. Sometimes they ran clean away; sometimes they ran away

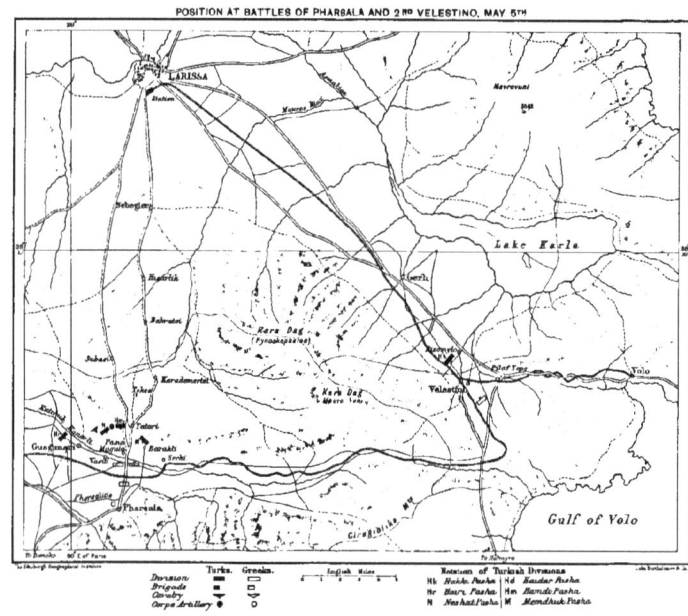

POSITION AT BATTLES OF PHARSALA AND 2ᴺᴰ VELESTINO, MAY 5ᵀᴴ

after a pretence at a fight just before the real fight was going to begin. Of the first branch of their tactics Mati is a good example; of the second both Pharsala and Domoko. Both were most enjoyable battles—battles at which it was possible to understand the plan and watch its developments; both furnished bits of very fine fighting. But both left off just when the real killing of Greeks was about to begin.

Pharsala was beyond question the most interesting battle we had yet had—would have been, that is, if it had been a battle at all. The force was large, the position open, and the combinations interesting. But as a matter of fact Pharsala, which began as a Gravelotte and was meant to develop into a Sedan, ended as a rear-guard engagement on a large scale to cover a retreat. The Greeks came out to fight, and they had to fight to get back. Therein consisted the battle.

The town—it is no more than a big village, but as the other villages near are all little ones, let it pass for a town—is huddled at the very foot of the broad band of mountains which kilts Southern Thessaly: it goes there by the name of Kasiardiari, but is really an outcrop of Mount Othrys. In front of it is the Volo-Trikkala railway; in front of that the half dried-up river, Kutchuk Kanarli; in front of that a broad belt, studded with villages,

—four miles or so of upward sloping ground; in front of that a long row of low hills; and in front of that again the rolling miles of the plain of Thessaly. That was the Greek position, and an army that was set on fighting might have searched half Europe for a better. The range of low hills offered unnumbered positions for artillery; it had to be attacked up a long incline absolutely naked of cover; there was plenty of room to make the very uttermost of all the force they had, and good artillery with good infantry behind it would have stood against ten times their number at least until they had done slaughter that would bid most armies pause. Good judges told me again and again that it was a position which would have cost the Turkish army at least five thousand men.

The Greeks abandoned it. They seem to abandon everything. The battle was not timed for the day it happened, but that seems little enough excuse. The Greeks had been there for a fortnight. They were no doubt inferior in numbers. On the showing of correspondents on their own side, they had—allowing amply for reinforcements sent to Velestino—25,000 men and 50 guns to about 40,000 Turks. But even that they might have known beforehand. They knew presumably that they would be outnumbered when they took up their position, and the position was good enough to go far to redeem the balance. Still they abandoned it, and from that moment the battle degenerated into a rear-guard engagement to cover the habitual retreat. Velestino had not stiffened them much after all.

On our left was the division of Memdhuk Pasha, in the centre those of Hamdi and Neshat Pasha, on the right, coming down from Trikkala, along the line of the railway, was Hairi Pasha, of whom more later. Memdhuk, Hamdi, and Neshat had been advancing southward in a slow and intermittent fashion during the fortnight since the taking of Larissa. There are two roads—or cart-tracks—to Pharsala from Larissa over the endless corn-waves, each one exactly like the last, that make the plain of Thessaly. The westermost, which was said to be the shortest, though there is very little in it either way, passes through no village till it reaches Subasi, nearly fifteen miles out of Larissa; I always preferred the other, as the villages of Nebegler, Hisarlik, Bakratsi, and Karademirtsi punctuate at nearly equal intervals the tedious five-and-twenty miles, and encourage you with the knowledge that you really are getting forward. You begin to ascend the line of low hills which was the Greek first position about Subasi and Karademitsi, on either side respectively, distant from Pharsala some eight to ten miles; at Tatari, five miles north of the town, where the two roads join, you are over the ridge and down on the plain of Pharsala. Memdhuk was on the eastern road, and by this road Edhem followed him and I followed Edhem; Hamdi and Neshat were on the western. Edhem only contemplated a reconnaissance in force for the 5th; simultaneous attacks on Pharsala and Velestino were to follow on the 6th. The Greeks, however, were in line at daybreak. They had two brigades in the first line with two half brigades in support; a brigade was supposed to number 8000 men, so that it was nearly equivalent to a Turkish division.

The battle may be divided into three parts— the reconnaissance, the retreat, and the fight. Finding Greeks on the crest of the ridge, Edhem sent his advanced-guard against them, with a view presumably to occupying it as an admirable position for his artillery in the morrow's engagement. I fancy that nobody quite knew—except, of course, Seyfoullah, who knew every tree and stone, and could have walked to Athens blindfold—that the army was almost tumbling on to the top of Pharsala. Later I pointed the place out to Memdhuk Pasha when he was over the ridge and in full view of it, and asked him its name : he had not the least idea. As the Turks advanced the Greek artillery opened about nine in the morning and the fire was returned. Then followed the usual artillery duel—bang, puff, and a bursting shell from our side; puff, bang, and a bursting shell from theirs. The Greek practice was the best they had yet made—probably they had measured off the ranges beforehand; but even so, it could afford to be better than usual and yet not do very much harm. The Turkish was not so good as usual; but even so it was good enough, or else some unexplained cause was good enough to persuade the Greeks to retire.

Retire at least they did, after about two hours cannonade, and the second phase of the fight began. By this time Memdhuk and his Albanians—advancing to the left of the Eastern road past the hill of Tekes—had got well into touch with their right wing and were beginning to outflank it. The artillery of the two central divisions with the corps artillery was advancing on to and over the heights. Memdhuk may not be much of a scientific soldier, but he is a fighter, and it was impossible to keep him back; plainly now the battle must be fought to-day or not at all.

The Greeks, on their right at least, retired very well: I learned afterwards that the rear-guard— as usual in moments of retreat—was the Foreign

P

Legion. It was good to see the way the little turbaned, grey-bearded, pot-bellied hero, Memdhuk,
hammered into them as they withdrew past
Tatari towards the bridge over the river and the
railway station. He pushed forward battery
after battery to the edge of the hills, and sent
battalion after battalion down into the plain.
The shells seemed to burst right into the firing
figures lined up across the brown fallows on
either side the road. As the columns of infantry
crested the ridge and saw the enemy they broke
into a run and whooped like bank-holiday
makers; as they went down they spread steadily
into line and went on firing steadily as if there
were no stubbornly-firing enemy at all. I saw
three, who had gone on faster than their comrades, standing coolly upright on the road and
answering the fire of the whole Legion. None
the less the Foreign Legion fired stubbornly and
retired swiftly, but without ever breaking into
a run. The smoke of their fire wafted backwards
over the fired, and ours wafted forwards. But
they got back over the river, and they did not
lose many men.

I had read of retreats over bridges, and I
expected horrible slaughter. But the truth was
that the river was easily fordable at almost every
point, and the Greek centre and left walked over

it easily enough : the Foreign Legion retired over
the bridge only because it covered the railway
station and the direct road into Pharsala. The
Greeks, it seemed, had made a hideous blunder—
supposing they wished to win the battle, which
apparently they did not—in leaving their open
position. They were now narrowing into a
semicircle, whose arc passed through the villages
of Pasia Megula, north of the Kutchuk Kanarli,
near the bridge, and Vasili south of the river.
These they still held and must hold if they were
to get away to Domoko. For behind Pharsala
ran a wall of grey mountains, and the guns could
not pass over it. The main road of retreat to
Domoko was by their left.

So now began the third stage of the battle—
the fight. Memdhuk now went down to the
centre to confer with Edhem, and I went with
him. On the way we passed an Albanian—a
boy of about seventeen—who had been hit in the
foot. He was standing on one leg just inside the
zone of fire, and appeared to be pointing out to a
boy of twenty—his brother, Charlie said—that it
was not worth while going back for a little thing
like that. His brother solved the question by
taking him on his back and carrying him away.
When we got to the Marshal we could see that
the enemy was being swept back across all the

plain. It remained for the Turks to pummel the Greeks as they cramped themselves up round Pharsala; it remained for them to hold back the Turks as they could, so as to get away the guns and decamp under cover of night into the mountains. It was a race between night and victory, and night won. But here comes the stroke of bad luck—or bad management. Hairi Pasha's division on the extreme right was to have worked round behind Pharsala, on to the Domoko road. That road skirts the mountains all the way on its left; about a mile out of Pharsala mountains rise upon its right also. But three or four miles on the right mountains sink again: they are a kind of island in the plain, and it is perfectly easy to march past them from the north and come down on the road ten miles or so from Domoko. Had Hairi done this, night would not have saved the Greeks; they were surrounded, annihilated. Hairi in the first place was late; true he had had a thirty-mile march from Kardista. And, in the second place, he missed his direction, and so he appeared towards nightfall on the Greek left front instead of their left rear. And that for them made all the difference between retreat and annihilation.

It was a battle that just failed. Yet all the same, before it failed there was one very fine bit of fighting which it was worth coming all the way from England to see. By this time Memdhuk had worked round to Barakli and Sechi; Hamdi had closed in on the arc of the semicircle; Neshat was a little further out. The artillery of the whole army had advanced till the Greeks were the centre of a ring of batteries, all belching shell into the villages and the railway station and the plain beyond, whence the Greek gunners sent a half-hearted reply. Pasia Megula was shelled and fusiladed and taken about four in the afternoon. But in the centre of the Greek position, just across the river and blocking our central advance on Pharsala, was a little village called Vasili. That village the Greeks were defending and the Turks were attacking. I rode carefully all round it the next day—I remember there was a big house flaming in the middle of it which must have been full of cartridges: they went off like crackers — and it was an awful village to attack. You approached it over half a mile of ploughed field, and as infantry laboured through it they might have been shot down as wheat goes down under the reaping-machine. Arrived at the end of that the storming-party had to get down a six-foot bank into the river, which here was nearly waist-deep and twenty yards across. Then there was a ten-foot bank to scramble up, and then the village, embanked everywhere, trenched everywhere, loopholed everywhere. It was a place that in anything but a toy war would have murdered regiments. Yet the Turks went at it not only without flinching back, but, more difficult still, without hurrying forward. Probably they did not guess how strong it was; but, on the other hand, they might have guessed it to be even stronger. Anyhow, they heard the bullets cracking past like whips, and the shells screaming like mad horses; they saw their comrades fling wild arms abroad and lurch forward on to their faces. Yet these indomitable men never once moved out of their steady slouch. "Allah! Allah! Allah!" they cried, with a fierce but very self-contained enthusiasm, as they tramped first through deep corn and then out over the bare plough. "Allah! Allah! Allah!" the sound swelling and mingling to a hoarse roar as they lined out into open order and began firing quickly, but not hurriedly. "Allah! Allah! Allah!" as the jets of fire ran more clearly round the village, and men went down beside them, and the bullets kicked up little dust-devils between their legs.

And Allah saw them through. The Greeks bolted. I doubt if they lost even a man, for the Turks looked to shoot very high. But they saw their masters coming, and they went to kennel. They could not stand there and face those slip-shod heroes shambling composedly forward past death to victory.

They took the village as darkness settled down from the western mountains. By this time the shells had cleared the railway station also, and our skirmishers were over the river. When the dawn came Pharsala was empty, and we went in. The battle of Pharsala was a very important action, though comparatively a bloodless one. Our loss was possibly 200; the Greeks owned to the same, but probably lost more; we took four guns and 50 prisoners. But after this action the Greeks could not hold Velestino, outflanked on their left, and Velestino lost meant Volo lost. The Greeks were still in line through Halmyro and Domoko; but they had lost the strategic advantage of the railway from wing to wing. Yet that was all nothing. The real battle of Pharsala was those squat, heavy, dirty, sloppy, ragged-bearded, Allah-inspired invincibles strolling upon Vasili.

XXIII.

THE COMEDY OF VOLO.

" By the Lord, there's the British flag ! " And by the Lord there it was—the glorious, imperturbable, confident Union Jack waving opposite the booking-office of Velestino railway station in the very middle of the Turkish army.

It was four in the morning ; we were looking for water to make tea. But the three Englishmen present—and also, please observe, a free but most fraternal citizen of the United States—got up and rushed at the flag. And there holding it was a white-ducked, clean-faced, clear-skinned, straight-eyed bluejacket of twenty. There were some other men there, and some other flags, but I stood for a little space to cool my eyes with the bluejacket. How good he looked ! How honest and steady and trim and fearless, and what dumpy ruffians the dear, fearless, good-natured, dishevelled Turks looked by the side of him. I was almost relieved; I had not turned into a Turk after all.

But what was it all about? Had England annexed Greece, or had the Powers intervened to stop the war, or what? It soon came out. A deputation of the British and French Consuls, with several British and American correspondents, had come to tell us that Volo was evacuated and at our mercy, and to beg us not to hurt the peaceable inhabitants. We knew the fact, and the request was a good deal of an impertinence. But, of course, they didn't know that, poor dears; their minds were stuffed with Greek stories of Turkish ferocity, and their nerves were jumpy with recollections of a fortnight's panic. They never stopped to ask themselves whether any sane man, to put it no higher, would massacre the shopkeepers of Volo within sight of warships from half Europe.

I ought to tell you, meantime, what had been happening since Pharsala. Pharsala was fought on the 5th of May, and this was the morning of the 8th. On the 6th, according to Turkish etiquette after victory, nothing was done; on the 7th we rode to Velestino. Just as we were starting in the morning came news that Hakki had forced back Smolenski from Velestino, and was on the road to Volo. There had been skirmishing nearly every day in front of this position, but the main action appears to have been on the 5th. As the battle of Pharsala was going on the same day, I could not be also at Velestino : I was lucky in that this was the only considerable engagement of the war I missed. For the sake of the connected story, I take what seem to be the main outlines of the fighting from the reports of correspondents with the Greeks ; there was no correspondent on the 5th with Hakki.

The fighting appears to have opened at half-past six in the morning. The attack, as in the first action, was chiefly directed against the Greek left : on the other wing Laka Karla prevented any turning movement, and the steep and lofty Pilaf Tepe had to be attacked, if at all, in front. About eleven o'clock the Turks began to gain ground on the spurs of the Kara Dagh : the Greeks opened on them with a mountain battery, but it was silenced by Turkish shrapnel. About noon the Greeks began to retreat, but Hakki did not follow his advantage—either because he did not know of it or on general Turkish grounds. By two the Greeks had left all their trenches, and were in full retreat. Their left was turned, and their retreat in danger of being cut along the railway from Pharsala. Colonel Smolenski therefore evacuated Velestino on the afternoon

of the 5th. He fired a few shots at the Turkish
advanced-guard on the morning of the 6th, and
in the afternoon retreated, apparently in good
order, towards Halmyro, which he reached next
morning. Edhem had sent off Memdhuk's division
from Pharsala to reinforce Hakki on the night of
the 6th ; it arrived next afternoon, but the fighting was over. Edhem himself, with the Headquarters Staff, arrived towards evening the same
day. So did I—little dreaming of the intoxicating eminence that awaited me on the morrow.

It was highly informal, no doubt, for Consuls
and journalists to come out waving flags of truce
and ensigns of the Powers and negotiate for the
surrender of the second port in Greece. It was
also, as I have suggested, something of an impertinence. But the Turks were the last people on
earth to object to anything on the score of informality, and as they are not always on the look-
out for offence, are the last people to take it.
Informal or not, let it be put on record that
British journalists came out to save Greeks when
the Greek army had left them to their fate, and
the Greek mayor and corporation stayed dither-
ing at home.

However, it was not so bad as that. Captain
Nedjib Bey was sent off with a proclamation
assuring peace to the peaceable and evil to the

evildoer. I galloped out after him : if war-cor-
respondents were to be elevated into high con-
tracting parties, why not even I with the rest ?
In fact Nedjib welcomed my two friends and me
most eagerly, and took no single step in the
capitulation without consulting us. It is a shame
to be looking always on the weakest side of
human nature; but it did occur to me that this
was Nedjib's richest day in the whole war, and
that he looked to us to immortalise it. But what
of that ? Was that any reason for not taking a
hand in the surrender when it was offered ? It
would be rather a fine thing to negotiate a
capitulation between two correspondents of the
'Daily Mail.' True, it was not exactly a capitulation, since the town was not militarily occupied.
But there was still one military, or naval, element
left. The Greek fleet, true to the last to the
national tradition, was not going to be left out
when there was any talking to be done. It appeared that there lay in Volo harbour a battleship—the *Psara*, flagship of Admiral Something-
opoulos or Tweedledouris or another—two sloops,
and an armed transport. What were they going
to do ? They might shell us as we went in,
and we could do nothing. On the other hand,
that would surely justify us in reprisals in the
way of smashing up public buildings, and other

things that the Greeks would hardly like. The
question altogether was a queer one. Did Volo
surrender, or did it not? If it did, the Greek
ships could do nothing. If it did not, we were
justified in shelling defenceless citizens. What
would the Greek fleet do?

But the question solved itself like all the other
questions of this wonderful war. We strolled on,
and the Greeks went away. The Consuls had
gone on ahead, feeling that the Greek fleet, which
at the moment had not gone away as it was told
to, might cut up nasty. We went in steadily—
the flags of the Great Powers in an aureole round
the fez of the Sultan's aide-de-camp, and three
correspondents, two Albanian cavasses, and a
stray cavalry trooper, who had come to see the
fun, riding behind like the general, and staff, and
army. That was the invading army—an officer,
a man, and five Bashi-Bazouks. It was the most
ridiculous and yet the most sublime thing in the
world. For absurd as we were, we carried with
us the life or death of a town. And as we drew
near to it this became very clear. The outskirts
of Volo are obscure, and as you ride in there are
gasworks on the right-hand side, but beyond this
I am bound to own I noticed Volo very little.
I was looking at the people. For as we got into
the town we passed through lanes of them—

shaggy, dirty, dumpy people, banked up on the
roadsides, with obsequiousness in their mien and
terror in their faces. There was no doubt about
it—the people of Volo were most horribly afraid.
I don't know what tales they had been told, but
I am pretty sure they would have left if they
could. Only they were at the end of their tether,
in a corner of their country, and they had to wait
there for their fate.

So we went on towards the centre of the town
—always the same grotesque mixture, with five-
sevenths of the invading army made up of correspondents and their servants. As we got towards
the central streets the populace seemed reassured ;
we had not massacred anybody so far, and they
began to think they had a chance. They still
took off their hats most obediently. Many had
bought fezzes for the occasion, and I saw one so
uninstructed in the use of that symbol of victory
as to take it off, which the Turk never does, indoors or out. Women appeared presently on the
balconies with smirks of welcome. The substantial
inhabitants began to meet us—that is to say, the
inhabitants not quite substantial enough to command a passage to Athens. They also smirked
uneasily.

As we passed each group of kow-tow it fell in
behind us till we were the head of a procession

half a mile long. It looked like a great festival. But except the invading seven I don't think anybody quite enjoyed it except the boys. They trooped in and scuttled on with a will—brush-haired, smug-faced little ragamuffins with no school open to-day. Through war and panic, bloodshed and ruin, the boy, thank God, remains the boy. The pity was that they could only grow up into Greeks after all.

And so, the centre of a scraping, quaking city, we arrived at the town-hall. We jumped down carelessly off our horses, and flung the reins into crowds that competed for the honour of holding them. Then up into the council-chamber, or whatever they call it. Who cared what conquered Greeks call it? There was a crowd of jabbering Greeks inside; we pushed them out of the way. Who cared what conquered Greeks had to say?

"Is the Mayor here?" Not he. "Where is the representative of the Mayor?" Not here. "Where—is—the—representative—of—the—Mayor?" Now they comprehended that there had to be a representative of the Mayor. "You." "No, you." At last they produced a bald-headed, grey-bearded, quaking little man, and he trembled up to the table. "Listen to this: 'The town of Volo is now under the humane and puissant pro-

tection of his Imperial Majesty the Sultan Abdul
Hamid II.'" And so on. "Does the town submit?" The town submits. "Then sign your
name there." Then the bald-heads began to wag
again. "You sign." "No, you." At last they
produced a man to sign. I don't know who he
was, and I'm sure nobody cared.

Now on to the balcony. Here is a grey-bearded
elder; no doubt he is a leading citizen. "Do
you understand French? Very well; then translate this aloud to the people. 'The town of Volo
is now———'" and so on. I looked down arrogantly
at the people as he translated. "Louder," said
I, as if I were the governor of the town, and
obediently he raised his voice. The people looked
up timorously; there were only a thousand of
them, and there were four fezzes on the balcony,
with two and a trooper's sheepskin cap in reserve
in the refreshment-room. But as they listened
their cowed faces lightened. They were spared;
they lived again. And then a Greek on the
balcony called for three cheers for the Sultan.
How they rang! All the Greeks who called him
a monster at dawn that morning emptied their
lungs with a relish. Faugh! All the same, I
suppose conquered townsmen have their feelings,
and it is a relief to hear that you are to be neither
robbed nor killed. But you can't expect the

conquerors to think much of that. To us it appeared just despicable sycophancy.

And then a shuffling rattle down the street, and in came the Turks. They had not waited to hear whether the town capitulated,—why should they? The Greek admiral had tried to bluff it out, but already his smoke was trailing behind him. And in came the Turks. One battalion only—but what a battalion! Dusty, ragged, probably hungry, they strode in with shuffling strides, but very long ones, looking neither to left nor to right, desiring no pillage nor ravishment, doing what their officers told them. They had marched through Thessaly at the word of command; at the word of command they would march through the fires of hell as long as there was a man who could step. Were they elated, triumphant, arrogant, intoxicated, like us? Dear, no! They just shambled in as always. They had conquered, but what of that? How should they do else than conquer?

Q

XXIV.

ON THE ART OF CAMPAIGNING.

It is a noteworthy phenomenon of war that time goes with it about a dozen times as slowly as anywhere else. Perhaps it would be more correct to say that there is a dozen times as much time packed into it. Pharsala and Volo gave such crowded, glorious hours. But Pharsala was now a week old and Volo two days, and Volo had dwindled a generation back and Pharsala a century. There had been nothing since of interest to the world. But there had been a vast deal of interest to me.

In war, when no arrangements hold, when all rules of life are cancelled, and all institutions of society hung up in abeyance, when you come down to the very bed-rock and bottom of things, and all the little, contemptible, convenient arrangements called civilisation suddenly vanish clean away, and leave you to depend for your bare necessities upon your bare naked self—in short, when it comes to this, that if you are hungry you have got to find a sheep and kill it and cook it before you can fill your stomach, and if you are sleepy you have to find something to keep out cold and wet enough to let you sleep, and you don't care in the least whose sheep it is, or whose shelter—why, when it comes to all this, there are events happening once and twice and all day long far more important than scores of battles and captured cities. There had been half a dozen milestones in my life since Pharsala and Volo.

The night after the battle of Pharsala I was too tired to do anything but eat all the food I had and drink all the drink my numerous friends left me. How well I knew them by now! "*Ha, ha, vous avez du vin: quelle chance!*" and up went the full bottle to the dry lips, and down with "*Merci beaucoup, cher ami,*" it came empty. Lucky were you if the emptier was endowed with censorial powers and you could improve the occasion by getting your telegram countersigned. After meat and drink I had just energy left to trudge to the village of Tatari, see the horses into an empty stable, and then lie down and sleep on a solid mud-bank—I learn they are neither less nor more civilised than similar erections in Ashanti—such as the peasantry of this country build outside their hovels.

But then there was the night after that. I had ridden all day over a quarter-county or so of battle-field—for a correspondent, unlike the Turks, cannot do nothing on the morrow of victory—and I was hungry and I had nothing to eat. I must own that I was not quite so much alone with my bed-rock self as I have suggested above. I had Charlie and Aslan, who had just returned from taking a telegram to Larissa, and Georghi. And I must also own that my part in the struggle with the naked forces of nature was rather that of the directing mind than the executing hand.

I called to Charlie and gave him a Medjidieh, value 3s. 2d. " Get a lamb, Charlie," I said with Homeric simplicity. " No got," was Charlie's ready response. " Then get." " Where I get ? No can buy." " Then steal." " Very well, sir," and Charlie mounted the galumphing, flea-bitten, grey baggage-pony which he regarded as the best horse in the Turkish army. He galumphed away with a vague but watchful eye fixed speculatively on the horizon. In half an hour he returned with, not one, but two black lambs slung in front of his saddle. Of one he tied the legs together and left it bleating on the ground ; the other he carried away. " What have you done with it ? " I asked when he came back. " Give him to the servant of the one Pasha," he cried, with a grin of expansive triumph ; " ten piastres backsheesh." In the art of making war support war, and hedging loot therewith, Charlie could learn nothing from Hannibal or Napoleon.

But let us eat. There was no difficulty about the killing, and skinning, and cutting up, and cooking. A podgy, brown-bearded soldier appeared from nowhere, stripped off his coat, and cut off the lamb's head. The little black head still bleated and the little black body still kicked, and it was the most grotesquely pathetic sight, bar the Karya hospital, I had seen in the whole war. Then the soldier made an incision in the skin of one leg, and blew into it till the little black lamb was like a full-grown water-skin. Then he slit up the skin and ripped it off in a wink. " Every man to his trade," he grinned, and went off well satisfied with his work and sixpence. He was a butcher from Angora. That is the blessing of a conscriptive army ; you need never go far for any tradesman you may be pleased to want.

Meanwhile they lit brushwood in a hole, ripped the rafters from a convenient barn,—

the proprietor will miss them if he ever comes back, but what would you? War is war, and soldiers must eat, and even correspondents— and we had a glorious fire. We thrust the ends of the beams into the fire till they got charred, then broke off the charred ends and rammed the beams in again. When there was a good deal of live wood we let the fire out; Aslan slashed up the lamb with his yataghan, and propped the pieces on crooked sticks over the embers; Charlie cut up the liver into little bits, strung them on a string, and roasted them likewise. Aslan preferred the lights, which he dumped down frankly in the ashes. Then we assembled our company in a deserted stable— three English, two Americans, and a German— and established a table out of the broken door. Then with jack-knives and fingers we fell to and ate gloriously. It was burnt outside, and raw inside, very tough and very greasy. But it was glorious, and in the fierce glutting of animal needs the very water—what had become of that last flask of whisky?—for the moment seemed almost sanitary. Then we wrapped ourselves up in our capotes, and went to sleep on fresh-cut rye in the stable till the dawn crept bashfully in through the broken roof. Who said that war is not all glory?

But all evenings are not like that. For example, there was the cold night in Velestino station; no rye there, and nothing but the hard gravel platform to sleep on. There was the night at Volo—a bed to sleep on certainly, but no bed-clothes, and I had had a horse roll over my legs in the afternoon, and the night was a sleepless alternation of sweat and shiver and aches and mosquitoes. There was the next day, going back to Larissa, with a twenty-mile gallop in a Greek springless waggon over a Greek highroad. I sat and lay and stood and knelt, but I could not get away from the agonising jolts without getting out of the carriage. It was the worst hardship of the whole war, but after all that was my own fault. What business had I to let my horse get himself lost—hastily ridden off by the conscientious Georghi, of course, who found it too good an opportunity of a mount that could gallop—while I was lunching?

But the next night was not my fault. Why must his Excellence choose to make his head-quarters on an out-of-the-way hill by a desolate ruined shrine called Tekes? Why, as I followed him, must inky rain-clouds beat up from over Meluna to bring on nightfall an hour too soon, and swallow up the baggage from sight of me and of the headquarters? Why must the clouds immediately thereupon dissolve into streams of dogged rain? Who was to have foreseen a December night in the middle of the dog-day heat of Thessalian May? There was corn fit to cut even now, if there was anybody to cut it; why should winter dip down over it so suddenly?

There was a tent, to be sure. In theory, I own, no man need wish for more than a tent, even when its door will not shut, and its canvas lets in water. I know that thousands of Turkish soldiers spent an uncomplaining night without a tent, many without an overcoat, and some without the egg and bit of cheese, the last cigarette, and liqueur-glass of resinous red wine that I had. In theory the war correspondent wraps his shaggy coat round him and sleeps peacefully. In practice he hasn't got a shaggy coat; at least I hadn't that night—only a waterproof overcoat between myself and a friend, and that had to go on the dank ground. In the old story the Highland chieftain kicked away the lump of snow which his soft son was using for a pillow. In this new story, if anybody had kicked away my revolver, which was my simple cushion, I would have shot him with it. Moreover, the war correspondent of romance never buys a paste-board box of vaseline because the skin is peeling off his nose; and if he did the box would never telescope in his pocket while he was asleep, and let out the vaseline over his long-cold pipe, and his long-stopped watch, and his last two matches. All trifles, of course. Hunger and thirst, cold and wet, dirt and stickiness, pain and sleeplessness—they are none of them any real hardship when you are in fair condition; and by this time I was as lean as Greek mutton, and as hard as soldier's biscuit. But taking hunger, thirst, cold, wet, dirt, stickiness, pain, and sleeplessness all together, they are so near an approach to hardship that they begin to tell on the temper.

When I got up next morning, and there was no great inducement to be abed, the rain had stopped. But a clammy mist was sucking at the wringing ground. There was a half-view over the rolling ridges of Southern Thessaly— for the plain of Thessaly is no more level than Salisbury Plain, or any other plain—and you could see bedraggled horses plucking hopelessly at sun-dried grass, and bedraggled soldiers puffing hopelessly at sodden brushwood. The path up to the little hill had turned to a slide you could have tobogganed down. And as I shivered and stamped the wet out of my boots came the cheering news that nothing

was to be done to-day in the way of war, and
I might just as well have stayed in Larissa.

But, after all, the worse off you are the more
room there is for improvement. The baggage
had turned up in the night — that wonderful
baggage, which never could be persuaded to
arrive anywhere before one o'clock in the morning. The men would waste hours after sunrise,
so as to time their arrival accurately for the
small hours of the morrow. But if the baggage
came late, it always came, and that could be
said of nobody else's. It was almost pathetic to
see the Germans. In hours of ease they were
always giving us little lectures about commissariat,
and explaining how in the German army the
trooper's saddle and the private's knapsack contained everything that man or horse could possibly want, in a weight of I forget how few
kilos. Next morning you would find the German
shivering on a bare hill and devil a kilo about
him. His *verfluchter* dragoman had not turned
up, and he didn't know where his servant was,
and he had mislaid his horse. Meantime he
was sucking at a peppermint-drop : they were
found most effective in the German manœuvres,
he assured you, for keeping out hunger, thirst, and
cold. All the same he accepted an invitation to
breakfast.

For the excellent fellows had annexed a tent belonging to the military attachés and had made a fire in it, and Andreas was cooking breakfast. Andreas could never be persuaded to go into action. Not that he was afraid—had he not seen Kassassin and Tel-el-Kebir?—but war bored him, and he preferred the kitchen-fire. We had tried Dimitri once in action—at Velestino, in the unavoidable absence of Charlie, gone to Elassona to try and cash a cheque and pay up the long-outstanding telegram account—but Dimitri was not a success. Dimitri was the elderly Greek who looked like a divine and spoke French like a raven. His pony came down on the road and Dimitri came over his head. It was the horse's fault, he explained, for he prided himself much on his knowledge of horses: *Moi, z'ai acété beaucoup de cevaux*, he would croak. He rode slowly and miserably, with sticking-plaster on his nose, as far as Rizomylo. And there the first thing he saw was a group of Albanians, of whom he was ever in hideous terror, and a blazing Greek house. That was Dimitri's first sight of war, but it was enough. "*Ze suis malade*," he explained, and we were constrained to send him back with telegrams. He asked for an escort of cavalry, but Mahmud Bey had used up all the superfluous troopers that day, and he had to quake in alone.

However, we were now going south to Domoko —at least we thought so, poor innocents!—and had to have a line of communication between it and the telegraphic base. So Charlie, with a telegram-rider for each man, was to be the advanced guard, and Andreas, with telegram - riders in Pharsala, was to be the point, and Dimitri—so he persuaded himself—was the main body and remount and veterinary officer in Larissa. But meanwhile Andreas was cooking breakfast. They had brought a bucket of water to wash in. Then tea and tinned sausages and a bor-rowed cigarette—what more do you want? How anxious was the Herr Hauptmann not to eat a whole sausage to himself, lest we went short! But when we succeeded in proving that four ones were three, his appetite seemed to sug-gest that even the regulation peppermint-drop left an unfilled space somewhere.

Then the rain soaked in a little and a little sun came out. The come-and-go of the soldiers began to be interesting. A bronze - skinned, smooth - faced boy fired off his rifle — partly because it was the feast of Bairam, partly out of wantonness. His major called him up and rated him a little in Turkish, then slashed him

three times across the face with a riding-whip;
the boy saluted, and was taken down the hill
under arrest. It looked brutal, but it would do
him good: it is boys like that who set fire to
cottages. However, that was not my affair: no
more, for the moment, were the operations—if
any—of to-day and to-morrow. I was happy
again, and could lie down peaceably on a horse-
rug in front of the tent and write down my views
on the art of campaigning.

XXV.

AT TEKES.

MONDAY, Tuesday, Wednesday, Thursday, Friday, Saturday, Sunday—seven mortal days in a tent on a little hill by a ruined shrine in Thessaly. I suppose when the real history of this war comes to be written — assuming that anybody ever thinks he knows enough about it to tackle the task—the grave historian will take the week at Tekes as a matter of course. "After the occupation of Volo it was found necessary to recruit the energies of the troops, and to perfect the transport arrangements: it was not until May 17th, exactly a month after the opening of hostilities, that Edhem once more moved forward." That will be quite enough for the week, unless the grave historian should chance to be a German. In that case he will describe how the reserve division, Haidar Pasha, was moved up from Meluna through Larissa to the front; how a brigade of Nizam, or troops with the colours, from the Second or Adrianople Army Corps, armed with the Mauser rifle, likewise reached the front; how many baggage-animals loaded with what sort of stores started out of Larissa, and where, if anywhere, they arrived,—all that and more he will tell you, and I, for one, shall read it with the greatest interest.

But to the ordinary correspondent, to whom one division is very much like another, and one baggage-animal does not differ in glory from another, the week at Tekes was a little uneventful. The Mauser rifles were something to talk about certainly: the whole camp was full of stories as to how many Greeks one bullet would kill at 2000 yards. But for the rest — you crawled out of your tent in the morning: anything to-day? No; not to-day. To-day it is Bairam; to-day it is raining; to-day we are awaiting reinforcements; to-day we have not got quite all our supplies. Have a little patience: you Europeans are always in a hurry. Wait till the day after to-morrow. It is a bad sign when the Turk abandons to-morrow and seeks refuge in the day after. For if to-morrow never comes, how can you ever possibly win through to the next day?

Of course the young enthusiast following his

first campaign expects a battle every day. Meluna and the following week set a bad precedent,
for we never lacked at least a little pot-shooting
with artillery. Certainly it was unreasonable
to expect general engagements and captured
cities for a whole month on end. Yet when all
that was allowed, it was impossible not to feel
that the Turks were very slow. Was it not their
old fault to throw away victory by sloth? For
we were now, after a month of war, pretty well
where we might have been at the end of the first
week. If we had gone straight forward after
Meluna, if we had harried the Greeks on their
flight from Larissa with cavalry and horse-artillery and flying columns of infantry, they would
never have concentrated at Pharsala, would have
needed no beating there, and we might have been
at Domoko three weeks back instead of hoping to
be there the day after to-morrow. But setting
all that aside, we were doing with Domoko exactly
what we had done with Pharsala. We were giving the Greeks about a week to talk themselves
into self-confidence, to bring up reinforcements,
to throw up entrenchments, to mount guns of
position, to measure off ranges. Of course it may
have been unfair, both here and elsewhere, to
blame Edhem for delay. It was said the Sultan
had given him a free hand; but in Turkey, where

personal government is really personal, and you will do well not to forget it, a free hand is not quite so free as it is in other countries. Free or not, it was noteworthy that Edhem had never yet gone forward faster than the field-telegraph, whose other end was in the Yildiz. But the field-telegraph had been up along the road into Pharsala for nearly a week now—up in the true Turkish fashion, at just the level where an unwary rider might cut his throat on it. It was true, too, though we at Tekes did not know it, that the air was full of proposals for peace; but the Yildiz would consent to no armistice as yet. Why could we not have either peace or war? We might have had three divisions before Domoko on May 6, the morrow of Pharsala, and yet have sent a division to strengthen Hakki on the left wing, and had also a division and a brigade coming up in reserve.

Instead, on May 16, we were at last going to advance to-morrow. To-morrow very early, said the staff-officers reassuringly—as if it were any consolation for a week of idleness to go to your bed in spurs and be hauled off it at two in the morning. We were advancing, of course, on Domoko. What force we might find there, and in what state, we did not know. Less than 30,000, and those deserting fast, said the Greek

R

sergeant—a Volo Jew—who had deserted two
days ago; they had suffered much from the
week's rain, having no tents and next to no
rations. But then it was plainly the deserter's
game—even supposing him not to be a spy, which
was always possible—to magnify the hardships
which had been too much for himself. There
had, indeed, been a tardy reconnaissance three
days back and a little shooting, but we knew
nothing of any information that might have been
gathered. We might find the Greeks in force
at Domoko, fifteen miles south of Pharsala; we
might find only a rear-guard, the main body
holding the Furka Pass, a dozen miles further on.
And when we did find them—who knew? Would
they fight at last? Of course the army hoped so.
But the Crown Prince, we heard, had telegraphed
to Athens that the army was prepared to resist
to the last: that looked bad. Only if the Greeks
did not defend the Othrys line they would never
defend anything at all. There were magnificent
positions, said Seyfoullah—nothing like them between us and Athens. It was Greece's third
chance, and her last.

, We should once more have a vast superiority
in numbers. I gathered the plan to be this.
Hairi's division was to advance by his right front
across the tongue of plain which runs southward

into the Othrys from the line of the Kutchuk Kanarli, and has its extremity at Domoko. He would thus get on to the hills and advance on the left flank of the Greeks by Amarlar, Velisiotæ and Skarmitsa. Neshat, with the newly arrived Mauser brigade from Adrianople added to his division, was to advance in front by the main road along the plain: behind him was the corps artillery, and behind the artillery Haidar's division in reserve. Hamdi's division was to march over the eastward heights by Tsiatma and Gerakli, so as to come in on the right flank of Domoko. The Crown Prince would thus be simultaneously attacked in front and on both flanks by something like 45,000 men. Meanwhile Memdhuk's division advanced wide to the eastward upon the foot of the Furka Pass to cut the Greek retreat. Hakki simultaneously advanced through Halmyro, presumably to get round the Greek extreme right, and, if possible, cut them off from Stylida and Lamia. The plan, no doubt, was Seyfoullah's: he was the only man who knew the country well enough to frame it. But it was Edhem's old strategy—turning and cutting the retreat. The plan was sound enough, only it presupposed intelligence, energy, and resolution on the part of the generals of division who were to put it into execution.

With this force and these dispositions there was no need to feel uneasy about the result. Yet we remembered that war, after all, is not a sum in arithmetic. If we were attacking under 30,000 men with three to two, and more to meet him when the three had done with him, it was only just to Turkish valour to bear in mind that we were attacking. The defensive positions of the Othrys were worth regiments on regiments. The Greek engineers were very good, and they had been allowed plenty of time. Unless the complex scheme of action were timed and worked out to a nicety, the Greeks might put Edhem to loss and trouble even yet.

In the meantime, whatever you might say of his Excellency's energy as a general, there can be no question about his taste in the selection of a camp. His green tent stood on the summit of the hill of Tekes in a circle of nine cypress-trees. Inside the tent was half taken up by the only civilised bed in camp, and the half which was not bed was half table. But outside the sight was glorious. Down the long slopes of the hill and along the ridge to its left the green had been freshened and the tents whitened by the rain until they shone in the sun like diamonds among emeralds. At the elbow of the ridge and the hill was the tomb of two holy Mussulmans—a round grey building also girdled with cypresses, and with many-coloured threads twined round its window-bars, as testimony to the devotion of the faithful. The shrine had gone to rack and ruin ever since Greece took Thessaly. The little caravanserai where pilgrims lodged was half tumbled down; the horses of the General Staff were stabled in its courtyard, and at sundown owls screeched a mournful croon in the crumbling chambers.

But now the holy men of Islam were having their revenge. They must have laughed in their graves to hear the old fanfare at five in the evening, when the soldiers get their bread and the hills ring with cheers for the Padishah. They must have joined keenly in the wailing lilt of the Albanian songs at sundown. Even the gun-horses plucking at their pickets among their supper of chopped straw, and neighing through the night when the rest of us wished to sleep, must have been pleasant music to those holy men. If they could only have risen up with us in the morning and seen the sheen of dawn over the green plain, on the grey houses of Pharsala, and over the checkered light-and-shade of the mauve mountains! Right and left, on the plain and before the town and on the mountains, gleamed acres of white tents—all full of conquering Turks.

They would be straggling out of the tents now
at sunrise, serene in their shabby middle - aged
confidence of victory, chopping wood for fires,
drawing water from the springs to soak their dry
biscuit, weaving branches into little round bowers
to shield them from the midday sun. There is
nothing like the lazy industry of the Turkish
soldier : he never hurries, but war has yet to
invent the task that will find him wanting.
There was only one thing that might be too
much for him—that beautiful, diaphanous, soft-
shining belt of mist stretched over the plain.
That was the fever of Thessaly squeezing itself
out into the morning. Perhaps it was as well
that we were to strike camp and be moving
again.

So we rode down to Pharsala on the evening
of May 16, and established our depot there in a
house we found empty. Next morning we rode
out and overtook the first brigade of the central
advance ; then rode on into the narrowing plain
and sat down to see the battle of Domoko.

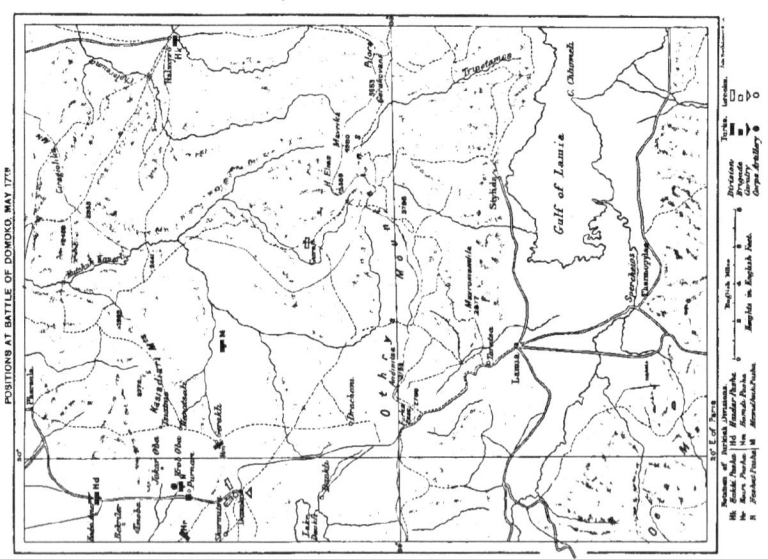

POSITIONS AT BATTLE OF DOMOKO, MAY 17th

XXVI.

MAUSER RIFLES.

A BAND! I had an idea that bands never went into action nowadays, but this was unquestionably a band. Rather a good band, too—not the barbaric clash and blare of the usual Turkish music, but something with a melody as well as a rhythm! As I marvelled it swung round the little hill where I sat—sure enough a real complete military band. And behind it, striding out, erect, elastic, almost supernaturally un-Turk, came the brigade from Adrianople. All young men, for they were of the Nizam, or regular army, whereas nearly all the regiments in action hitherto have been of the Redif. All had white canvas knapsacks; all the fezzes were in shape; all the rifles were Mauser repeaters, not Martinis, and all were sloped at the same angle; all the uniforms were uniform, clean, well-fitting; all the men kept step, long and brisk. The army corps of Adrianople is the pick of the Turkish army. It was a revelation after the sloppy, ragged-bearded Redifs. Here were battalions both Turk and un-Turk—Turk in the solid, dogged resolution of their advance, un-Turk in the spick-and-span smartness of their gear, in the springing, swinging smartness of their gait. With the music swelling and dwindling at their head, and the dancing rifles swaying up and down with it along the column, quivering with the expectancy of their first battle, the young men strode along the dusty road towards Domoko.

It was the last Greek stronghold this side of the old frontier—by nature the strongest hold of all, and by circumstances that which they were like to hold most strongly. I am no expert in military positions, but I should doubt if there could be found a stronger in the whole world. Domoko stands at the head of a pass which climbs from the Thessalian plain on to a little tableland, which is really one of the mountains of Othrys. We could see the town miles above us, as it seemed—broad, flat, white houses, one storey with a door for the stables below, one storey with many windows for the living rooms above — hanging in the air, clinging round a sugar-loaf peak, with a flat, battlemented, medi-eval-Venetian fortress like a diadem on the top.

From the fortress and from a peak above, behind
and to the left of the town, thundered two big
fortress guns, five or six inches apiece. From
positions right and left of the winding road,
which zigzags up the cleft between two mountain
masses, thundered the guns of four field-batteries.
On the lowest slopes, across the road and to right
and left of it, bending forward so as to converge
a fire on any front advance, ran the dim, grey-
yellow streaks which I had learned to know for
entrenchments, held by infantry. Against all
this—against six times their force, against a
sheer two thousand feet of death — marched
buoyantly the Mauser rifles.

It was a hideous bungle from start to finish.
To attack such a place in front was staring madness, as Edhem saw quite clearly. But to attack
it he had five divisions and a brigade. Of course
it was necessary to deliver a feint in front to
keep the Greeks to their guns and their trenches,
and the Mauser rifles, with a division of Redif
behind them, were there to do it. But who could
have ever thought that on seven battalions out
of seventy would be laid the burden of fighting
the whole battle ? The plan, if you remember,
was this. Haidar Pasha's division was in reserve.
The division of Neshat Pasha, with the Adrianople brigade—which was, in fact, only seven bat-

talions—took the main front road along the valley
to the foot of the ascent to Domoko. Hairi was
to march along the hills on our right, and Hamdi
on the left; thus the position would be turned
on both sides. Meanwhile Memdhuk was to pass
right by Domoko, and occupy the Furka Pass
behind it. It was one more attempt to surround
the Greek army—to destroy or capture it. And
once more the attempt failed.

Hairi Pasha was the first to appear. At eleven
o'clock the head of his advance-guard came into
view of the little eminence where I sat and
watched between the two armies. First a group
of loose skirmishers; then, after an interval, a
little group of men—the point; then the solid
mass of the main body of the advance-guard;
then the connecting-link with the main body;
then, with no more interval, but steadily blackening the plain, trooping on, till they seemed to
swallow it up in their multitude, came the masses
of Hairi's infantry and the long trails of Hairi's
guns. But Hairi—first blunder—was marching
in the plain in such a line that he must either
clog Neshat at the bottom of the pass, or get up
into the mountains in face of the Greek left.
And Hairi—second blunder—did not start till
six in the morning, so that the Greeks could
watch every step of his advance, and his men

had to fight after five hours' march under the sun. Neshat started about the same time and came into action a couple of hours later. Memdhuk himself only started in earnest—he was posted forward on the left and some say he broke camp earlier, but what matter?—at four in the morning and Hamdi at five, though he too had to make a long circuit over a perpetual seesaw of rugged hills. A night-march would have brought the troops into action fresh, and after all they could not have missed their times and their directions much worse in the dark than they did in the day. But there was no night-march; divisions arrived, not together, but dropping in one after another. And for the third, and blackest blunder of all—but that presently.

Hairi found the enemy at eleven. We could see the Greek cavalry cantering about in the village of Tsioba, but his skirmishers could not. They crawled on—when would they be fired on? On and on, till they looked to be shambling on to certain death. Then the half-dozen horsemen between us and the village galloped violently back, making signals. Surely the skirmishers would see them. No; they shambled on. Then suddenly the white smoke shot out from behind a hedge in front of the huddle of red roofs. Half the squadron had dismounted, and were using their carbines; the other half were already mustering for retreat in a court at the back of the village. But even when the fire came—even then the skirmishers did not seem to notice. They only spread out a little to left of the village, and shambled on. Crack, crack, crackle —the troopers were putting it in very briskly, but not one of the twenty-odd shambling figures either went down or stopped. Then the smoke drifted lazily away, more figures dashed into the court behind Tsioba, and then the whole group streamed out in mad gallop across the plain. Then, when we could see that the village was empty, the twenty-odd raised their rifles, and began to fire. Still firing they shambled into the village, and they shambled out of it the other side. The division, which had halted, crawled on again, crawled through Tsioba, crawled on an hour across the plain. There it came to the foot of the hills, and there again it met with a feeble fire. And there it stayed.

There it stayed. Hairi was ordered to advance, but there was a battalion or so in front of his sixteen; he said he would lose too many men, and there he stayed. Neshat Pasha also was ordered to advance with his twenty-three battalions, of which the men from Adrianople were the leading brigade. He had come up with his staff to the rocky slope where I sat. The brave old man was in boisterously high spirits, as always in action; he laughed and clapped his hands like a boy when the advance-guard flushed a hare. But he seemed to have no idea at all of the part he was expected to take in the battle. When the order came to advance, he did not like it. Already he had got his men huddled up in the road in front of the Greek guns, till a shell or two, well planted, hurried them at the double under the shelter of a huge granite wedge that cropped up out of the plain. There they had waited, about a mile or over from the enemy, while Neshat tardily sent a couple of batteries forward to his left on the open plain and attempted a fire against batteries behind earthworks, hundreds of feet above. But now, at half-past three, Neshat was ordered to advance, and what wonder if he did not like it? Hairi was standing still, his battalions black and motionless upon the plain. He had brought one battery into action, which kept up a lazy fire, more by way of requesting the Greeks to let the division pass than of driving them before it. Now he could hardly make himself felt before dark. We had heard a little intermittent firing on the left, which must be Hamdi; from its position, and from the rugged way he had to come, it was pretty clear that he, too, could not get at the enemy before dark. Neshat had sent the second of his three brigades up towards the hills on his left, presumably with a vague idea of supplementing Hamdi's flank attack, or of replacing it with one of his own. But this had already halted, and even it could not conceivably make itself felt for an hour or more. Some one had blundered; every one had blundered. And about half-past four or five, to retrieve the blunders, to make one attempt to get something done before nightfall, against that terrible tier of entrenched fire they slammed in the Mauser rifles.

They brought up all their available guns to help the boys in their desperate venture. As the carriages of the corps artillery clattered and roared along the road, I galloped beside them, and scrambled up on to the granite hill just as the brigade was deploying from behind it. They trooped out into the tall corn-fields in an order which showed that, with all their smartness, they had been taught little enough of the methods of war. They trooped out like draughts-men on a draught-board. In this loose order the rear ranks must needs shoot the front ranks, while no possible volley could be fired to terrify an enemy they could hardly hope to hit. As

they moved confidently forward under their first
fire, a shell, with an angry, spiteful "phutt,"
burst in the middle of a clump of them not yet
deployed. All went down; half stayed down,
but the other half sprang to their feet again,
shook themselves, and moved confidently forward
again. More shells fell among them; more little,
dark, motionless blots drilled holes in the green
wheat-field. But always they moved on.

And now began the most furious fight of all
the war. Ten batteries to right and left of our
little hill hammered away at the Greek guns.
The Greek guns sometimes whizzed a shell over
our rock and sometimes dropped one into the
gun-horses to left and right of it. But in the
main they relentlessly hammered away at the
men from Adrianople. They went on. One of
our guns blew up a Greek limber full of shell;
there was a geyser of flame, then a geyser of
grey smoke, spreading very slowly out into a
mushroom. But the other batteries still peppered
the men from Adrianople, and the men from
Adrianople still went on. They came up to a
thousand yards of the entrenchments, and curling
blue lines of smoke showed that their skirmishers
had opened fire—opened fire against three-foot
banks of earth. And then there burst from the
Greek lines a hellish storm. Savage volleys

snarled along the trenches in front and left and right. They came so fast that you would have said it was the Greeks who had repeating Mausers, instead of our dotted brigade. The flashes ran like red lightning along the works; the dull smoke rose from them in rolls, and hung sullenly on the skirts of the hills. Still the young men went on. How pitifully their poor little individual puffs showed by the side of the smashing, crashing hail of the Greeks! Yet they went on. And now, on the Greek right, we saw figures hurrying helter-skelter back from the most advanced trenches. They were Italian red-shirts, we found out next day, and they left their dead behind them. But from the Greek centre and left the lead came thicker yet, as the brigade pushed on and on — and then, at five hundred yards or so, coming out of the corn-field into the fallow, it stopped. On the low ground, before that torrent of fire, every man must have been swept down. Still they clung on.

But now their only hope was either night or Hairi or Hamdi. Night would save them from annihilation: Hairi or Hamdi might lift them to victory. " *O das Kamel, das Kamel,*" screamed a German captain between his clenched teeth, and shook his fist away towards the right : " *der*

brillianteste Brigad der ganzen Armee!" But
Hairi was still black and motionless on the plain.
Will he never move? Is he not moving now—
no; not there—further on the right? No; he
is not moving, damn him, and he will never
move. The trickle of fire from the young
men in front is getting feebler. The sun is
dipping down over the hills, though, and the
shadows are slanting right across the plain. And
there is Hamdi coming in—at least, there is a
brisk fire on the hills leftward—and is that not
Hamdi's men answering it from the other hill?
Yes, it is Hamdi, and it is miles and miles away.
It is all over. Now we can hardly see the smoke,
it is getting so dark. Hairi is blotted out in the
shadow; may he never leave it! And now there
is nothing left but the flashes in front. The
guns have said their say; they are limbering
up and drawing back for the night. And in
front are still the belching spurts of fire from
the Greeks; and in front still—how pitifully
few and far apart—the distressful, desperate,
defeated, dauntless sparks from what is left of
the Mauser rifles.

Out of 4000 or so that went into action, they
lost, killed and wounded, more than 1000.
Two battalions out of the seven lost their
commanding officers. One battalion lost all its

s

officers but two. They came limping and groaning past my fire all night. The Greeks went in the night, of course. Hamdi had done that : he came late, but he came in time to turn the murderous bungle into an empty victory. But in the morning the field was like a sieve with those little black holes. In the morning I saw twenty of the boys just being covered up in one shelter-trench—arms and legs cramped as in the sleep of nightmare. In the morning the corn-field was sown anew before it was reaped, with dead young men in new uniforms, and beside them, just out of reach of clutching, blackening fingers, Mauser rifles.

XXVII.

THE GHEGAS.

THEY turned up somewhere about a week after we occupied Larissa. They wore a neat enough blue uniform along with the white pointed Pierrot-fez of Albania, but they were not regular troops. They were all volunteers; they came to the war from the north of Albania, of all whose clans the Ghegas are reputed the most tameless. They came unpaid for the fighting, the glory— and the loot. It is a mistake to suppose that the Albanians refuse to serve in the Sultan's army; there are battalions on battalions of Albanian regiments. So that the irregulars had few men of military age. About two-thirds were in their teens—some of them smooth, open-faced boys, who looked as if they might be in the Fifth Form; others larrikins of twenty, hair shaved in front, and one tuft hanging out raggedly behind like a Red Indian's scalping-lock; but for that and their straight lithe bodies they might have come straight out of Bethnal Green. Half the remainder were old, old men of sixty or seventy or eighty; fierce browed fathers and grand-fathers, who had tramped down from the mountains to show the boys the way to glory—and loot.

Larissa they drew blank. They spent a day or two on its pavements looking hungrily at the tight shop-shutters; there were too many sentries. But they gutted about a third of Pharsala after the battle, and Domoko they turned into a little hell. They did not loot much—the Greeks had not left much to loot; but they burned and they shot at large about the streets. Some of them made a hollow pretence of shooting pigs, but most loosed off at random, aiming at nothing, for the pure delight of the thing. Bullets whistled as joyously as cocoa-nuts on a bank holiday; it was splendid fun—only about half as dangerous as a battle.

But the burning became a nuisance. It was said the Greek irregulars burned a mosque as they retreated; certainly the mosque was burned, and I saw a great fire in Domoko before daybreak, before as yet our men had gone in. But whether the Greeks burned the mosque, or it caught fire from the next houses, the Albanians did the rest.

It was all I could do to get my pony through the
live embers the morning after the fight. Half
the village by the afternoon was empty shells.
And at eleven that night the nuisance became a
curse. I had taken an empty house, having
declined, in view of the Ghegas, an invitation to
sleep in the same building as the deserted Greek
ammunition. I was sleeping peacefully on the
floor after three nights' bivouac. Suddenly I heard
the voice of Charlie. "I'm fright," he hoarsely
exclaimed; "'ouse on fire: come on boys." Sure
enough the house—or to be quite literal, the adjoin-
ing one—was on fire, flaming to heaven and sending a Niagara of sparks on to our roof. As I put
on my clothes again and went to finish the night
on the road, I damned all white fezzes with a
will. And all up and down the hot streets these
tireless Fifth Form boys and bank-holiday 'Arries
went on shooting, shooting, shooting at nothing
till dawn.

But next day I had my revenge. I saw the
Ghegas in action. First, however, I must explain what had happened on the 18th, the day
after the battle. I spent it myself about Domoko,
riding round the Greek positions and chasing
the censor. The Greeks, we found, had left
one gun of position behind them—also two big
houses full of ammunition, estimated by the en-

thusiastic captors at a million rounds.   They had
also found letters on the dead red-shirts which
they were wholly unable to read, but which filled
them with mingled indignation and pride.   There
were half-a-dozen of them, mostly half illiterate.
Here was one just written from a son to his
father, which would now never be sent, thanking
him for twenty lire, and wishing that he had
never been such a fool as to come to Greece ;
here was one from a wife to her husband, thanking God that the war was over and that he would
soon return.   Here was the passport of Robert
Sinclair, lieutenant in one of his Majesty of
Norway's dragoon regiments—made out for a
journey through Germany, Austria, and Italy.
The owners were all lying dead on the slopes of
the road up to Domoko.

Meanwhile the Greeks were making the best
of their way over the Furka Pass to Lamia.
Memdhuk, of course, arrived too late to cut them
off at its foot.   His skirmishers just got up in
time to fire a few shots at them, and then they
were off and over the heights.   In the afternoon Seyfoullah took the Turkish advance-
guard up to the Pass ; but he only found a rear-
guard in occupation of it, and after an hour's
desultory firing they withdrew down the southern
slopes.   Seyfoullah had only one battery of moun-

tain-guns with him; the Greeks for a wonder had broken the road up to Domoko in two places, where it passed over mountain-burns, and it was not till well after mid-day that the field-artillery got up to the village. In the early morning of the 19th the guns were sent on over the ten miles of fairly level table-land between Domoko and the Pass. The divisions of Memdhuk, Haidar, Hairi, and Hamdi were by this time gone forward also, though I do not think either of the latter went up the pass: in the evening they were camped, at any rate, Hamdi to the left of the ascent, and Hairi at the village of Daukli to its right.

I rode out in the early morning, passing much infantry and artillery on the road, and began to ascend the wooded serpentine of the Pass. Nobody expected any fighting; everybody believed the war over. But half-way up I met the advanced batteries of the corps artillery coming down. A little farther on I met his Excellency the Commander-in-Chief coming down. Mahmud Bey was with him, and had important news to tell: the advance-guard was in the plain of Lamia; the cavalry had occupied Thermopylæ; the Greeks were in full retreat over Oeta to Athens. I ought to have known better at this time of day than to believe Turkish information, but to-day this seemed not so unlikely : if it was true, this was indeed the end. However, the Marshal said I could go on to the top of the Pass if I liked, and I went—not so much in the hope of seeing any Greeks as with the wish to look down on the other side. At the top I found Haidar and Memdhuk ; Memdhuk, too, was just going down. He was not in the least abashed by his failure to cut off the enemy. " There was an English journalist," said the jolly little General, "came to Elassona before the war, and advised us not to try to beat the Greeks : go home and tell him you saw Memdhuk Pasha sitting on the top of the Furka Pass." Memdhuk belongs to the school which regards the occupation of territory as the one end of war : here was he on the Furka Pass, and whether the Greeks had been smashed or not was all one to him. The war was over, said Memdhuk and Haidar also. Nevertheless, I just went down a little way to look round the elbow of the Pass at Thermopylæ.

From one of the little hawthorn-grown promontories that jut out over the winding road I saw a line of black heads breaking the curve of a round hill below. A battalion of Reserves was struggling up a larger hill which commanded it. Somebody remarked that the men on the lower hill wore no fezzes. By George, they're Greeks !

With the word came a crack and a splutter, and then the familiar snarl of a volley. The battalion on the upper hill hesitated; some of the Turkish officers looked grave. But Seyfoullah Pasha was in command, and Seyfoullah is no disciple of the Turkish school which enjoins a week's rest to give a retreating enemy time to take himself together again. A company of Turks was lying behind the promontory on which I was. I thought they were in reserve, but they may have been shirking. Seyfoullah galloped right into the middle of them on his big chestnut, lashing out with his riding-whip. They slouched moodily round the hill into action.

Then down came the Ghegas. A whoop and a yell and a dozen rifle-shots behind us, and they were streaming down the slopes like a couple of football teams when a fast man has got away with the ball. No pretence of order; no officers visible, though a standard was tossing about somewhere in the middle of the scrimmage; no care to see where the enemy was, before opening fire; no effort not to shoot their brothers in the back. A couple of staff-officers rode furiously up to them; they raced on without a moment's heed. Seyfoullah rode at them with an oath to try to form them in line, to turn them leftwards to cut off the enemy. But not they.

They scampered straight down the slope in a long, loose trail, and began to bound up the higher hill straight for the enemy. Every man was yelling; everybody was firing fast and joyously into the backs of his brethren. It was not war; it was just fighting—blind, deaf, mad, lustful fighting. The croakers who complain that war is turning into mathematics never saw the Ghegas going into action.

Of course the Greeks took no notice of them; why should they? A few spent bullets may have come their way, but that was nothing. They kept up their volley-firing at the battalion above them. They were reinforced; the growling volleys swelled. It looked as if the little rear-guard skirmish might grow into a general action. And our field-guns were all the other side of the Furka, and our infantry was somewhere on the rearward slopes also—only nobody quite knew where. They routed up a mountain battery, but it was slow and opened too far in rear. Haidar Pasha hurried down to command, but he did not seem quite to realise what was going on. Time went on, but the Greeks did not go back. More than one eye turned anxiously back up the pass.

But other eyes happened to light on the gold and crimson standard of the Ghegas. They were not scampering now like boys on a football field.

The standard was not dancing ; it was going very sober and steady and slow—but it was going on. The Ghegas were all going on. Bent half double, they were striding with lithe stealthiness over the rocks, following the standard, firing. They were firing slower now,—they were firing at the enemy. The crimson bunting and the white fezzes crawled on with caution, yet with swiftness : here a quick glide forward, there a shot or two behind cover. And so the red and white stole on. Now it was at the corner of the big hill round which, between it and the Greek hill, ran the road. And now I woke up to the fact that the volleys had suddenly ceased.

The Greeks were in retreat. And the Ghegas had done it — the worst soldiers and the best fighters in the world. They never came back nor halted, nor formed up into any kind of formation. They strode on like young roes down the Pass after the Greeks. As I followed them down I found plenty of hard-faced boys tossed aside on the road with bullet-holes through their faces. I found a white-headed old man coughing and choking on a rock, with his four sons supporting him, and perplexedly wondering whether anything could be done that he should not die. But if the sons stayed behind, the cousins and nephews went on. So they pushed the Greeks down. They were still a sort of football team, only better together. Till the armistice came up with the white flag they dribbled the Greeks down towards Lamia.

The next day they took away the Ghegas' rifles, and confidence revived. They disbanded them and sent them home. The Ghegas trailed off as they had come, back to their happy valleys, to fill up the interval to the next war as best they can with blood - feuds and any stranger-shooting that may offer itself. Some trailed after the broad-shouldered young ruffians who marched with the standard, whose braided trousers and embroidered gaiters proclaimed them chiefs. Others went quite alone and unarmed, sleeping carelessly in the middle of the road : who would dare lay finger on a Gheg ? One smiling, white-haired, turbaned, spectacled patri-arch of eighty rode all by himself on a bare-backed donkey—probably the last loot of a well-spent life. And though from the point of view of loot the campaign had been a string of un-redeemed disasters, I incline to think, on a general view, that donkeys, and even ponies, will be plenty this season in the happy valleys of Albania.

XXVIII.

HOMEWARD.

THE armistice came up with the white flag from somewhere about Lamia. We could see the grey town at the bottom of the Pass; we could see the black columns of the Greek main body heading across the plain for the snow-crested wall of Oeta opposite us; we could see the broad miles of sea-lapped flat which they absurdly call the Pass of Thermopylæ. The Greeks' rear-guard was on the last slope—the Ghegas were driving it down; the one mountain battery had come forward and was shelling it merrily; the cavalry was just behind us on the winding road; it was only two o'clock. At last, thanks to Seyfoullah's energy, we should get at the Greeks retreating along the level, with four hours of good day-light to cut them up in. And then, of course, up came the white flag.

The guns sank into sulky silence. With diffi-

culty they silenced even the Ghegas. Up came
the tall officer in green with a crooked sabre, and
the strutting little man in black; never did I
see—small blame to him—so queer a mixture
of embarrassment and swagger. From Haidar
Pasha in nominal command to the powder-black-
ened bombardiers, we crowded round to see what
they had to say to Seyfoullah. Seyfoullah led
them aside awhile and spoke Greek: they saluted
and started back down the pass. Then it came
out. They said that an armistice was made—
an armistice when we were all but into the plain
of pursuit. Seyfoullah replied that he knew
nothing about that, but he would cease firing
until he heard from Edhem. And on the top
of that comes a message from Edhem to say the
armistice is concluded indeed; we must cease
firing and go no further down the Pass. And
that was the end of the Turko-Grecian war.

So find the ponies, Charlie, and let us mount
and get back over to Domoko before it is dark.
In one way the end of all things came none too
soon. For lunch that day we had just one tin
of corned beef—the tin painfully torn asunder
with a pocket-knife—between four owners. To
the four we had to add a Swiss officer, who gave
us a little, little slice of black bread apiece, and
had, of course, to be thanked in beef; and

Seyfoullah, who for his share of the feast con-
tributed a soldier's biscuit and half-a-pint of
water. The horses had nothing at all, neither
drink nor fodder, for the slopes of the Pass were
long burned bare by the May sun. The most of
Seyfoullah's half-pint of water went to moisten
the biscuit to breaking-point, and Charlie refused
point-blank to ask the soldiers for any more.
"You ask the one soldier, 'e give it," explained
Charlie, "then 'im no got it water for 'isself,"—
and who could press the point? Perhaps it was
just as well the war was over. But it was possible that supplies had come up from the depot at
Pharsala during the day : let us hurry home.

Of course we lost ourselves that night. We
had added a dishevelled landau to our caravan
during the days at Tekes, and we left it at the
foot of the Pass to fill itself up with green
corn for the horses; there was not a bite in
Domoko. And half-way across the table-land it
was unanimously declared by the soldiers that
the Mushir Pasha had not gone back to Domoko
at all, but was now in the village of Daukli, away
westward. It might be true. You never knew
what his Excellency would do : his Excellency
had a very educated taste in water, and was
accustomed to go where the spring was good.
So we sent back the disgusted Charlie to head

off the carriage, and back across country in the
gathering dark we headed for Daukli. The
ponies were faint and starving, but the game
little men took ditches with a will, and only
snatched a little in passing even at the tall
barley. And so we got to the blazing bivouac,
where the Albanians were building up screens
of brushwood to keep off the cold night wind.
"Mushir Pasha here?" "No; Mushir Pasha
not here; Ferik Pasha there." Ten thousand
imprecations: it was only a—well, a General of
Division. It turned out to be Hairi Pasha; and
recalling what I had sent off the day before about
Hairi's conduct in action, it was almost a relief
that he did not offer dinner.

And then a cheery "M'Seevens" out of the
dark, and the admirable Charlie was there with
the carriage, and the carriage was full to over-
flowing with green corn. Charlie had been
boarded on the way by Ghegas demanding bread,
but he readily answered that this carriage belonged to the Marshal. The ponies would just
submit to wait a second while we slipped off the
bridles, and then how they fell to! Meanwhile
we ate bread and cheese—what bread! what
cheese!—and conversed with an officer of the
Ghegas. He gave us tobacco—no Albanian is ever
short of tobacco, as the Sultan's customs-officers

can tell you. Not quite realising who he was, we offered to pay him, whereat he opened the door of a little hovel close by and disappeared. But he came out again and relented when we apologised, and offered to show us his horse. He had brought a small horse from Albania, he explained, but it had died; but now the Pasha had given him a good horse. We said we were always delighted to see a good horse. Solemnly he opened the door of the hovel. It was a windowless cellar—perhaps fifteen feet by ten. From one corner a fire drenched it in bitter smoke. In front of it on the damp earth, one rolling over the other, lay eight of the Ghegas asleep, and snoring like electric tramcars. Behind, rifles between their knees, binding filthy rags on to raw wounds, were two more. And at the very back, leaning faintly against the wall, a running sore on its back and its hip-bones sticking through its skin, eleven-two in its shoes, loomed the good horse. We thanked him much for showing it, and got out into the air again; but all the same it was interesting to have seen the quarters of a gentleman of the Ghegas.

It was too late to try and catch the censor now. Hairi kindly lent us a cellar to sleep in; it was all he had to lend, and they brought us a most adorable dish of mutton-fat after we had half

T

gone to sleep. We rode back to Domoko in the grey dawn next morning. A day to rest and write, and call finally on Edhem Pasha, and then I was off to ride home. I had only been away ten weeks, and only half of it war, but I felt as if I had not been in England since I was a boy. One long look from the top of the pass at the flat carpet of the Thessalian Plain, in its walls of mountain—and it looked yet more beautiful than it had done on the first day from Meluna. Then down, down, and through the strings of disbanded Ghegas and ponies still bringing up precautionary ammunition from Pharsala. Two hours' shelter from the mid-day sun in Pharsala, picking up the depot, and then out again to Larissa. Was the Thessalian Plain ever so rollingly, damnably interminable ?

It was the campaign all over backwards. Here was the grey granite wedge whence we watched the Mauser rifles go down before Domoko. There the corn-fields where we followed the attack upon Vasili. There on the left was the barn where we roasted the lamb ; above the Marshal's Bairam camp at the shrine of Tekes. Larissa now, to pack up the traps. Who is it coming in ? Saad-ed-Din Bey to borrow a tin of butter ? Give him three, God bless him ! Then we came to the spring whence we started to ride into Larissa.

Then up the winding reaches—and here was dear old Meluna—how absurdly desolate and naked now, with only one captured siege - gun on its way to Constantinople. And now dear old Elassona, with six hours' sleep on a Wallach's un-Keatinged divan. Out again next morning. Serfidje now, with the dear old Mutessarif, as kindly a gentleman as ever, cooking a royal dinner at three in the afternoon. Over the pass again to Karaveria—who would have thought it was so far up when we cantered down in half an hour: there is the very place where Andreas came off—and then lunch with real cherries! And then the train, and then once more—was it not years ago?—the first hotel in Salonica. It was almost impertinent in Salonica to be so obtrusively the same age as it was two months before. The train once more—don't cry, Charlie; we'll meet again, and you shall be my dragoman again when Austria comes down to Salonica— and lunch at Uskub once more, and the frontier, and Vienna, and Dover, and London.

XXIX.

A SUMMARY.

IT would have been more impressive as a war if it had been less delicious as a comic opera. It had its solemn moments, no doubt. Nobody has yet invented a kind of war which can be conducted without hurting somebody sometimes, although Prince Konstantinos came nearer to it than had ever seemed possible. For, whereas we had believed that the object in war was to destroy the enemy's army, what we saw looked more like a benevolent conspiracy between the two generals commanding-in-chief to spare innocent blood. The Greeks hurried away the moment it threatened to be necessary to start shooting Turks in earnest. Upon that the Turks held back for a week, apprehensive lest the men might forget themselves, and do irreparable hurt to the Greeks. Domoko and the pursuit over the Furka were the only exceptions on either side.

It was a race for defeat between cowardice and apathy, and cowardice won. Cowardice—it is useless to try and explain facts away with any other word. It is true that Europeans from both sides have said that the Greek rank and file fought well; others, more discreet, have said that they would have fought well if they had been given a chance. Perhaps a correspondent following his first campaign has no right to dogmatise. But even he has one standard of comparison — the Turks — and it is impossible to imagine the Turks breaking in panic after three days of intermittent ineffective shelling, as did the Greeks. Unless the Greeks have enormously understated their own losses—which is likely—and unless the Turks have enormously underrated their own success—which is not—the Greeks left one magnificent position after another before they had so much as begun to suffer. The rank and file were ordered to retreat, no doubt; but they were not ordered to retreat in disorder and throw away their ammunition. They were not ordered, it may be presumed, to evacuate Deliler or Vasili before they were driven out—yet out they went when they got under fire and saw the Turks coming.

The truth seems to be that they made a mistake, which in a less conceited people would

perhaps be pardonable : they underestimated
their power of enduring the strain of continued
fighting. They did not realise what fighting
meant. They fought well the first day, at
Meluna, and never once afterwards. The great
battle of Mati, which broke them down, was not
a battle at all. Until I saw the descriptions of
it in the newspapers I did not know that anybody ever thought it was a battle. The real
battle was for Saturday, and the Greeks bolted
on Friday night. After that they were quite
done with. A regiment retreated very steadily
and well at Pharsala, and I complimented them,
thinking them to be Greeks, but next thing I
learned that they were the Foreign Legion, placed,
as usual, in the post of danger. Then, at Velestino and Domoko, they fired good volleys at a
weaker enemy from behind earthworks. But at
Velestino they could have cut Naim's brigade to
pieces if they had dared break his feeble centre ;
at Domoko they were off the moment they began
to be outflanked. So they were always. And
why not ? say their friends. Outflanked by a
superior enemy, what could they do but retreat ?
Strategically the Crown Prince was, first and
last, in the right. Yes ; but they knew when
they went to war that the enemy would be
superior ; they knew that the strongest position

could be turned. If their object was not to fight, it would have been best attained by remaining at peace. Once at war, nations of spirit believe it their duty to fight—to fight at strategical advantage, if possible, but always to fight. At Plevna Osman was not only outflanked, but surrounded. He deliberately stayed to be surrounded, and he nearly saved Turkey. But such deeds as those of Plevna are to the Greeks foolishness. They strove not to die for their country, and they succeeded.

The Turks gave them every chance. It was amusing to find people in England thinking that the Turkish army was officered and directed by Germans. How many German officers were there really with the Turks? asked all my friends when I returned. And I answered confidently: not one. Grumbkow Pasha arrived on the third day of the war, and he left on the eighth; after him I am sure there was not one single German. Certainly I did not know all the officers in the Turkish army; but I do know that if Germans had been directing the campaign they must occasionally have shown themselves in the neighbourhood of the General Staff, and they never did. But, indeed, the silly fiction is its own refutation. Nobody except a Turk could possibly have conducted a campaign with such consideration for a beaten enemy. Ask the German correspondents. Disillusioned enthusiasts—how reverently they approached a real war, conducted by the army of the Kaiser's friend! How eagerly they watched the movements, and with what joyful recognition they labelled them with their technical names! And then—then, when there were movements, and nothing to develop them, and often when there were no movements at all—then to see doubt and perplexity melt into contempt, and laughter, and tears! How they swore, and wept; and called a pasha—a German captain, mark you, called a general—"*das Kamel!*" No, no; if it had been a German army in disguise, there would have been some order and system in it. Movements would have been timed; operations would have been carried right through; and generals would have been degraded and shot nearly every day.

The Turkish army beat the Greeks in its own wonderful way. To what extent it beat them is almost more difficult to explain than it is to say why it beat them. Never was there a war about which it was so heart-breakingly impossible to be sure of a name or a number or a date. Names of places you could generally identify on the map; if you could not, it was hopeless to ask them of anybody but Seyfoullah. Even Seyfoullah has been spelt on half-a-dozen different systems since he attained a European reputation, and I am only moderately confident of my own rendering because I have seen him spell it thus himself. For dates the Turk seldom goes beyond yesterday and to-morrow; hours of the day the Turkish system rules out altogether. Numbers were, if possible, more hopeless still. To expect the Turkish army to know what force it had, and what men it lost, is to ask grapes of thistles. You can make rough guesses. For instance, I know on European authority that after Domoko 800 to 900 men came into hospital; so that with killed and wounded who never came into hospital, but just left themselves to get well, the loss was probably from 1200 to 1500. On a very rough calculation the losses of the whole campaign—including sick—may have mounted up to 7000. But no Turk would ever put it at anything so unsensational. Most would probably answer with perfect truth, "It is not known." Others, as a low or a high figure appealed to their momentary sense of the fitness of things, would answer a hundred or a hundred thousand.

Really nobody knows. I suppose there must be some sort of untrustworthy roll-call kept somewhere, but I never saw any sign of it in Thessaly. Even if there had been, it would be impossible

within a matter of weeks to find out whether a
man was killed, wounded, or only missing. Nobody knew the country; nobody knew the disposition of the country. Men lost their battalions
by the score, and strolled over the Thessalian
Plain by the day looking for them. "Have you
seen my battalion?"—the question has been put
to me a dozen times in a day's ride. Of course
Charlie always directed the straggler to the last
battalion we had met. Ten to one it was the
wrong one—in which case off went the wanderer
on his travels again—ten to one in the wrong
direction. One day on the Meluna an Albanian
private—dirty, dust-stained, white-capped, rifle·
slung over shoulder—stalked the headquarters,
and asked if anybody there could kindly direct
him to his battalion. He had got separated from
it, he explained, with a comrade or two, and he
wanted to get back quickly, as he had heard there
was fighting. I expected to see him shot or
confined to barracks—except that there were no
barracks to confine him to. But oh dear no! A
colonel politely pointed.out the direction of his
battalion, and he went off and beckoned to his
friends below the hill. But evidently they backed
their opinion against the staff; they strolled off
their way and he his. When you get little
incidents of this kind day by day, how can you

possibly tell the strength of an army or the tale
of its losses?

The Turkish army is summed up in the Turkish
transport service; it is like the pack-horse, which
brings up its ammunition and bread and water.
Strong, patient, stupid, slow, and indomitable, it
goes its own way, whoever tries to guide it. Nobody is responsible for it; nobody knows who
organises it; it knows not itself whence it comes,
nor whither it goes; when it set out, nor when
it means to arrive. Untroubled, it stumbles and
blunders on, and somehow Allah brings it straggling into camp at nightfall. So it is with the
Turkish army. It makes wonderful marches;
only it starts at the wrong time, and arrives at
the wrong place. It walks unafraid into a blizzard
of bullets; only it has no firing-line and no fire-
discipline, and the rear ranks shoot down the front
ranks, and the artillery shells both. The cavalry
cheerfully charges earthworks with other earthworks on its flank; only when the enemy is retreating the cavalry is held religiously back from
pursuit. Engineers there were none at all: crossing the line one day to Pharsala, I came on a
couple of Italian engineers whom they had to
import from Salonica to patch up a Greek railway-
engine. Infantry battalions were taken from the
fighting-line by half-dozens for road-making and

transport. Thus the Turkish army shambled on to victory.

In fine, the Turks have the best soldiers and the worst officers in the world. The Turkish soldier is titanically enduring, heroically fearless, angelically disciplined. He obeys his officer like a good child; he will walk starving through a street of bread-shops if his officer but says " Don't touch." Albanians are different — neater and quicker in body, impetuous and uncontrollable in spirit. But with the Turks, even as they stand, good officers could do anything in the world, and good officers are what they lack. For if the Turkish soldier is the raw material of the finest fighting in the world, his officer is the finished product of one of the worst Governments in the world. Nobody becomes a scoundrel in a moment, but it must be owned that his career leaves him very little alternative in the long-run. He is not, of course, the monster of cruel iniquity which British fancy often paints him. Outwardly he is a nearer approach to the British idea of a gentleman than the Briton will often encounter between Dover and Zibeftche. Courteous, dignified, hospitable, often vain, but never a swaggerer, he has the root of gentlemanliness in him—a sure self-confidence and self-respect. You will not find in him the jerky self-assertiveness of many Continental officers. He can maintain his dignity without any duello or court of honour. He is quite sure of himself.

You may divide the Turkish officer into two clearly marked types—each with virtues, each with vices. As favourable examples I cannot do better than take two I knew fairly well—Hussein Avni Bey and Yunus Effendi. Avni was a Constantinopolitan, Yunus a Gheg from the wilds of Albania. Avni was a man of wealth. One uncle was a Pasha; two others owned extensive property in Thessaly; Avni himself had an estate there. Yunus hadn't a penny to bless himself with: he dressed in rags, and the reason he longed for promotion was that he had a wife and two children, and could hardly keep them from starving. Talat Pasha, he told me, gave him a pound for distinguishing himself at Meluna, but even a pound would not last for ever. Try to imagine a general tipping a subaltern a sovereign for gallantry in action, and you will get a better idea of the two classes of Turkish officer than I can give you in pages of comparison. Avni, to resume, was twenty-three; Yunus was on the fringe of fifty, but Avni, being a full lieutenant, was Yunus's superior officer. Avni was a man of refinement and education: he spoke and read French very well; he was quite emancipated from fanatical Mohammedanism, and carried his bottle of sweet champagne like a man. He was well-read in his profession, and spoke of "*les lois de la tactique*" with the same hushed awe as of "*sa Majesté Impériale.*" One of these laws, I remember, was that you must never on any account attack the enemy unless with at least double his force. Nor can I imagine Avni doing any such thing, for he had not even the makings of a real soldier. He had never been out of a town in his life before : I don't believe he had even seen his estate in Thessaly, although he had once visited Larissa. He was a wobbly and tact-less horseman : he puffed heavily uphill ; he could ride along a road twice daily for a week, and then not recognise it when he struck it in the middle. He could live on next to nothing—apparently all Turks can—but he was more than a bit of a slug-a-bed. He never did anything on his own re-sponsibility. Although he had no duties to speak of—he spent two days map-making at Larissa, and complained that it told heavily on his eyes— he preferred to go off for a picnic on his estate to waiting to see what happened after the repulse at Velestino. One day I was riding with him up to the Meluna, when there came down a pony with baggage, which he thought he recognised. "The Marshal is in retreat, the Greeks are advancing,"

he cried, and without another word whipped round
and was well on his way down the Pass before he
could be persuaded to ask whether his fears were
not groundless.

Yunus, on the other hand, would have attacked
an army of the enemy by himself if there had
been nobody else present to help him. He was
as brave as a bull-dog and as wiry as a ferret.
He knew every stone of his mountains, and went
over them like a hart. He could live for ever on
dry biscuit and water, and sooner than touch wine
he would have read a book. Only I don't think
he could read, nor yet write his name. He knew
his men and his men knew him, and obeyed him;
but except this I am afraid he had not the least
possible qualification to command them. Take
him out of the mountains he knew, and I doubt
if he could have led his men straight. Certainly
he could not if an enemy to be gone for had presented himself on the way; to go for the enemy
was the beginning and the end of Yunus's tactics.
He had no field-glass—though he could see better
without than I could with one of Ross's best—
and had not the vaguest idea of what was going
on: if he had got his men into a hole he would
have left them there shooting till the last man
dropped.

Such were Avni and Yunus. If Avni has luck

he will die a Pasha—a well-meaning but incompetent Vali, or a safe but timid General of Division. If Yunus has luck he will be shot in a frontier scrimmage, a captain at seventy. Remember that both these men—in that both were honest, and sincere, and good-hearted—were exceptionally favourable specimens of their class. Some of the other Yunuses whimpered over wounds that would not take a private out of the firing-line. Some of the other Avnis were rank cowards. There was a high-officer whom we used to call the Turkish military attaché, because he was always sitting about with us taking notes, and never took any other part in the campaign. Riding with him one day from Pharsala to Velestino, we came on a village that had not yet been occupied by the Turks. We were about a dozen armed men—but nothing would persuade him to go through the village, and he implored us not to go. Of course the Greeks came out and salaamed and brought us milk to drink, and even Aslan, who had promised himself at last the bit of Bashi-Bazouking which his soul longed for, was constrained to put his revolver back again. But the Turk had galloped round behind a hill—and met us quite unashamed on the other side. Besides this, the worse sort of Constantinopolitan was idle, an intriguer, a peculator, and a spy; and so, according to his opportunities, was the worse sort of provincial.

As for the Generals—excepting only Edhem, Seyfoullah, and Riza—they were hopeless, especially the Generals of Divisions. All were excellent, good fellows; all were insubordinate, sluggish, absolutely incapable of combination, ignorant of the very range of their guns. When they ought to have cut off the Greeks and the Greeks got off, they were as pleased as little children. Quite honestly they could see no difference between destroying the enemy and merely forcing him to retreat. Quite honestly they believed each time that the Greeks had had a tremendous thrashing, and were all but annihilated. They had not the least idea of their own losses: how could you expect them to estimate those of the enemy?

It was a war of hyperbole — a page out of 'Tartarin de Tarascon.' It had been planned—nobody quite knew how—that the enemy was to be surrounded and annihilated; the enemy was not to be seen anywhere, the Turk was occupying his position, and the sun was very hot—why, surely, yes, he had been surrounded and annihilated. Of course. "*Oui, oui, mon cher ami, je vous donne ma parole d'honneur, la parole d'un aide-de-camp de sa Majesté: l'armée de l'ennemi n'existe plus.*" You want to see the dead and

U

prisoners with your own eyes? Dear, dear, these English! why, I tell you it is so: yes, I saw it myself. Dear, dear, these English are never satisfied—strange creatures. For himself, the Turk was quite satisfied. He believed his own fictions whole-heartedly. He sat down, looked at his beard for days together, and smoked cigarettes and drank coffee until some day somebody discovered that the enemy was not annihilated after all. Then the Turk got up, collected any troops that were lying about, spent a week in making a plan, forgot it as soon as it was made, and let the Greeks go again. Then again he quite sincerely gave his word of honour there were no more Greeks left, and fell to contemplating his beard again.

And the Greeks were scurrying across country for their little lives, screaming, "The Turks are upon us!" Queer war.

XXX.

WHAT WAR FEELS LIKE.

THE strange thing about war is that it is so wonderfully like peace.

Going to war is like coming of age. You expect to wake up one morning and find everything changed — a new self in a new world. You do wake up, and you are very much the same sort of boy at twenty-one as at twenty. So with war. You are rather disappointed to find yourself doing exactly the same things in war as you do in peace. You wear very much the same clothes; you eat—when you can get it —rather more than the same amount of breakfast; your disposition is no harder nor bloodthirstier than before. The horrors of war, of which you expected so much, leave you quite unmoved—just because you did expect so much.

You wondered whether you would be sick when you came across the dead, and you were

not even sorry. They were so still and restful
—neither hot nor cold, nor hungry nor thirsty,
nor tired nor famishing for sleep any more; it
was not possible to be very sorry for them.
Even when death had caught them unawares,
twisting them awry and gnarling arms and legs,
they only looked like strange shapes turned out
of a mould, and you cannot weep for a shape out
of a mould. When a shell had ripped all the
features off a face, it was not pleasant to look
at; but there was nothing human left about
it to stir compassion. Put it in a Greek trench
and cover it up; hang up its fez on a peg at
its head. The poor crumpled fez that used to
get so carefully blocked and ironed every morning in Elassona,—it was so much more pathetic
than the body. Somebody will cry for the body,
but not us. There are plenty of bayonets left
in its battalion; roll up your overcoats, and
sling on your water-cans, and march, and leave
it behind.

The wounded were worse, but even with them
tragedy soon lost its poignancy. In any other
army the treatment of them would have been
an atrocity. As soon as the war was general
and wounded were plenty the ambulance service
broke down utterly. A man was hit at six in
the morning. One of the rare surgeons, or else

a comrade, tied up the place with a handkerchief, and left water, if there was any, at his
side. There he lay in the sun till nightfall.
When it was dark, and the Greeks had begun
retreating, his comrades came back with a pony
and a pack - saddle. The wounded man was
hoisted on — clinging with his hands to the
pommel if he could; if not, spread - eagled on
his belly and tied with ropes. So he stumbled
on all night, ten or twenty or thirty miles to
the hospital. Arrived there—unless he had the
luck to get into the Ottoman Bank Hospital,
with expert Swiss and French and Turkish surgeons—the army doctor prodded at him with
a probe. By the time the limb was a bundle
of bleeding ribbons it was nearly an even chance
that the bullet would be worried out. And when
he saw the bullet the bleeding bundle turned
peacefully over and went to sleep. He had seen
with his own eyes that the bullet was out,—that
was all right. And in three weeks he was on
his legs again. Why not? He never touched
liquor in his life, and seldom saw meat; his
blood was clean and sweet, his muscles lean and
hard, his nerves he had never heard of in his
life. Why should he ever die?

With the dead gone out of the world of human
sympathy, and the wounded beginning to heal

up from the moment they were hit, there was little enough left to draw the line between war and peace. Not even in action. It was interesting to see masses of men trying to kill each other, but not surprising : you knew before that this was what they did in war. It was more surprising to see them sit about and talk and smoke through the best part of an engagement, quite unperturbed. And a cigarette tasted no better and no worse in war than in peace.

I had a sort of silly idea that they put civilians away during war-time. It was pleasant, then, to see elderly gentlemen in flame-coloured night-gowns and rainbow-coloured turbans, sitting about watching the battle, smoking cigarettes, and applauding well-placed shells as if they were late cuts to the boundary. One day when I was watching a side-issue of a fight on a stony hill, a slim gentleman with an umbrella came up and saluted me. It was my banker, who had shut up his bank and his tobacco-monopoly business and come out to spend a quiet afternoon with the war.

Yet war was still like coming of age. One day you start thinking and you suddenly see that some time, somehow—you don't know when or how—you have really become a man : the boy of twenty is gone, and there is a new self in his place. So once more with war. Gradually, imperceptibly, there was an utter difference after all. You saw it much better when you got into the enemy's country. The preoccupations of peace had imperceptibly ceased to preoccupy; things that mattered everything had ceased to matter in the least. The sum of it was that everything artificial, conventional, social, had vanished, and you were left the bare, natural man. Not absolutely so, perhaps, in a correspondent's case, for civilisation naturally hung longest round headquarters; but even for a correspondent very nearly so. It no longer mattered what your clothes looked like; but it mattered as it had never mattered before that they were not too hot in the sun and not too cold in the night wind. Bread was a food that you never set much store by before, and perhaps it may be true that it contains less nourishment than cocoa, chocolate, or beef-lozenges. But bread fills up the empty stomach while the other things do not, and the empty stomach howled aloud to be filled. And so you searched diligently for common, vulgar bread, or soldier's dog-biscuit for that matter. Your stomach had to be filled. In peace there are hosts of people whose business it is to make it easy for you to fill your stomach at the proper time. In war they are all gone, and you have got to see to filling it yourself when it needs it.

In peace, if you have rheumatism, you remember Elliman's Embrocation and St Jacob's Oil. You buy some, and presently say it has cured you. In war you haven't got Elliman's Embrocation and St Jacob's Oil, so you just leave it alone and let nature cure you—like a savage.

You come back to the common, natural division of day and night. We civilised English people have superseded day and night. We have got curtains to shut out the morning sun and electric lamps to supplement the stars. But in war marching and shooting can only be satisfactorily done by daylight, and there is no daylight to spare. So marching and shooting begin as soon as there is light to march and shoot by, and if you are not awake by then you will miss it. And if you have not suppered yourself and found your sleeping-place and looked to your horses by nightfall, you will lose supper and bed and horses together. There is nothing left then but to go to sleep, which you have been hungering to do half the day. So you go to sleep when it begins to get dark, and you get up as soon as it begins to get light—just like a savage.

It is in this return to the naked state of nature

that consist both the charm and the devilishness
of war. The charm you will understand readily.
War is the only quite complete holiday that has
yet been invented. Perhaps you realise it best
when your tailor's bill, after a devious and pre-
carious journey of three weeks or so, is delivered
to you on the morning of an engagement. How
utterly pointless is the absurd little scrawl!
What in the world has it to do with anybody?
Bills, debts, taxes, business—yes, and engagements, etiquette, matters of public interest, meal-
times, the law of the land, respectable clothes,
return of post, hours of the day, days of the
week, days of the month — all the complex
civilised tyranny summed up in the word
"arrangements"—you are free of it all. You
have to eat and drink, to keep yourself warm, to
get from one place to another, and, so far as is
compatible with doing your duty, to avoid being
shot. That is all. You feel in war as you feel
when you have got your clothes off—alone with
your naked untrammelled self.

Yet it is this suspension of everything which
has validity in time of peace that makes the
devilish cruelty of war. If nature, in the
absence of Elliman and St Jacob, cannot keep
you from rheumatic fever, why, then, as like as
not, you have to die. You never did any harm

to the Greek gunners over there, but their shell won't turn aside from you for that. You get rid of arrangements when you don't want them, but then they won't come and help you when you do.

Crueller still is it to see peace trying to go on by the side of war. It is an intoxicating privilege to be able to ride straight across a field of young vines in war-time, but after all the vines were planted for purposes of peace. You cut green corn for your horses—you have to—but you can't help thinking of the man who ploughed and sowed and will never reap. During the first battle of Velestino I saw a hen go, business-like, into a barn, and after a little while come out, her cackle shrilling triumphantly over the grinding musketry and banging guns. By evening the barn was burned, and the egg with it; the hen was plucked and on the fire. It was a small thing, but it seemed hard that she should have been put to the trouble of laying that last purposeless egg.

Saddest of all were the foals. The new-dropped foals, whose mothers had been taken straight away to carry cartridges, went trotting up and down the line of march calling for them. You knew the slightly querulous, expectant expression of a foal's hairy little face. The baby was getting very hungry and tired. He was quite confident of finding his mother,—she was there only an hour ago. But where could she have got to meanwhile, and why didn't she come to comfort him when he cried? They all starved. And I saw one little bit of a chestnut filly foal trying to struggle up a slope of the Furka with a forefoot lopped off at the pastern. Some devil must have done it to prevent her from following her dam. She tumbled over and whinnied, jumped up and hobbled a foot or two, tumbled over again and moaned. Yet the soldier was only a devil in that he should have shot her through the heart instead of cutting off her foot. For the chestnut filly had to die anyhow. She was part of what we call the inevitable wastage of war.

THE END.

PRINTED BY WILLIAM BLACKWOOD AND SONS

NEW BOOKS.

POPULAR NOVELS.

DARIEL: A ROMANCE OF SURREY.
> By R. D. BLACKMORE, Author of 'Lorna Doone,' &c. With 14 Page Illustrations by CHRIS. HAMMOND. Crown 8vo, 6s.

THE MAID OF SKER.
> By the SAME AUTHOR. Cheaper Edition. Crown 8vo, 3s. 6d.

PEACE WITH HONOUR.
> By SYDNEY C. GRIER. Crown 8vo, 6s.

HIS EXCELLENCY'S ENGLISH GOVERNESS.
> By the SAME AUTHOR. Second Edition. Crown 8vo, 6s.

AN UNCROWNED KING: A ROMANCE OF HIGH POLITICS. By the SAME AUTHOR. Second Edition. Crown 8vo, 6s.

IN FURTHEST IND: AN HISTORICAL ROMANCE.
> By the SAME AUTHOR. Post 8vo, 6s.

AUDREY CRAVEN.
> By MAY SINCLAIR. Second Edition. Crown 8vo, 6s.

MONA MACLEAN, MEDICAL STUDENT.
> By GRAHAM TRAVERS. Twelfth Edition. Crown 8vo, 6s.

FELLOW TRAVELLERS.
> By the SAME AUTHOR. Fourth Edition. Crown 8vo, 6s.

SARACINESCA.
> By F. MARION CRAWFORD, Author of 'Mr Isaacs,' &c. Cheaper Edition. Crown 8vo, 3s. 6d.

IN VARYING MOODS.
> By BEATRICE HARRADEN. Twelfth Edition. Crown 8vo, 3s. 6d.

HILDA STRAFFORD, AND THE REMITTANCE MAN.
> TWO CALIFORNIAN STORIES. By the SAME AUTHOR. Tenth Edition. Crown 8vo, 3s. 6d.

POPULAR NOVELS—*continued.*

THE KNIGHT'S TALE.

By F. EMILY PHILLIPS, Author of 'The Education of Antonia.'
Crown 8vo, 3s. 6d.

THE LOST PIBROCH, AND OTHER SHEILING STORIES.

By NEIL MUNRO. Crown 8vo, 6s.

A SPOTLESS REPUTATION.

By D. GERARD (MADAME LONGARD DE LONGGARDE), Author of
'Lady Baby,' 'The Wrong Man,' &c. Third Edition. Crown
8vo, 6s.

AN ELECTRIC SHOCK; AND OTHER STORIES.

By E. GERARD (MADAME DE LASZOWSKA), Author of 'A
Foreigner,' &c. ; Joint-Author of 'Reata,' &c. Crown 8vo, 6s.

THE STORY OF MARGRÉDEL; BEING A FIRESIDE HIS-
TORY OF A FIFESHIRE FAMILY. By D. STORRAR MELDRUM.
Cheap Edition. Crown 8vo, 3s. 6d.

GREY MANTLE AND GOLD FRINGE.

By the SAME AUTHOR. Crown 8vo, 6s.

MIRIAM CROMWELL, ROYALIST: A ROMANCE OF THE
GREAT REBELLION. By DORA GREENWELL M^CCHESNEY.
Crown 8vo, 6s.

KATHLEEN CLARE: HER BOOK, 1637-41.

By the SAME AUTHOR. With Frontispiece and Five Full-page
Illustrations by JAMES A. SHEARMAN. Crown 8vo, 6s.

A PRINCE OF TYRONE.

By CHARLOTTE FENNELL and J. P. O'CALLAGHAN. Crown
8vo, 6s.

WILLIAM BLACKWOOD & SONS, EDINBURGH AND LONDON.

Catalogue

of

Messrs Blackwood & Sons'

Publications

PHILOSOPHICAL CLASSICS FOR ENGLISH READERS.

EDITED BY WILLIAM KNIGHT, LL.D.,
Professor of Moral Philosophy in the University of St Andrews.

In crown 8vo Volumes, with Portraits, price 3s. 6d.

Contents of the Series.

DESCARTES, by Professor Mahaffy, Dublin.—BUTLER, by Rev. W. Lucas Collins, M.A.—BERKELEY, by Professor Campbell Fraser.—FICHTE, by Professor Adamson, Glasgow. — KANT, by Professor Wallace, Oxford.—HAMILTON, by Professor Veitch, Glasgow.—HEGEL, by the Master of Balliol. —LEIBNIZ, by J. Theodore Merz.—VICO, by Professor Flint, Edinburgh.—HOBBES, by Professor Croom Robertson.--HUME, by the Editor. — SPINOZA, by the Very Rev. Principal Caird, Glasgow.—BACON: Part I. The Life, by Professor Nichol.—BACON: Part II. Philosophy, by the same Author.—LOCKE, by Professor Campbell Fraser.

FOREIGN CLASSICS FOR ENGLISH READERS.

EDITED BY MRS OLIPHANT.

In crown 8vo, 2s. 6d.

Contents of the Series.

DANTE, by the Editor. — VOLTAIRE, by General Sir E. B. Hamley, K.C.B. —PASCAL, by Principal Tulloch. — PETRARCH, by Henry Reeve, C.B.—GOETHE, by A. Hayward, Q.C.—MOLIÈRE, by the Editor and F. Tarver, M.A.—MONTAIGNE, by Rev. W. L. Collins, M.A.—RABELAIS, by Sir Walter Besant. — CALDERON, by E. J. Hasell. — SAINT SIMON, by Clifton W. Collins, M.A. — CERVANTES, by the Editor. — CORNEILLE AND RACINE, by Henry M. Trollope. — MADAME DE SÉVIGNÉ, by Miss Thackeray.—LA FONTAINE, AND OTHER FRENCH FABULISTS, by Rev. W. Lucas Collins, M.A.—SCHILLER, by James Sime, M.A., Author of 'Lessing, his Life and Writings.'—TASSO, by E. J. Hasell.—ROUSSEAU, by Henry Grey Graham.—ALFRED DE MUSSET, by C. F. Oliphant.

ANCIENT CLASSICS FOR ENGLISH READERS.

EDITED BY THE REV. W. LUCAS COLLINS, M.A.

CHEAP RE-ISSUE.   In limp cloth, fcap. 8vo, price 1s. each.

Two Volumes will be issued Monthly in the following order :—

HOMER: ILIAD, . . The Editor.	} *Ready.*	HESIOD AND THEOGNIS, J. Davies.	} *Sept.*	
HOMER: ODYSSEY, . The Editor.		PLAUTUS AND TERENCE, The Editor.		
HERODOTUS, . . . G. C. Swayne.	} *Ready.*	TACITUS, ... W. B. Donne.	} *Oct.*	
CÆSAR, . . Anthony Trollope.		LUCIAN, ... The Editor.		
VIRGIL, ... The Editor.	} *Ready.*	PLATO, ... C. W. Collins.	} *Nov.*	
HORACE, . Sir Theodore Martin.		GREEK ANTHOLOGY, Lord Neaves.		
ÆSCHYLUS, . Bishop Copleston.	} *May.*	LIVY, ... The Editor.	} *Dec.*	
XENOPHON, . . Sir Alex. Grant.		OVID, ... Rev. A. Church.		
CICERO, ... The Editor.	} *June.*	CATULLUS, TIBULLUS, AND PROPERTIUS, ... J. Davies.	} 1898. *Jan.*	
SOPHOCLES, . . . C. W. Collins.		DEMOSTHENES, . W. J. Brodribb.		
PLINY, . Church and Brodribb.	} *July.*	ARISTOTLE, . . Sir Alex. Grant.	} *Feb.*	
EURIPIDES, . . . W. B. Donne.		THUCYDIDES, . . . The Editor.		
JUVENAL, ... E. Walford.	} *Aug.*	LUCRETIUS, . . . W. H. Mallock.	} *March.*	
ARISTOPHANES, . . The Editor.		PINDAR, . . Rev. F. D. Morice.		

CATALOGUE

OF

MESSRS BLACKWOOD & SONS'

PUBLICATIONS.

ALISON.
History of Europe. By Sir ARCHIBALD ALISON, Bart., D.C.L.

1. From the Commencement of the French Revolution to the Battle of Waterloo.
LIBRARY EDITION, 14 vols., with Portraits. Demy 8vo, £10, 10s.
ANOTHER EDITION, in 20 vols. crown 8vo, £6.
PEOPLE'S EDITION, 13 vols. crown 8vo, £2, 11s.

2. Continuation to the Accession of Louis Napoleon.
LIBRARY EDITION, 8 vols. 8vo, £6, 7s. 6d.
PEOPLE'S EDITION, 8 vols. crown 8vo, 34s.

Epitome of Alison's History of Europe. Thirtieth Thousand, 7s. 6d.

Atlas to Alison's History of Europe. By A. Keith Johnston.
LIBRARY EDITION, demy 4to, £3, 3s.
PEOPLE'S EDITION, 31s. 6d.

Life of John Duke of Marlborough. With some Account of his Contemporaries, and of the War of the Succession. Third Edition. 2 vols. 8vo. Portraits and Maps, 30s.

Essays: Historical, Political, and Miscellaneous. 3 vols. demy 8vo, 45s.

ACROSS FRANCE IN A CARAVAN: BEING SOME ACCOUNT OF A JOURNEY FROM BORDEAUX TO GENOA IN THE "ESCARGOT," taken in the Winter 1889-90. By the Author of 'A Day of my Life at Eton.' With fifty Illustrations by John Wallace, after Sketches by the Author, and a Map. Cheap Edition, demy 8vo, 7s. 6d.

ACTA SANCTORUM HIBERNLÆ; Ex Codice Salmanticensi. Nunc primum integre edita opera CAROLI DE SMEDT et JOSEPHI DE BACKER, e Soc. Jesu, Hagiographorum Bollandianorum; Auctore et Sumptus Largiente JOANNE PATRICIO MARCHIONE BOTHAE. In One handsome 4to Volume, bound in half roxburghe, £2, 2s.; in paper cover, 31s. 6d.

ADOLPHUS. Some Memories of Paris. By F. ADOLPHUS. Crown 8vo, 6s.

AIKMAN.
Manures and the Principles of Manuring. By C. M. AIKMAN, D.Sc., F.R.S.E., &c., Professor of Chemistry, Glasgow Veterinary College; Examiner in Chemistry, University of Glasgow, &c. Crown 8vo, 6s. 6d.

Farmyard Manure: Its Nature, Composition, and Treatment. Crown 8vo, 1s. 6d.

AIRD. Poetical Works of Thomas Aird. Fifth Edition, with Memoir of the Author by the Rev. JARDINE WALLACE, and Portrait. Crown 8vo, 7s. 6d.

ALLARDYCE.
The City of Sunshine. By ALEXANDER ALLARDYCE, Author of 'Earlscourt,' &c. New Edition. Crown 8vo, 6s.
Balmoral : A Romance of the Queen's Country. New Edition. Crown 8vo, 6s.

ALMOND. Sermons by a Lay Head-master. By HELY HUTCH-INSON ALMOND, M.A. Oxon., Head-Master of Loretto School. Crown 8vo, 5s.

ANCIENT CLASSICS FOR ENGLISH READERS. Edited by Rev. W. LUCAS COLLINS, M.A. Price 1s. each. *For List of Vols. see p. 2.*

ANDERSON. Daniel in the Critics' Den. A Reply to Dean Farrar's 'Book of Daniel.' By ROBERT ANDERSON, LL.D., Barrister-at-Law, Assistant Commissioner of Police of the Metropolis; Author of 'The Coming Prince,' 'Human Destiny,' &c. Post 8vo, 4s. 6d.

AYTOUN.
Lays of the Scottish Cavaliers, and other Poems. By W. EDMONDSTOUNE AYTOUN, D.C.L., Professor of Rhetoric and Belles-Lettres in the University of Edinburgh. New Edition. Fcap. 8vo, 3s. 6d.
ANOTHER EDITION. Fcap. 8vo, 7s. 6d.
CHEAP EDITION. 1s. Cloth, 1s. 3d.
An Illustrated Edition of the Lays of the Scottish Cavaliers. From designs by Sir NOEL PATON. Cheaper Edition. Small 4to, 10s. 6d.
Bothwell : a Poem. Third Edition. Fcap., 7s. 6d.
Poems and Ballads of Goethe. Translated by Professor AYTOUN and Sir THEODORE MARTIN, K.C.B. Third Edition. Fcap., 6s.
The Ballads of Scotland. Edited by Professor AYTOUN. Fourth Edition. 2 vols. fcap. 8vo, 12s.
Memoir of William E. Aytoun, D.C.L. By Sir THEODORE MARTIN, K.C.B. With Portrait. Post 8vo, 12s.

BEDFORD & COLLINS. Annals of the Free Foresters, from 1856 to the Present Day. By W. K. R. BEDFORD, W. E. W. COLLINS, and other Contributors. With 55 Portraits and 59 other Illustrations. Demy 8vo, 21s. *net.*

BELLAIRS. Gossips with Girls and Maidens, Betrothed and Free. By LADY BELLAIRS. New Edition. Crown 8vo, 3s. 6d. Cloth, extra gilt edges, 5s.

BELLESHEIM. History of the Catholic Church of Scotland. From the Introduction of Christianity to the Present Day. By ALPHONS BELLESHEIM, D.D., Canon of Aix-la-Chapelle. Translated, with Notes and Additions, by D. OSWALD HUNTER BLAIR, O.S.B., Monk of Fort Augustus. Cheap Edition. Complete in 4 vols. demy 8vo, with Maps. Price 21s. net.

BENTINCK. Racing Life of Lord George Cavendish Bentinck, M.P., and other Reminiscences. By JOHN KENT, Private Trainer to the Goodwood Stable. Edited by the Hon. FRANCIS LAWLEY. With Twenty-three full-page Plates, and Facsimile Letter. Third Edition. Demy 8vo, 25s.

BEVERIDGE.
Culross and Tulliallan ; or, Perthshire on Forth. Its History and Antiquities. With Elucidations of Scottish Life and Character from the Burgh and Kirk-Session Records of that District. By DAVID BEVERIDGE. 2 vols. 8vo, with Illustrations, 42s.
Between the Ochils and the Forth ; or, From Stirling Bridge to Aberdour. Crown 8vo, 6s.

BICKERDYKE. A Banished Beauty. By JOHN BICKERDYKE, Author of ' Days in Thule, with Rod, Gun, and Camera,' ' The Book of the All-Round Angler,' ' Curiosities of Ale and Beer,' &c. With Illustrations. Crown 8vo, 6s.

BIRCH.

Examples of Stables, Hunting-Boxes, Kennels, Racing Establishments, &c. By JOHN BIRCH, Architect, Author of ' Country Architecture,' &c. With 30 Plates. Royal 8vo, 7s.

Examples of Labourers' Cottages, &c. With Plans for Improving the Dwellings of the Poor in Large Towns. With 34 Plates. Royal 8vo, 7s.

Picturesque Lodges. A Series of Designs for Gate Lodges, Park Entrances, Keepers', Gardeners', Bailiffs', Grooms', Upper and Under Servants' Lodges, and other Rural Residences. With 16 Plates. 4to, 12s. 6d.

BLACK. Heligoland and the Islands of the North Sea. By WILLIAM GEORGE BLACK. Crown 8vo, 4s.

BLACKIE.

Lays and Legends of Ancient Greece. By JOHN STUART BLACKIE, Emeritus Professor of Greek in the University of Edinburgh. Second Edition. Fcap. 8vo, 5s.

The Wisdom of Goethe. Fcap. 8vo. Cloth, extra gilt, 6s.

Scottish Song: Its Wealth, Wisdom, and Social Significance. Crown 8vo. With Music. 7s. 6d.

A Song of Heroes. Crown 8vo, 6s.

John Stuart Blackie: A Biography. By ANNA M. STODDART. With 3 Plates. Third Edition. 2 vols. demy 8vo, 21s.
POPULAR EDITION. With Portrait. Crown 8vo, 6s.

BLACKMORE. The Maid of Sker. By R. D. BLACKMORE, Author of ' Lorna Doone,' &c. New Edition. Crown 8vo, 6s. Cheaper Edition. Crown 8vo, 3s. 6d.

BLACKWOOD.

Annals of a Publishing House. William Blackwood and his Sons; including a History of their Magazine and Friends. By Mrs OLIPHANT. With Four Portraits, demy 8vo. [*Vols. I. and II. in the press.*

Blackwood's Magazine, from Commencement in 1817 to May 1897. Nos. 1 to 979, forming 160 Volumes.

Index to Blackwood's Magazine. Vols. 1 to 50. 8vo, 15s.

Tales from Blackwood. First Series. Price One Shilling each, in Paper Cover. Sold separately at all Railway Bookstalls.
They may also be had in 12 vols., cloth, 18s. Half calf, richly gilt, 30s. Or the 12 vols. in 6, roxburghe, 21s. Half red morocco, 28s.

Tales from Blackwood. Second Series. Complete in Twenty-four Shilling Parts. Handsomely bound in 12 vols., cloth, 30s. In leather back, roxburghe style, 37s. 6d. Half calf, gilt, 52s. 6d. Half morocco, 55s.

Tales from Blackwood. Third Series. Complete in Twelve Shilling Parts. Handsomely bound in 6 vols., cloth, 15s.; and in 12 vols., cloth, 18s. The 6 vols. in roxburghe, 21s. Half calf, 25s. Half morocco, 28s.

Travel, Adventure, and Sport. From ' Blackwood's Magazine. Uniform with ' Tales from Blackwood.' In Twelve Parts, each price 1s. Handsomely bound in 6 vols., cloth, 15s. And in half calf, 25s.

BLACKWOOD.

New Educational Series. *See separate Catalogue.*

New Uniform Series of Novels (Copyright).

Crown 8vo, cloth.   Price 3s. 6d. each.   Now ready :—

THE MAID OF SKER. By R. D. Blackmore.
WENDERHOLME. By P. G. Hamerton.
THE STORY OF MARGRÉDEL. By D. Storrar Meldrum.
MISS MARJORIBANKS. By Mrs Oliphant.
THE PERPETUAL CURATE, and THE RECTOR. By the Same.
SALEM CHAPEL, and THE DOCTOR'S FAMILY. By the Same.
A SENSITIVE PLANT. By E. D. Gerard.
LADY LEE'S WIDOWHOOD. By General Sir E. B. Hamley.
KATIE STEWART, and other Stories. By Mrs Oliphant.
VALENTINE AND HIS BROTHER. By the Same.
SONS AND DAUGHTERS. By the Same.
MARMORNE. By P. G. Hamerton.

REATA. By E. D. Gerard.
BEGGAR MY NEIGHBOUR. By the Same.
THE WATERS OF HERCULES. By the Same.
FAIR TO SEE. By L. W. M. Lockhart.
MINE IS THINE. By the Same.
DOUBLES AND QUITS. By the Same.
ALTIORA PETO. By Laurence Oliphant.
PICCADILLY. By the Same. With Illustrations.
LADY BABY. By D. Gerard.
THE BLACKSMITH OF VOE. By Paul Cushing.
THE DILEMMA. By the Author of 'The Battle of Dorking.'
MY TRIVIAL LIFE AND MISFORTUNE. By A Plain Woman.
POOR NELLIE. By the Same.

Standard Novels. Uniform in size and binding. Each complete in one Volume.

FLORIN SERIES, Illustrated Boards. Bound in Cloth, 2s. 6d.

TOM CRINGLE'S LOG. By Michael Scott.
THE CRUISE OF THE MIDGE. By the Same.
CYRIL THORNTON. By Captain Hamilton.
ANNALS OF THE PARISH. By John Galt.
THE PROVOST, &c. By the Same.
SIR ANDREW WYLIE. By the Same.
THE ENTAIL. By the Same.
MISS MOLLY. By Beatrice May Butt.
REGINALD DALTON. By J. G. Lockhart.

PEN OWEN. By Dean Hook.
ADAM BLAIR. By J. G. Lockhart.
LADY LEE'S WIDOWHOOD. By General Sir E. B. Hamley.
SALEM CHAPEL. By Mrs Oliphant.
THE PERPETUAL CURATE. By the Same.
MISS MARJORIBANKS. By the Same.
JOHN: A Love Story. By the Same.

SHILLING SERIES, Illustrated Cover. Bound in Cloth, 1s. 6d.

THE RECTOR, and THE DOCTOR'S FAMILY. By Mrs Oliphant.
THE LIFE OF MANSIE WAUCH. By D. M. Moir.
PENINSULAR SCENES AND SKETCHES. By F. Hardman.

SIR FRIZZLE PUMPKIN, NIGHTS AT MESS, &c.
THE SUBALTERN.
LIFE IN THE FAR WEST. By G. F. Ruxton.
VALERIUS: A Roman Story. By J. G. Lockhart.

BON GAULTIER'S BOOK OF BALLADS. Fifteenth Edition. With Illustrations by Doyle, Leech, and Crowquill. Fcap. 8vo, 5s.

BRADDON. Thirty Years of Shikar. By Sir EDWARD BRADDON, K.C.M.G. With Illustrations by G. D. Giles, and Map of Oudh Forest Tracts and Nepal Terai. Demy 8vo, 18s.

BROUGHAM. Memoirs of the Life and Times of Henry Lord Brougham. Written by HIMSELF. 3 vols. 8vo, £2, 8s. The Volumes are sold separately, price 16s. each.

BROWN. The Forester: A Practical Treatise on the Planting and Tending of Forest-trees and the General Management of Woodlands. By JAMES BROWN, LL.D. Sixth Edition, Enlarged. Edited by JOHN NISBET, D.Œc., Author of 'British Forest Trees,' &c. In 2 vols. royal 8vo, with 350 Illustrations, 42s. net.

Also being issued in 15 Monthly parts, price 2s. 6d. net each.

[Parts 1 to 4 ready.

BROWN. Stray Sport. By J. MORAY BROWN, Author of 'Shikar Sketches,' 'Powder, Spur, and Spear,' 'The Days when we went Hog-Hunting.' 2 vols. post 8vo, with Fifty Illustrations, 21s.

BROWN. A Manual of Botany, Anatomical and Physiological. For the Use of Students. By ROBERT BROWN, M.A., Ph.D. Crown 8vo, with numerous Illustrations, 12s. 6d.

BRUCE.

In Clover and Heather. Poems by WALLACE BRUCE. New and Enlarged Edition. Crown 8vo, 3s. 6d.
A limited number of Copies of the First Edition, on large hand-made paper, 12s. 6d.

Here's a Hand. Addresses and Poems. Crown 8vo, 5s. Large Paper Edition, limited to 100 copies, price 21s.

BUCHAN. Introductory Text-Book of Meteorology. By ALEXANDER BUCHAN, LL.D., F.R.S.E., Secretary of the Scottish Meteorological Society, &c. New Edition. Crown 8vo, with Coloured Charts and Engravings. *[In preparation.*

BURBIDGE.

Domestic Floriculture, Window Gardening, and Floral Decorations. Being Practical Directions for the Propagation, Culture, and Arrangement of Plants and Flowers as Domestic Ornaments. By F. W. BURBIDGE. Second Edition. Crown 8vo, with numerous Illustrations, 7s. 6d.

Cultivated Plants: Their Propagation and Improvement. Including Natural and Artificial Hybridisation, Raising from Seed, Cuttings, and Layers, Grafting and Budding, as applied to the Families and Genera in Cultivation. Crown 8vo, with numerous Illustrations, 12s. 6d.

BURGESS. The Viking Path: A Tale of the White Christ. By J. J. HALDANE BURGESS, Author of 'Rasmie's Büddie,' 'Shetland Sketches,' &c. Crown 8vo, 6s.

BURKE. The Flowering of the Almond Tree, and other Poems. By CHRISTIAN BURKE. Pott 4to, 5s.

BURROWS.

Commentaries on the History of England, from the Earliest Times to 1865. By MONTAGU BURROWS, Chichele Professor of Modern History in the University of Oxford; Captain R.N.; F.S.A., &c.; "Officier de l'Instruction Publique," France. Crown 8vo, 7s. 6d.

The History of the Foreign Policy of Great Britain. Demy 8vo, 12s.

BURTON.

The History of Scotland: From Agricola's Invasion to the Extinction of the last Jacobite Insurrection. By JOHN HILL BURTON, D.C.L., Historiographer-Royal for Scotland. Cheaper Edition. In 8 monthly vols. Crown 8vo, 3s. 6d. each. *[Vols. I. to III. ready.*

History of the British Empire during the Reign of Queen Anne. In 3 vols. 8vo. 36s.

The Scot Abroad. Third Edition. Crown 8vo, 10s. 6d.

The Book-Hunter. New Edition. With Portrait. Crown 8vo, 7s. 6d.

BUTCHER. Armenosa of Egypt. A Romance of the Arab Conquest. By the Very Rev. Dean BUTCHER, D.D., F.S.A., Chaplain at Cairo. Crown 8vo, 6s.

BUTE. The Altus of St Columba. With a Prose Paraphrase and Notes. In paper cover, 2s. 6d.

BUTT.

Theatricals: An Interlude. By BEATRICE MAY BUTT. Crown 8vo, 6s.

Miss Molly. Cheap Edition, 2s.

Eugenie. Crown 8vo, 6s. 6d.

Elizabeth, and other Sketches. Crown 8vo, 6s.

Delicia. New Edition. Crown 8vo, 2s. 6d.

CAIRD. Sermons. By JOHN CAIRD, D.D., Principal of the University of Glasgow. Seventeenth Thousand. Fcap. 8vo, 5s.

CALDWELL. Schopenhauer's System in its Philosophical Significance (the Shaw Fellowship Lectures, 1893). By WILLIAM CALDWELL, M.A., D.Sc., Professor of Moral and Social Philosophy, Northwestern University, U.S.A.; formerly Assistant to the Professor of Logic and Metaphysics, Edin., and Examiner in Philosophy in the University of St Andrews. Demy 8vo, 10s. 6d. net.

CALLWELL. The Effect of Maritime Command on Land Campaigns since Waterloo. By Major C. E. CALLWELL, R.A. With Plans. Post 8vo, 6s. *net.*

CAMPBELL. Sermons Preached before the Queen at Balmoral. By the Rev. A. A. CAMPBELL, Minister of Crathie. Published by Command of Her Majesty. Crown 8vo, 4s. 6d.

CAMPBELL. Records of Argyll. Legends, Traditions, and Recollections of Argyllshire Highlanders, collected chiefly from the Gaelic. With Notes on the Antiquity of the Dress, Clan Colours, or Tartans of the Highlanders. By Lord ARCHIBALD CAMPBELL. Illustrated with Nineteen full-page Etchings. 4to, printed on hand-made paper, £3, 3s.

CANTON. A Lost Epic, and other Poems. By WILLIAM CANTON. Crown 8vo, 5s.

CARSTAIRS.
Human Nature in Rural India. By R. CARSTAIRS. Crown 8vo, 6s.
British Work in India. Crown 8vo, 6s.

CAUVIN. A Treasury of the English and German Languages. Compiled from the best Authors and Lexicographers in both Languages. By JOSEPH CAUVIN, LL.D. and Ph.D., of the University of Göttingen, &c. Crown 8vo, 7s. 6d.

CHARTERIS. Canonicity; or, Early Testimonies to the Existence and Use of the Books of the New Testament. Based on Kirchhoffer's 'Quellensammlung.' Edited by A. H. CHARTERIS, D.D., Professor of Biblical Criticism in the University of Edinburgh. 8vo, 18s.

CHENNELLS. Recollections of an Egyptian Princess. By her English Governess (Miss E. CHENNELLS). Being a Record of Five Years' Residence at the Court of Ismael Pasha Khédive. Second Edition. With Three Portraits. Post 8vo, 7s. 6d.

CHESNEY. The Dilemma. By General Sir GEORGE CHESNEY, K.C.B., M.P., Author of 'The Battle of Dorking,' &c. New Edition. Crown 8vo, 3s. 6d.

CHRISTISON. Life of Sir Robert Christison, Bart., M.D., D.C.L. Oxon., Professor of Medical Jurisprudence in the University of Edinburgh. Edited by his Sons. In 2 vols. 8vo. Vol. I.—Autobiography. 16s. Vol. II.—Memoirs. 16s.

CHURCH. Chapters in an Adventurous Life. Sir Richard Church in Italy and Greece. By E. M. CHURCH. With Photogravure Portrait. Demy 8vo, 10s. 6d.

CHURCH SERVICE SOCIETY.
A Book of Common Order: being Forms of Worship issued by the Church Service Society. Seventh Edition, carefully revised. In 1 vol. crown 8vo, cloth, 3s. 6d.; French morocco, 5s. Also in 2 vols. crown 8vo, cloth, 4s.; French morocco, 6s. 6d.
Daily Offices for Morning and Evening Prayer throughout the Week. Crown 8vo, 3s. 6d.
Order of Divine Service for Children. Issued by the Church Service Society. With Scottish Hymnal. Cloth, 3d.

CLOUSTON. Popular Tales and Fictions: their Migrations and Transformations. By W. A. CLOUSTON, Editor of 'Arabian Poetry for English Readers,' &c. 2 vols. post 8vo, roxburghe binding, 25s.

COCHRAN. A Handy Text-Book of Military Law. Compiled chiefly to assist Officers preparing for Examination; also for all Officers of the Regular and Auxiliary Forces. Comprising also a Synopsis of part of the Army Act. By Major F. COCHRAN, Hampshire Regiment Garrison Instructor, North British District. Crown 8vo, 7s. 6d.

COLQUHOUN. The Moor and the Loch. Containing Minute Instructions in all Highland Sports, with Wanderings over Crag and Corrie, Flood and Fell. By JOHN COLQUHOUN. Cheap Edition. With Illustrations. Demy 8vo, 10s. 6d.

COLVILE. Round the Black Man's Garden. By Lady Z. COLVILE, F.R.G.S. With 2 Maps and 50 Illustrations from Drawings by the Author and from Photographs. Demy 8vo, 16s.

CONDER. The Bible and the East. By Lieut.-Col. C. R. CONDER, R.E., LL.D., D.C.L., M.R.A.S., Author of 'Tent Work in Palestine,' &c. With Illustrations and a Map. Crown 8vo, 5s.

CONSTITUTION AND LAW OF THE CHURCH OF SCOTLAND. With an Introductory Note by the late Principal Tulloch. New Edition, Revised and Enlarged. Crown 8vo, 3s. 6d.

COTTERILL. Suggested Reforms in Public Schools. By C. C. COTTERILL, M.A. Crown 8vo, 3s. 6d.

COUNTY HISTORIES OF SCOTLAND. In demy 8vo volumes of about 350 pp. each. With Maps. Price 7s. 6d. net.

Fife and Kinross. By ÆNEAS J. G. MACKAY, LL.D., Sheriff of these Counties.

Dumfries and Galloway. By Sir HERBERT MAXWELL, Bart., M.P.

Moray and Nairn. By CHARLES RAMPINI, LL.D., Sheriff-Substitute of these Counties.

Inverness. By J. CAMERON LEES, D.D.   [*Others in preparation.*

CRAWFORD. Saracinesca. By F. MARION CRAWFORD, Author of 'Mr Isaacs,' &c., &c. Eighth Edition. Crown 8vo, 6s.

CRAWFORD.

The Doctrine of Holy Scripture respecting the Atonement. By the late THOMAS J. CRAWFORD, D.D., Professor of Divinity in the University of Edinburgh. Fifth Edition. 8vo, 12s.

The Fatherhood of God, Considered in its General and Special Aspects. Third Edition, Revised and Enlarged. 8vo, 9s.

The Preaching of the Cross, and other Sermons. 8vo, 7s. 6d.

The Mysteries of Christianity. Crown 8vo, 7s. 6d.

CROSS. Impressions of Dante, and of the New World; with a Few Words on Bimetallism. By J. W. CROSS, Editor of 'George Eliot's Life, as related in her Letters and Journals.' Post 8vo, 6s.

CUMBERLAND. Sport on the Pamirs and Turkistan Steppes. By Major C. S. CUMBERLAND. With Map and Frontispiece. Demy 8vo, 10s. 6d.

CURSE OF INTELLECT. Third Edition. Fcap. 8vo, 2s. 6d. net.

CUSHING. The Blacksmith of Voe. By PAUL CUSHING, Author of 'The Bull i' th' Thorn,' 'Cut with his own Diamond.' Cheap Edition. Crown 8vo, 3s. 6d.

DAVIES.

Norfolk Broads and Rivers; or, The Waterways, Lagoons, and Decoys of East Anglia. By G. CHRISTOPHER DAVIES. Illustrated with Seven full-page Plates. New and Cheaper Edition. Crown 8vo, 6s.

Our Home in Aveyron. Sketches of Peasant Life in Aveyron and the Lot. By G. CHRISTOPHER DAVIES and Mrs BROUGHALL. Illustrated with full-page Illustrations. 8vo, 15s. Cheap Edition, 7s. 6d.

DE LA WARR. An Eastern Cruise in the 'Edeline.' By the Countess DE LA WARR. In Illustrated Cover. 2s.

DESCARTES. The Method, Meditations, and Principles of Philosophy of Descartes. Translated from the Original French and Latin. With a New Introductory Essay, Historical and Critical, on the Cartesian Philosophy. By Professor VEITCH, LL.D., Glasgow University. Eleventh Edition. 6s. 6d.

DOGS, OUR DOMESTICATED: Their Treatment in reference to Food, Diseases, Habits, Punishment, Accomplishments. By 'MAGENTA.' Crown 8vo, 2s. 6d.

DOUGLAS.

The Ethics of John Stuart Mill. By CHARLES DOUGLAS, M.A., D.Sc., Lecturer in Moral Philosophy, and Assistant to the Professor of Moral Philosophy in the University of Edinburgh. Post 8vo, 6s. net.

John Stuart Mill: A Study of his Philosophy. Crown 8vo, 4s. 6d. net.

DOUGLAS. Chinese Stories. By ROBERT K. DOUGLAS. With numerous Illustrations by Parkinson, Forestier, and others. New and Cheaper Edition. Small demy 8vo, 5s.

DOUGLAS. Iras: A Mystery. By THEO. DOUGLAS, Author of 'A Bride Elect.' Cheaper Edition, in Paper Cover specially designed by Womrath. Crown 8vo, 1s. 6d.

DU CANE. The Odyssey of Homer, Books I.-XII. Translated into English Verse. By Sir CHARLES DU CANE, K.C.M.G. 8vo, 10s. 6d.

DUDGEON. History of the Edinburgh or Queen's Regiment Light Infantry Militia, now 3rd Battalion The Royal Scots; with an Account of the Origin and Progress of the Militia, and a Brief Sketch of the Old Royal Scots. By Major R. C. DUDGEON, Adjutant 3rd Battalion the Royal Scots. Post 8vo, with Illustrations, 10s. 6d.

DUNSMORE. Manual of the Law of Scotland as to the Relations between Agricultural Tenants and the Landlords, Servants, Merchants, and Bowers. By W. DUNSMORE. 8vo, 7s. 6d.

DZIEWICKI. Entombed in Flesh. By M. H. DZIEWICKI. In 1 vol. crown 8vo. [*In the press.*

ELIOT.

George Eliot's Life, Related in Her Letters and Journals. Arranged and Edited by her husband, J. W. CROSS. With Portrait and other Illustrations. Third Edition. 3 vols. post 8vo, 42s.

George Eliot's Life. With Portrait and other Illustrations. New Edition, in one volume. Crown 8vo, 7s. 6d.

Works of George Eliot (Standard Edition). 21 volumes, crown 8vo. In buckram cloth, gilt top, 2s. 6d. per vol.; or in roxburghe binding, 3s. 6d. per vol.

ADAM BEDE. 2 vols.—THE MILL ON THE FLOSS. 2 vols.—FELIX HOLT, THE RADICAL. 2 vols.—ROMOLA. 2 vols.—SCENES OF CLERICAL LIFE. 2 vols.—MIDDLEMARCH. 3 vols.—DANIEL DERONDA. 3 vols.—SILAS MARNER. 1 vol.—JUBAL. 1 vol.—THE SPANISH GIPSY. 1 vol.—ESSAYS. 1 vol.—THEOPHRASTUS SUCH. 1 vol.

Life and Works of George Eliot (Cabinet Edition). 24 volumes, crown 8vo, price £6. Also to be had handsomely bound in half and full calf. The Volumes are sold separately, bound in cloth, price 5s. each.

ELIOT.

Novels by George Eliot. Cheap Edition.
Adam Bede. Illustrated. 3s. 6d., cloth.—The Mill on the Floss. Illustrated. 3s. 6d., cloth.—Scenes of Clerical Life. Illustrated. 3s., cloth.—Silas Marner: the Weaver of Raveloe. Illustrated. 2s. 6d., cloth.—Felix Holt, the Radical. Illustrated. 3s. 6d., cloth.—Romola. With Vignette. 3s. 6d., cloth.

Middlemarch. Crown 8vo, 7s. 6d.

Daniel Deronda. Crown 8vo, 7s. 6d.

Essays. New Edition. Crown 8vo, 5s.

Impressions of Theophrastus Such. New Edition. Crown 8vo, 5s.

The Spanish Gypsy. New Edition. Crown 8vo, 5s.

The Legend of Jubal, and other Poems, Old and New. New Edition. Crown 8vo, 5s.

Wise, Witty, and Tender Sayings, in Prose and Verse. Selected from the Works of GEORGE ELIOT. New Edition. Fcap. 8vo, 3s. 6d.

ESSAYS ON SOCIAL SUBJECTS. Originally published in the 'Saturday Review.' New Edition. First and Second Series. 2 vols. crown 8vo, 6s. each.

FAITHS OF THE WORLD, The. A Concise History of the Great Religious Systems of the World. By various Authors. Crown 8vo, 5s.

FALKNER. The Lost Stradivarius. By J. MEADE FALKNER. Second Edition. Crown 8vo, 6s.

FENNELL AND O'CALLAGHAN. A Prince of Tyrone. By CHARLOTTE FENNELL and J. P. O'CALLAGHAN. Crown 8vo, 6s.

FERGUSON. Sir Samuel Ferguson in the Ireland of his Day. By LADY FERGUSON, Author of 'The Irish before the Conquest,' 'Life of William Reeves, D.D., Lord Bishop of Down, Connor, and Drumore,' &c., &c. With Two Portraits. 2 vols. post 8vo, 21s.

FERRIER.

Philosophical Works of the late James F. Ferrier, B.A. Oxon., Professor of Moral Philosophy and Political Economy, St Andrews. New Edition. Edited by Sir ALEXANDER GRANT, Bart., D.C.L., and Professor LUSHINGTON. 3 vols. crown 8vo, 34s. 6d.

Institutes of Metaphysic. Third Edition. 10s. 6d.

Lectures on the Early Greek Philosophy. 4th Edition. 10s. 6d.

Philosophical Remains, including the Lectures on Early Greek Philosophy. New Edition. 2 vols. 24s.

FLINT.

Historical Philosophy in France and French Belgium and Switzerland. By ROBERT FLINT, Corresponding Member of the Institute of France, Hon. Member of the Royal Society of Palermo, Professor in the University of Edinburgh, &c. 8vo, 21s.

Agnosticism. Being the Croall Lecture for 1887-88.
[*In the press.*

Theism. Being the Baird Lecture for 1876. Ninth Edition, Revised. Crown 8vo, 7s. 6d.

Anti-Theistic Theories. Being the Baird Lecture for 1877. Fifth Edition. Crown 8vo, 10s. 6d.

FOREIGN CLASSICS FOR ENGLISH READERS. Edited by Mrs OLIPHANT. Price 2s. 6d. *For List of Volumes, see page 2.*

FOSTER. The Fallen City, and other Poems. By WILL FOSTER. Crown 8vo, 6s.

FRANCILLON. Gods and Heroes ; or, The Kingdom of Jupiter.
By R. E. FRANCILLON. With 8 Illustrations. Crown 8vo, 5s.

FRANCIS. Among the Untrodden Ways. By M. E. FRANCIS
(Mrs Francis Blundell), Author of 'In a North Country Village,' 'A Daughter of
the Soil,' 'Frieze and Fustian,' &c. Crown 8vo, 3s. 6d.

FRASER.
Philosophy of Theism. Being the Gifford Lectures delivered
before the University of Edinburgh in 1894-95. First Series. By ALEXANDER
CAMPBELL FRASER, D.C.L. Oxford; Emeritus Professor of Logic and Metaphysics in the University of Edinburgh. Post 8vo, 7s. 6d. net.

Philosophy of Theism. Being the Gifford Lectures delivered
before the University of Edinburgh in 1895-96. Second Series. Post 8vo,
7s. 6d. *net.*

FRASER. St Mary's of Old Montrose : A History of the Parish
of Maryton. By the Rev. WILLIAM RUXTON FRASER, M.A., F.S.A. Scot.,
Emeritus Minister of Maryton; Author of 'History of the Parish and Burgh of
Laurencekirk.' Crown 8vo, 3s. 6d.

FULLARTON.
Merlin : A Dramatic Poem. By RALPH MACLEOD FULLAR-
TON. Crown 8vo, 5s.

Tanhäuser. Crown 8vo, 6s.

Lallan Sangs and German Lyrics. Crown 8vo, 5s.

GALT.
Novels by JOHN GALT. With General Introduction and
Prefatory Notes by S. R. CROCKETT. The Text Revised and Edited by D.
STORRAR MELDRUM, Author of 'The Story of Margrédel.' With Photogravure
Illustrations from Drawings by John Wallace. Fcap. 8vo, 3s. net each vol.

ANNALS OF THE PARISH, and THE AYRSHIRE LEGATEES. 2 vols.—SIR ANDREW
WYLIE. 2 vols.—THE ENTAIL; or, The Lairds of Grippy. 2 vols.—THE PRO-
VOST, and THE LAST OF THE LAIRDS. 2 vols.

See also STANDARD NOVELS, *p. 6.*

GENERAL ASSEMBLY OF THE CHURCH OF SCOTLAND.
Scottish Hymnal, With Appendix Incorporated. Published
for use in Churches by Authority of the General Assembly. 1. Large type,
cloth, red edges, 2s. 6d.; French morocco, 4s. 2. Bourgeois type, limp cloth, 1s.;
French morocco, 2s. 3. Nonpareil type, cloth, red edges, 6d.; French morocco,
1s. 4d. 4. Paper covers, 3d. 5. Sunday-School Edition, paper covers, 1d.,
cloth, 2d. No. 1, bound with the Psalms and Paraphrases, French morocco, 8s.
No. 2, bound with the Psalms and Paraphrases, cloth, 2s.; French morocco, 3s.

Prayers for Social and Family Worship. Prepared by a
Special Committee of the General Assembly of the Church of Scotland. Entirely
New Edition, Revised and Enlarged. Fcap. 8vo, red edges, 2s.

Prayers for Family Worship. A Selection of Four Weeks'
Prayers. New Edition. Authorised by the General Assembly of the Church of
Scotland. Fcap. 8vo, red edges, 1s. 6d.

One Hundred Prayers. Prepared by the Committee on Aids
to Devotion. 16mo, cloth limp, 6d.

Morning and Evening Prayers for Affixing to Bibles. Prepared
by the Committee on Aids to Devotion. 1d. for 6, or 1s. per 100.

GERARD.
Reata : What's in a Name. By E. D. GERARD. Cheap
Edition. Crown 8vo, 3s. 6d.

Beggar my Neighbour. Cheap Edition. Crown 8vo, 3s. 6d.

The Waters of Hercules. Cheap Edition. Crown 8vo, 3s. 6d.

A Sensitive Plant. Crown 8vo, 3s. 6d.

GERARD.

A Foreigner. An Anglo-German Study. By E. GERARD. Crown 8vo, 6s.

The Land beyond the Forest. Facts, Figures, and Fancies from Transylvania. With Maps and Illustrations. 2 vols. post 8vo, 25s.

Bis : Some Tales Retold. Crown 8vo, 6s.

A Secret Mission. 2 vols. crown 8vo, 17s.

An Electric Shock, and other Stories. Crown 8vo, 6s.

GERARD.

A Spotless Reputation. By DOROTHEA GERARD. Third Edition. Crown 8vo, 6s.

The Wrong Man. Second Edition. Crown 8vo, 6s.

Lady Baby. Cheap Edition. Crown 8vo, 3s. 6d.

Recha. Second Edition. Crown 8vo, 6s.

The Rich Miss Riddell. Second Edition. Crown 8vo, 6s.

GERARD. Stonyhurst Latin Grammar. By Rev. JOHN GERARD. Second Edition. Fcap. 8vo, 3s.

GILL.

Free Trade : an Inquiry into the Nature of its Operation. By RICHARD GILL. Crown 8vo, 7s. 6d.

Free Trade under Protection. Crown 8vo, 7s. 6d.

GORDON CUMMING.

At Home in Fiji. By C. F. GORDON CUMMING. Fourth Edition, post 8vo. With Illustrations and Map. 7s. 6d.

A Lady's Cruise in a French Man-of-War. New and Cheaper Edition. 8vo. With Illustrations and Map. 12s. 6d.

Fire-Fountains. The Kingdom of Hawaii : Its Volcanoes, and the History of its Missions. With Map and Illustrations. 2 vols. 8vo, 25s.

Wanderings in China. New and Cheaper Edition. 8vo, with Illustrations, 10s.

Granite Crags : The Yō-semité Region of California. Illustrated with 8 Engravings. New and Cheaper Edition. 8vo, 8s. 6d.

GRAHAM. Manual of the Elections (Scot.) (Corrupt and Illegal Practices) Act, 1890. With Analysis, Relative Act of Sederunt, Appendix containing the Corrupt Practices Acts of 1883 and 1885, and Copious Index. By J. EDWARD GRAHAM, Advocate. 8vo, 4s. 6d.

GRAND.

A Domestic Experiment. By SARAH GRAND, Author of 'The Heavenly Twins,' 'Ideala : A Study from Life.' Crown 8vo, 6s.

Singularly Deluded. Crown 8vo, 6s.

GRANT. Bush-Life in Queensland. By A. C. GRANT. New Edition. Crown 8vo, 6s.

GRIER.

In Furthest Ind. The Narrative of Mr EDWARD CARLYON of Ellswether, in the County of Northampton, and late of the Honourable East India Company's Service, Gentleman. Wrote by his own hand in the year of grace 1697. Edited, with a few Explanatory Notes, by SYDNEY C. GRIER. Post 8vo, 6s.

His Excellency's English Governess. Crown 8vo, 6s.

An Uncrowned King : A Romance of High Politics. Second Edition. Crown 8vo, 6s.

GUTHRIE-SMITH. Crispus : A Drama. By H. GUTHRIE-SMITH. Fcap. 4to, 5s.

HAGGARD. Under Crescent and Star. By Lieut.-Col. ANDREW
HAGGARD, D.S.O., Author of 'Dodo and I,' 'Tempest Torn,' &c. With a
Portrait. Second Edition. Crown 8vo, 6s.

HALDANE. Subtropical Cultivations and Climates. A Handy
Book for Planters, Colonists, and Settlers. By R. C. HALDANE. Post 8vo, 9s.

HAMERTON.

Wenderholme: A Story of Lancashire and Yorkshire Life.
By P. G. HAMERTON, Author of 'A Painter's Camp.' New Edition. Crown
8vo, 3s. 6d.

Marmorne. New Edition. Crown 8vo, 3s. 6d.

HAMILTON.

Lectures on Metaphysics. By Sir WILLIAM HAMILTON,
Bart., Professor of Logic and Metaphysics in the University of Edinburgh.
Edited by the Rev. H. L. MANSEL, B.D., LL.D., Dean of St Paul's; and JOHN
VEITCH, M.A., LL.D., Professor of Logic and Rhetoric, Glasgow. Seventh
Edition. 2 vols. 8vo, 24s.

Lectures on Logic. Edited by the SAME. Third Edition,
Revised. 2 vols., 24s.

Discussions on Philosophy and Literature, Education and
University Reform. Third Edition. 8vo, 21s.

Memoir of Sir William Hamilton, Bart., Professor of Logic
and Metaphysics in the University of Edinburgh. By Professor VEITCH, of the
University of Glasgow. 8vo, with Portrait, 18s.

Sir William Hamilton: The Man and his Philosophy. Two
Lectures delivered before the Edinburgh Philosophical Institution, January and
February 1883. By Professor VEITCH. Crown 8vo, 2s.

HAMLEY.

The Operations of War Explained and Illustrated. By
General Sir EDWARD BRUCE HAMLEY, K.C.B., K.C.M.G. Fifth Edition, Revised
throughout. 4to, with numerous Illustrations, 30s.

National Defence; Articles and Speeches. Post 8vo, 6s.

Shakespeare's Funeral, and other Papers. Post 8vo, 7s. 6d.

Thomas Carlyle: An Essay. Second Edition. Crown 8vo,
2s. 6d.

On Outposts. Second Edition. 8vo, 2s.

Wellington's Career; A Military and Political Summary.
Crown 8vo, 2s.

Lady Lee's Widowhood. New Edition. Crown 8vo, 3s. 6d.
Cheaper Edition, 2s. 6d.

Our Poor Relations. A Philozoic Essay. With Illustrations,
chiefly by Ernest Griset. Crown 8vo, cloth gilt, 3s. 6d.

The Life of General Sir Edward Bruce Hamley, K.C.B.,
K.C.M.G. By ALEXANDER INNES SHAND. With two Photogravure Portraits and
other Illustrations. Cheaper Edition. With a Statement by Mr EDWARD
HAMLEY. 2 vols. demy 8vo, 10s. 6d.

HARE. Down the Village Street: Scenes in a West Country
Hamlet. By CHRISTOPHER HARE. Second Edition. Crown 8vo, 6s.

HARRADEN.

In Varying Moods: Short Stories. By BEATRICE HARRADEN,
Author of 'Ships that Pass in the Night.' Twelfth Edition. Crown 8vo, 3s. 6d.

Hilda Strafford, and The Remittance Man. Two Californian
Stories. Tenth Edition. Crown 8vo, 3s. 6d.

HARRIS.

From Batum to Baghdad, *via* Tiflis, Tabriz, and Persian
Kurdistan. By WALTER B. HARRIS, F.R.G.S., Author of 'The Land of an
African Sultan; Travels in Morocco,' &c. With numerous Illustrations and 2
Maps. Demy 8vo, 12s.

HARRIS.

Tafilet. The Narrative of a Journey of Exploration to the Atlas Mountains and the Oases of the North-West Sahara. With Illustrations by Maurice Romberg from Sketches and Photographs by the Author, and Two Maps. Demy 8vo, 12s.

A Journey through the Yemen, and some General Remarks upon that Country. With 3 Maps and numerous Illustrations by Forestier and Wallace from Sketches and Photographs taken by the Author. Demy 8vo, 16s.

Danovitch, and other Stories. Crown 8vo, 6s.

HAWKER. The Prose Works of Rev. R. S. HAWKER, Vicar of Morwenstow. Including 'Footprints of Former Men in Far Cornwall.' Re-edited, with Sketches never before published. With a Frontispiece. Crown 8vo, 3s. 6d.

HAY. The Works of the Right Rev. Dr George Hay, Bishop of Edinburgh. Edited under the Supervision of the Right Rev. Bishop STRAIN. With Memoir and Portrait of the Author. 5 vols. crown 8vo, bound in extra cloth, £1, 1s. The following Volumes may be had separately—viz. :

The Devout Christian Instructed in the Law of Christ from the Written Word. 2 vols., 8s.—The Pious Christian Instructed in the Nature and Practice of the Principal Exercises of Piety. 1 vol., 3s.

HEATLEY.

The Horse-Owner's Safeguard. A Handy Medical Guide for every Man who owns a Horse. By G. S. HEATLEY, M.R.C.V.S. Crown 8vo, 5s.

The Stock-Owner's Guide. A Handy Medical Treatise for every Man who owns an Ox or a Cow. Crown 8vo, 4s. 6d.

HEDDERWICK. Lays of Middle Age ; and other Poems. By JAMES HEDDERWICK, LL.D., Author of 'Backward Glances.' Price 3s. 6d.

HEMANS.

The Poetical Works of Mrs Hemans. Copyright Editions. Royal 8vo, 5s. The Same with Engravings, cloth, gilt edges, 7s. 6d.

Select Poems of Mrs Hemans. Fcap., cloth, gilt edges, 3s.

HERKLESS. Cardinal Beaton : Priest and Politician. By JOHN HERKLESS, Professor of Church History, St Andrews. With a Portrait. Post 8vo, 7s. 6d.

HEWISON. The Isle of Bute in the Olden Time. With Illustrations, Maps, and Plans. By JAMES KING HEWISON, M.A., F.S.A. (Scot.), Minister of Rothesay. Vol. I., Celtic Saints and Heroes. Crown 4to, 15s. net. Vol. II., The Royal Stewards and the Brandanes. Crown 4to, 15s. net.

HIBBEN. Inductive Logic. By JOHN GRIER HIBBEN, Ph.D., Assistant Professor of Logic in Princeton University, U.S.A. Crown 8vo, 3s. 6d. net.

HILDEBRAND. The Early Relations between Britain and Scandinavia. Being the Rhind Lectures in Archæology for 1896. By Dr HANS HILDEBRAND, Royal Antiquary of Sweden. With Illustrations. In 1 vol. post 8vo. [*In the press.*

HOME PRAYERS. By Ministers of the Church of Scotland and Members of the Church Service Society. Second Edition. Fcap. 8vo, 3s.

HORNBY. Admiral of the Fleet Sir Geoffrey Phipps Hornby, G.C.B. A Biography. By Mrs FRED. EGERTON. With Three Portraits. Demy 8vo, 16s.

HUTCHINSON. Hints on the Game of Golf. By HORACE G. HUTCHINSON. Ninth Edition, Enlarged. Fcap. 8vo, cloth, 1s.

HYSLOP. The Elements of Ethics. By JAMES H. HYSLOP, Ph.D., Instructor in Ethics, Columbia College, New York, Author of 'The Elements of Logic.' Post 8vo, 7s. 6d. net.

IDDESLEIGH. Life, Letters, and Diaries of Sir Stafford Northcote, First Earl of Iddesleigh. By ANDREW LANG. With Three Portraits and a View of Pynes. Third Edition. 2 vols. post 8vo, 31s. 6d.

POPULAR EDITION. With Portrait and View of Pynes. Post 8vo, 7s. 6d.

INDEX GEOGRAPHICUS: Being a List, alphabetically arranged, of the Principal Places on the Globe, with the Countries and Subdivisions of the Countries in which they are situated, and their Latitudes and Longitudes. Imperial 8vo, pp. 676, 21s.

JEAN JAMBON.   Our Trip to Blunderland ; or, Grand Excursion to Blundertown and Back. By JEAN JAMBON. With Sixty Illustrations designed by CHARLES DOYLE, engraved by DALZIEL. Fourth Thousand. Cloth, gilt edges, 6s. 6d. Cheap Edition, cloth, 3s. 6d. Boards, 2s. 6d.

JEBB. A Strange Career. The Life and Adventures of JOHN GLADWYN JEBB. By his Widow. With an Introduction by H. RIDER HAGGARD, and an Electrogravure Portrait of Mr Jebb. Third Edition. Demy 8vo, 10s. 6d. CHEAP EDITION. With Illustrations by John Wallace. Crown 8vo, 3s. 6d.

Some Unconventional People. By Mrs GLADWYN JEBB, Author of 'Life and Adventures of J. G. Jebb.' With Illustrations. Crown 8vo, 3s. 6d.

JENNINGS.   Mr Gladstone: A Study.   By LOUIS J. JENNINGS, M.P., Author of 'Republican Government in the United States,' 'The Croker Memoirs,' &c. Popular Edition. Crown 8vo, 1s.

JERNINGHAM.

Reminiscences of an Attaché. By HUBERT E. H. JERNINGHAM. Second Edition. Crown 8vo, 5s.

Diane de Breteuille. A Love Story. Crown 8vo, 2s. 6d.

JOHNSTON.

The Chemistry of Common Life. By Professor J. F. W. JOHNSTON. New Edition, Revised. By ARTHUR HERBERT CHURCH, M.A. Oxon.; Author of 'Food: its Sources, Constituents, and Uses,' &c. With Maps and 102 Engravings. Crown 8vo, 7s. 6d.

Elements of Agricultural Chemistry. An entirely New Edition from the Edition by Sir CHARLES A. CAMERON, M.D., F.R.C.S.I., &c. Revised and brought down to date by C. M. AIKMAN, M.A., B.Sc., F.R.S.E., Professor of Chemistry, Glasgow Veterinary College. 17th Edition. Crown 8vo, 6s. 6d.

Catechism of Agricultural Chemistry. An entirely New Edition from the Edition by Sir CHARLES A. CAMERON. Revised and Enlarged by C. M. AIKMAN, M.A., &c. 95th Thousand. With numerous Illustrations. Crown 8vo, 1s.

JOHNSTON. Agricultural Holdings (Scotland) Acts, 1883 and 1889 ; and the Ground Game Act, 1880. With Notes, and Summary of Procedure, &c. By CHRISTOPHER N. JOHNSTON, M.A., Advocate. Demy 8vo, 5s.

JOKAI. Timar's Two Worlds. By MAURUS JOKAI. Authorised Translation by Mrs HEGAN KENNARD. Cheap Edition. Crown 8vo, 6s.

KEBBEL. The Old and the New: English Country Life. By T. E. KEBBEL, M.A., Author of 'The Agricultural Labourers,' 'Essays in History and Politics,' 'Life of Lord Beaconsfield.' Crown 8vo, 5s.

KERR. St Andrews in 1645-46. By D. R. KERR. Crown 8vo, 2s. 6d.

KINGLAKE.

History of the Invasion of the Crimea. By A. W. KINGLAKE. Cabinet Edition, Revised. With an Index to the Complete Work. Illustrated with Maps and Plans. Complete in 9 vols., crown 8vo, at 6s. each.

—— Abridged Edition for Military Students. Revised by Lieut.-Col. Sir GEORGE SYDENHAM CLARKE, K.C.M.G., R.E. In 1 vol. demy 8vo. [*In the press.*]

History of the Invasion of the Crimea. Demy 8vo. Vol. VI. Winter Troubles. With a Map, 16s. Vols. VII. and VIII. From the Morrow of Inkerman to the Death of Lord Raglan With an Index to the Whole Work. With Maps and Plans. 28s.

KINGLAKE.

Eothen. A New Edition, uniform with the Cabinet Edition
of the 'History of the Invasion of the Crimea.' 6s.
CHEAPER EDITION. With Portrait and Biographical Sketch of the Author.
Crown 8vo, 3s. 6d. Popular Edition, in paper cover, 1s. net.

KIRBY. In Haunts of Wild Game: A Hunter-Naturalist's
Wanderings from Kahlamba to Libombo. By FREDERICK VAUGHAN KIRBY,
F.Z.S. (Maqaqamba). With numerous Illustrations by Charles Whymper, and a
Map. Large demy 8vo, 25s.

KLEIN. Among the Gods. Scenes of India, with Legends by
the Way. By AUGUSTA KLEIN. With 22 Full-page Illustrations. Demy 8vo, 15s.

KNEIPP. My Water-Cure. As Tested through more than
Thirty Years, and Described for the Healing of Diseases and the Preservation of
Health. By SEBASTIAN KNEIPP, Parish Priest of Wörishofen (Bavaria). With a
Portrait and other Illustrations. Authorised English Translation from the
Thirtieth German Edition, by A. de F. Cheap Edition. With an Appendix, con-
taining the Latest Developments of Pfarrer Kneipp's System, and a Preface by
E. Gerard. Crown 8vo, 3s. 6d.

KNOLLYS. The Elements of Field-Artillery. Designed for
the Use of Infantry and Cavalry Officers. By HENRY KNOLLYS, Colonel Royal
Artillery; Author of 'From Sedan to Saarbrück,' Editor of 'Incidents in the
Sepoy War,' &c. With Engravings. Crown 8vo, 7s. 6d.

LANG. Life, Letters, and Diaries of Sir Stafford Northcote,
First Earl of Iddesleigh. By ANDREW LANG. With Three Portraits and a View
of Pynes. Third Edition. 2 vols. post 8vo, 31s. 6d.
POPULAR EDITION. With Portrait and View of Pynes. Post 8vo, 7s. 6d.

LEES. A Handbook of the Sheriff and Justice of Peace Small
Debt Courts. With Notes, References, and Forms. By J. M. LEES, Advocate,
Sheriff of Stirling, Dumbarton, and Clackmannan. 8vo, 7s. 6d.

LINDSAY.

Recent Advances in Theistic Philosophy of Religion. By Rev.
JAMES LINDSAY, M.A., B.D., B.Sc., F.R.S.E., F.G.S., Minister of the Parish of
St Andrew's, Kilmarnock. Demy 8vo, 12s. 6d. net.

The Progressiveness of Modern Christian Thought. Crown
8vo, 6s.

Essays, Literary and Philosophical. Crown 8vo, 3s. 6d.

The Significance of the Old Testament for Modern Theology.
Crown 8vo, 1s. net.

The Teaching Function of the Modern Pulpit. Crown 8vo,
1s. net.

LOCKHART.

Doubles and Quits. By LAURENCE W. M. LOCKHART. New
Edition. Crown 8vo, 3s. 6d.

Fair to See. New Edition. Crown 8vo, 3s. 6d.

Mine is Thine. New Edition. Crown 8vo, 3s. 6d.

LOCKHART.

The Church of Scotland in the Thirteenth Century. The
Life and Times of David de Bernham of St Andrews (Bishop), A.D. 1239 to 1253.
With List of Churches dedicated by him, and Dates. By WILLIAM LOCKHART,
A.M., D.D., F.S.A. Scot., Minister of Colinton Parish. 2d Edition. 8vo, 6s.

Dies Tristes: Sermons for Seasons of Sorrow. Crown 8vo, 6s.

LORIMER.

The Institutes of Law : A Treatise of the Principles of Jurisprudence as determined by Nature. By the late JAMES LORIMER, Professor of
Public Law and of the Law of Nature and Nations in the University of Edinburgh. New Edition, Revised and much Enlarged. 8vo, 18s.

LORIMER.

The Institutes of the Law of Nations. A Treatise of the Jural Relation of Separate Political Communities. In 2 vols. 8vo. Volume I., price 16s. Volume II., price 20s.

LUGARD. The Rise of our East African Empire : Early Efforts in Uganda and Nyasaland. By F. D. LUGARD, Captain Norfolk Regiment. With 130 Illustrations from Drawings and Photographs under the personal superintendence of the Author, and 14 specially prepared Maps. In 2 vols. large demy 8vo, 42s.

M'CHESNEY.

Miriam Cromwell, Royalist : A Romance of the Great Rebellion. By DORA GREENWELL M'CHESNEY. Crown 8vo, 6s.

Kathleen Clare: Her Book, 1637-41. With Frontispiece, and five full-page Illustrations by James A. Shearman. Crown 8vo, 6s.

M'COMBIE. Cattle and Cattle-Breeders. By WILLIAM M'COMBIE, Tillyfour. New Edition, Enlarged, with Memoir of the Author by JAMES MACDONALD, F.R.S.E., Secretary Highland and Agricultural Society of Scotland. Crown 8vo, 3s. 6d.

M'CRIE.

Works of the Rev. Thomas M'Crie, D.D. Uniform Edition. 4 vols. crown 8vo, 24s.

Life of John Knox. Crown 8vo, 6s. Another Edition, 3s. 6d.

Life of Andrew Melville. Crown 8vo, 6s.

History of the Progress and Suppression of the Reformation in Italy in the Sixteenth Century. Crown 8vo, 4s.

History of the Progress and Suppression of the Reformation in Spain in the Sixteenth Century. Crown 8vo, 3s. 6d.

M'CRIE. The Public Worship of Presbyterian Scotland. Historically treated. With copious Notes, Appendices, and Index. The Fourteenth Series of the Cunningham Lectures. By the Rev. CHARLES G. M'CRIE, D.D. Demy 8vo, 10s. 6d.

MACDONALD. A Manual of the Criminal Law (Scotland) Procedure Act, 1887. By NORMAN DORAN MACDONALD. Revised by the LORD JUSTICE-CLERK. 8vo, 10s. 6d.

MACDONALD AND SINCLAIR. History of Polled Aberdeen and Angus Cattle. Giving an Account of the Origin, Improvement, and Characteristics of the Breed. By JAMES MACDONALD and JAMES SINCLAIR. Illustrated with numerous Animal Portraits. Post 8vo, 12s. 6d.

MACDOUGALL AND DODDS. A Manual of the Local Government (Scotland) Act, 1894. With Introduction, Explanatory Notes, and Copious Index. By J. PATTEN MACDOUGALL, Legal Secretary to the Lord Advocate, and J. M. DODDS. Tenth Thousand, Revised. Crown 8vo, 2s. 6d. net.

MACINTYRE. Hindu - Koh : Wanderings and Wild Sports on and beyond the Himalayas. By Major-General DONALD MACINTYRE, V.C., late Prince of Wales' Own Goorkhas, F.R.G.S. *Dedicated to H.R.H. The Prince of Wales.* New and Cheaper Edition, Revised, with numerous Illustrations. Post 8vo, 3s. 6d.

MACKAY.

Elements of Modern Geography. By the Rev. ALEXANDER MACKAY, LL.D., F.R.G.S. 55th Thousand, Revised to the present time. Crown 8vo, pp. 300, 3s.

The Intermediate Geography. Intended as an Intermediate Book between the Author's 'Outlines of Geography' and 'Elements of Geography.' Eighteenth Edition, Revised. Fcap. 8vo, pp. 238, 2s.

Outlines of Modern Geography. 191st Thousand, Revised to the present time. Fcap. 8vo, pp. 128, 1s.

Elements of Physiography. New Edition. Rewritten and Enlarged. With numerous Illustrations. Crown 8vo.   [*In the press.*

MACKENZIE. Studies in Roman Law. With Comparative Views of the Laws of France, England, and Scotland. By Lord MACKENZIE, one of the Judges of the Court of Session in Scotland. Sixth Edition, Edited by JOHN KIRKPATRICK, M.A., LL.B., Advocate, Professor of History in the University of Edinburgh. 8vo, 12s.

MACPHERSON. Glimpses of Church and Social Life in the Highlands in Olden Times. By ALEXANDER MACPHERSON, F.S.A. Scot. With 6 Photogravure Portraits and other full-page Illustrations. Small 4to, 25s.

M'PHERSON. Golf and Golfers. Past and Present. By J. GORDON M'PHERSON, Ph.D., F.R.S.E. With an Introduction by the Right Hon. A. J. BALFOUR, and a Portrait of the Author. Fcap. 8vo, 1s. 6d.

MACRAE. A Handbook of Deer-Stalking. By ALEXANDER MACRAE, late Forester to Lord Henry Bentinck. With Introduction by Horatio Ross, Esq. Fcap. 8vo, with 2 Photographs from Life. 3s. 6d.

MAIN. Three Hundred English Sonnets. Chosen and Edited by DAVID M. MAIN. New Edition. Fcap. 8vo, 3s. 6d.

MAIR. A Digest of Laws and Decisions, Ecclesiastical and Civil, relating to the Constitution, Practice, and Affairs of the Church of Scotland. With Notes and Forms of Procedure. By the Rev. WILLIAM MAIR, D.D., Minister of the Parish of Earlston. New Edition, Revised. Crown 8vo, 9s. net.

MARCHMONT AND THE HUMES OF POLWARTH. By One of their Descendants. With numerous Portraits and other Illustrations. Crown 4to, 21s. net.

MARSHMAN. History of India. From the Earliest Period to the present time. By JOHN CLARK MARSHMAN, C.S.I. Third and Cheaper Edition. Post 8vo, with Map, 6s.

MARTIN.

The Æneid of Virgil. Books I.-VI. Translated by Sir THEODORE MARTIN, K.C.B. Post 8vo, 7s. 6d.

Goethe's Faust. Part I. Translated into English Verse. Second Edition, crown 8vo, 6s. Ninth Edition, fcap. 8vo, 3s. 6d.

Goethe's Faust. Part II. Translated into English Verse. Second Edition, Revised. Fcap. 8vo, 6s.

The Works of Horace. Translated into English Verse, with Life and Notes. 2 vols. New Edition. Crown 8vo, 21s.

Poems and Ballads of Heinrich Heine. Done into English Verse. Third Edition. Small crown 8vo, 5s.

The Song of the Bell, and other Translations from Schiller, Goethe, Uhland, and Others. Crown 8vo, 7s. 6d.

Madonna Pia: A Tragedy; and Three Other Dramas. Crown 8vo, 7s. 6d.

Catullus. With Life and Notes. Second Edition, Revised and Corrected. Post 8vo, 7s. 6d.

The 'Vita Nuova' of Dante. Translated, with an Introduction and Notes. Third Edition. Small crown 8vo, 5s.

Aladdin: A Dramatic Poem. By ADAM OEHLENSCHLAEGER. Fcap. 8vo, 5s.

Correggio: A Tragedy. By OEHLENSCHLAEGER. With Notes. Fcap. 8vo, 3s.

MARTIN. On some of Shakespeare's Female Characters. By HELENA FAUCIT, Lady MARTIN. Dedicated by permission to Her Most Gracious Majesty the Queen. Fifth Edition. With a Portrait by Lehmann. Demy 8vo, 7s. 6d.

MARWICK. Observations on the Law and Practice in regard to Municipal Elections and the Conduct of the Business of Town Councils and Commissioners of Police in Scotland. By Sir JAMES D. MARWICK, LL.D., Town-Clerk of Glasgow. Royal 8vo, 30s.

MATHESON.
Can the Old Faith Live with the New? or, The Problem of Evolution and Revelation. By the Rev. GEORGE MATHESON, D.D. Third Edition. Crown 8vo, 7s. 6d.

The Psalmist and the Scientist; or, Modern Value of the Religious Sentiment. Third Edition. Crown 8vo, 5s.

Spiritual Development of St Paul. Third Edition. Cr. 8vo, 5s.

The Distinctive Messages of the Old Religions. Second Edition. Crown 8vo, 5s.

Sacred Songs. New and Cheaper Edition. Crown 8vo, 2s. 6d.

MATHIESON. The Supremacy and Sufficiency of Jesus Christ our Lord, as set forth in the Epistle to the Hebrews. By J. E. MATHIESON, Superintendent of Mildmay Conference Hall, 1880 to 1890. Second Edition. Crown 8vo, 3s. 6d.

MAURICE. The Balance of Military Power in Europe. An Examination of the War Resources of Great Britain and the Continental States. By Colonel MAURICE, R.A., Professor of Military Art and History at the Royal Staff College. Crown 8vo, with a Map, 6s.

MAXWELL.
A Duke of Britain. A Romance of the Fourth Century. By Sir HERBERT MAXWELL, Bart., M.P., F.S.A., &c., Author of 'Passages in the Life of Sir Lucian Elphin.' Fourth Edition. Crown 8vo, 6s.

Life and Times of the Rt. Hon. William Henry Smith, M.P. With Portraits and numerous Illustrations by Herbert Railton, G. L. Seymour, and Others. 2 vols. demy 8vo, 25s.
POPULAR EDITION. With a Portrait and other Illustrations. Crown 8vo, 3s. 6d.

Scottish Land-Names: Their Origin and Meaning. Being the Rhind Lectures in Archæology for 1893. Post 8vo, 6s.

Meridiana: Noontide Essays. Post 8vo, 7s. 6d.

Post Meridiana: Afternoon Essays. Post 8vo, 6s.

Dumfries and Galloway. Being one of the Volumes of the County Histories of Scotland. With Four Maps. Demy 8vo, 7s. 6d. net.

MELDRUM.
The Story of Margrédel: Being a Fireside History of a Fifeshire Family. By D. STORRAR MELDRUM. Cheap Edition. Crown 8vo, 3s. 6d.

Grey Mantle and Gold Fringe. Crown 8vo, 6s.

MERZ. A History of European Thought in the Nineteenth Century. By JOHN THEODORE MERZ. Vol. I., post 8vo, 10s. 6d. net.

MICHIE.
The Larch: Being a Practical Treatise on its Culture and General Management. By CHRISTOPHER Y. MICHIE, Forester, Cullen House. Crown 8vo, with Illustrations. New and Cheaper Edition, Enlarged, 5s.

The Practice of Forestry. Crown 8vo, with Illustrations. 6s.

MIDDLETON. The Story of Alastair Bhan Comyn; or, The Tragedy of Dunphail. A Tale of Tradition and Romance. By the Lady MIDDLETON. Square 8vo, 10s. Cheaper Edition, 5s.

MIDDLETON. Latin Verse Unseens. By G. MIDDLETON, M.A., Lecturer in Latin, Aberdeen University; late Scholar of Emmanuel College, Cambridge; Joint-Editor of 'Student's Companion to Latin Authors.' In 1 vol. crown 8vo.   [*In the press.*]

MILLER. The Dream of Mr H——, the Herbalist. By HUGH MILLER, F.R.S.E., late H.M. Geological Survey, Author of 'Landscape Geology.' With a Photogravure Frontispiece. Crown 8vo, 2s. 6d.

MILLS. Greek Verse Unseens. By T. R. MILLS, M.A., late Lecturer in Greek, Aberdeen University; formerly Scholar of Wadham College, Oxford; Joint-Editor of 'Student's Companion to Latin Authors.' In 1 vol. crown 8vo.   [*In the press.*]

MINTO.

A Manual of English Prose Literature, Biographical and Critical: designed mainly to show Characteristics of Style. By W. MINTO, M.A., Hon. LL.D. of St Andrews; Professor of Logic in the University of Aberdeen. Third Edition, Revised. Crown 8vo, 7s. 6d.

Characteristics of English Poets, from Chaucer to Shirley. New Edition, Revised. Crown 8vo, 7s. 6d.

Plain Principles of Prose Composition. Crown 8vo, 1s. 6d.

The Literature of the Georgian Era. Edited, with a Biographical Introduction, by Professor KNIGHT, St Andrews. Post 8vo, 6s.

MOIR. Life of Mansie Wauch, Tailor in Dalkeith. By D. M. MOIR. With CRUIKSHANK'S Illustrations. Cheaper Edition. Crown 8vo, 2s. 6d. Another Edition, without Illustrations, fcap. 8vo, 1s. 6d.

MOLE. For the Sake of a Slandered Woman. By MARION MOLE. Fcap. 8vo, 2s. 6d. net.

MOMERIE.

Defects of Modern Christianity, and other Sermons. By Rev. ALFRED WILLIAMS MOMERIE, M.A., D.Sc., LL.D. Fifth Edition. Crown 8vo, 5s.

The Basis of Religion. Being an Examination of Natural Religion. Third Edition. Crown 8vo, 2s. 6d.

The Origin of Evil, and other Sermons. Eighth Edition, Enlarged. Crown 8vo, 5s.

Personality. The Beginning and End of Metaphysics, and a Necessary Assumption in all Positive Philosophy. Fifth Edition, Revised. Crown 8vo, 3s.

Agnosticism. Fourth Edition, Revised. Crown 8vo, 5s.

Preaching and Hearing; and other Sermons. Fourth Edition, Enlarged. Crown 8vo, 5s.

Belief in God. Third Edition. Crown 8vo, 3s.

Inspiration; and other Sermons. Second Edition, Enlarged. Crown 8vo, 5s.

Church and Creed. Third Edition. Crown 8vo, 4s. 6d.

The Future of Religion, and other Essays. Second Edition. Crown 8vo, 3s. 6d.

The English Church and the Romish Schism. Second Edition. Crown 8vo, 2s. 6d.

MONCREIFF.

The Provost-Marshal. A Romance of the Middle Shires. By the Hon. FREDERICK MONCREIFF. Crown 8vo, 6s.

The X Jewel. A Romance of the Days of James VI. Crown 8vo, 6s.

MONTAGUE. Military Topography. Illustrated by Practical Examples of a Practical Subject. By Major-General W. E. MONTAGUE, C.B., P.S.C., late Garrison Instructor Intelligence Department, Author of 'Campaigning in South Africa.' With Forty-one Diagrams. Crown 8vo, 5s.

MONTALEMBERT. Memoir of Count de Montalembert. A Chapter of Recent French History. By Mrs OLIPHANT, Author of the 'Life of Edward Irving,' &c. 2 vols. crown 8vo, £1, 4s.

MORISON.

Doorside Ditties. By JEANIE MORISON. With a Frontispiece. Crown 8vo, 3s. 6d.

Æolus. A Romance in Lyrics. Crown 8vo, 3s.

There as Here. Crown 8vo, 3s.

*** *A limited impression on hand-made paper, bound in vellum, 7s. 6d.*

Selections from Poems. Crown 8vo, 4s. 6d.

Sordello. An Outline Analysis of Mr Browning's Poem. Crown 8vo, 3s.

MORISON.

Of "Fifine at the Fair," "Christmas Eve and Easter Day,'
and other of Mr Browning's Poems. Crown 8vo, 3s.

The Purpose of the Ages. Crown 8vo, 9s.

Gordon : An Our-day Idyll. Crown 8vo, 3s.

Saint Isadora, and other Poems. Crown 8vo, 1s. 6d.

Snatches of Song. Paper, 1s. 6d. ; cloth, 3s.

Pontius Pilate. Paper, 1s. 6d. ; cloth, 3s.

Mill o' Forres. Crown 8vo, 1s.

Ane Booke of Ballades. Fcap. 4to, 1s.

MUNRO. The Lost Pibroch, and other Sheiling Stories. By
NEIL MUNRO. Crown 8vo, 6s.

MUNRO.

Rambles and Studies in Bosnia-Herzegovina and Dalmatia.
With an Account of the Proceedings of the Congress of Archæologists and
Anthropologists held at Sarajevo in 1894. By ROBERT MUNRO, M.A., M.D.,
F.R.S.E., Author of 'The Lake-Dwellings of Europe,' &c. With numerous Illus-
trations. Demy 8vo, 12s. 6d. net.

Prehistoric Problems. With numerous Illustrations. Demy
8vo, 10s. net.

MUNRO. On Valuation of Property. By WILLIAM MUNRO,
M.A., Her Majesty's Assessor of Railways and Canals for Scotland. Second
Edition, Revised and Enlarged. 8vo, 3s. 6d.

MURDOCH. Manual of the Law of Insolvency and Bankruptcy :
Comprehending a Summary of the Law of Insolvency, Notour Bankruptcy,
Composition-Contracts, Trust-Deeds, Cessios, and Sequestrations ; and the
Winding-up of Joint-Stock Companies in Scotland ; with Annotations on the
various Insolvency and Bankruptcy Statutes ; and with Forms of Procedure
applicable to these Subjects. By JAMES MURDOCH, Member of the Faculty of
Procurators in Glasgow. Fifth Edition, Revised and Enlarged. 8vo, 12s. net.

MURRAY. A Popular Manual of Finance. By SYDNEY J.
MURRAY. In 1 vol. crown 8vo.   [*In the press.*

MY TRIVIAL LIFE AND MISFORTUNE : A Gossip with
no Plot in Particular. By A PLAIN WOMAN. Cheap Edition. Crown 8vo, 3s. 6d.

By the SAME AUTHOR.

POOR NELLIE. Cheap Edition. Crown 8vo, 3s. 6d.

MY WEATHER-WISE COMPANION. Presented by B. T.
Fcap. 8vo, 1s. net.

NAPIER. The Construction of the Wonderful Canon of Loga-
rithms. By JOHN NAPIER of Merchiston. Translated, with Notes, and a
Catalogue of Napier's Works, by WILLIAM RAE MACDONALD. Small 4to, 15s.
A few large-paper copies on Whatman paper, 30s.

NEAVES. Songs and Verses, Social and Scientific. By An Old
Contributor to 'Maga.' By the Hon. Lord NEAVES. Fifth Edition. Fcap.
8vo, 4s.

NICHOLSON.

A Manual of Zoology, for the Use of Students. With a
General Introduction on the Principles of Zoology. By HENRY ALLEYNE
NICHOLSON, M.D., D.Sc., F.L.S., F.G.S., Regius Professor of Natural History in
the University of Aberdeen. Seventh Edition, Rewritten and Enlarged. Post
8vo, pp. 956, with 555 Engravings on Wood, 18s.

Text-Book of Zoology, for Junior Students. Fifth Edition,
Rewritten and Enlarged. Crown 8vo, with 358 Engravings on Wood, 10s. 6d.

Introductory Text-Book of Zoology, for the Use of Junior
Classes. New Edition, Revised and Enlarged.   [*In the press.*

NICHOLSON.

A Manual of Palæontology, for the Use of Students. With a General Introduction on the Principles of Palæontology. By Professor H. ALLEYNE NICHOLSON and RICHARD LYDEKKER, B.A. Third Edition, entirely Rewritten and greatly Enlarged. 2 vols. 8vo, £3, 3s.

The Ancient Life-History of the Earth. An Outline of the Principles and Leading Facts of Palæontological Science. Crown 8vo, with 276 Engravings, 10s. 6d.

On the "Tabulate Corals" of the Palæozoic Period, with Critical Descriptions of Illustrative Species. Illustrated with 15 Lithographed Plates and numerous Engravings. Super-royal 8vo, 21s.

Synopsis of the Classification of the Animal Kingdom. 8vo, with 106 Illustrations, 6s.

On the Structure and Affinities of the Genus Monticulipora and its Sub-Genera, with Critical Descriptions of Illustrative Species. Illustrated with numerous Engravings on Wood and Lithographed Plates. Super-royal 8vo, 18s.

NICHOLSON.

Thoth. A Romance. By JOSEPH SHIELD NICHOLSON, M.A., D.Sc., Professor of Commercial and Political Economy and Mercantile Law in the University of Edinburgh. Third Edition. Crown 8vo, 4s. 6d.

A Dreamer of Dreams. A Modern Romance. Second Edition. Crown 8vo, 6s.

NICOLSON AND MURE. A Handbook to the Local Government (Scotland) Act, 1889. With Introduction, Explanatory Notes, and Index. By J. BADENACH NICOLSON, Advocate, Counsel to the Scotch Education Department, and W. J. MURE, Advocate, Legal Secretary to the Lord Advocate for Scotland. Ninth Reprint. 8vo, 5s.

OLIPHANT.

Masollam : A Problem of the Period. A Novel. By LAURENCE OLIPHANT. 3 vols. post 8vo, 25s. 6d.

Scientific Religion; or, Higher Possibilities of Life and Practice through the Operation of Natural Forces. Second Edition. 8vo, 16s.

Altiora Peto. Cheap Edition. Crown 8vo, boards, 2s. 6d. ; cloth, 3s. 6d. Illustrated Edition. Crown 8vo, cloth, 6s.

Piccadilly. With Illustrations by Richard Doyle. New Edition, 3s. 6d. Cheap Edition, boards, 2s. 6d.

Traits and Travesties ; Social and Political. Post 8vo, 10s. 6d.

Episodes in a Life of Adventure; or, Moss from a Rolling Stone. Cheaper Edition. Post 8vo, 3s. 6d.

Haifa : Life in Modern Palestine. Second Edition. 8vo, 7s. 6d.

The Land of Gilead. With Excursions in the Lebanon. With Illustrations and Maps. Demy 8vo, 21s.

Memoir of the Life of Laurence Oliphant, and of Alice Oliphant, his Wife. By Mrs M. O. W. OLIPHANT. Seventh Edition. 2 vols. post 8vo, with Portraits. 21s.
POPULAR EDITION. With a New Preface. Post 8vo, with Portraits. 7s, 6d.

OLIPHANT.

Annals of a Publishing House. William Blackwood and his Sons ; including a History of their Magazine and Friends. By Mrs OLIPHANT. With Four Portraits. Demy 8vo. [*Vols. I. and II. in the press.*

Who was Lost and is Found. Second Edition. Crown 8vo, 6s.

Miss Marjoribanks. New Edition. Crown 8vo, 3s. 6d.

OLIPHANT.

The Perpetual Curate, and The Rector. New Edition. Crown 8vo, 3s. 6d.

Salem Chapel, and The Doctor's Family. New Edition. Crown 8vo, 3s. 6d.

Katie Stewart, and other Stories. New Edition. Crown 8vo, cloth, 3s. 6d.

Katie Stewart. Illustrated boards, 2s. 6d.

Valentine and his Brother. New Edition. Crown 8vo, 3s. 6d.

Sons and Daughters. Crown 8vo, 3s. 6d.

Two Stories of the Seen and the Unseen. The Open Door—Old Lady Mary. Paper covers, 1s.

OLIPHANT. Notes of a Pilgrimage to Jerusalem and the Holy Land. By F. R. OLIPHANT. Crown 8vo, 3s. 6d.

OSWALD. By Fell and Fjord; or, Scenes and Studies in Iceland. By E. J. OSWALD. Post 8vo, with Illustrations. 7s. 6d.

PAGE.

Introductory Text-Book of Geology. By DAVID PAGE, LL.D., Professor of Geology in the Durham University of Physical Science, Newcastle. With Engravings and Glossarial Index. New Edition. Revised by Professor LAPWORTH of Mason Science College, Birmingham.   [*In preparation.*

Advanced Text-Book of Geology, Descriptive and Industrial. With Engravings, and Glossary of Scientific Terms. New Edition. Revised by Professor LAPWORTH.   [*In preparation.*

Introductory Text-Book of Physical Geography. With Sketch-Maps and Illustrations. Edited by Professor LAPWORTH, LL.D., F.G.S., &c., Mason Science College, Birmingham. Thirteenth Edition, Revised and Enlarged. 2s. 6d.

Advanced Text-Book of Physical Geography. Third Edition. Revised and Enlarged by Professor LAPWORTH. With Engravings. 5s.

PATON.

Spindrift. By Sir J. NOEL PATON. Fcap., cloth, 5s.

Poems by a Painter. Fcap., cloth, 5s.

PATON. Body and Soul. A Romance in Transcendental Pathology. By FREDERICK NOEL PATON. Third Edition. Crown 8vo, 1s.

PATRICK. The Apology of Origen in Reply to Celsus. A Chapter in the History of Apologetics. By the Rev. J. PATRICK, D.D. Post 8vo, 7s. 6d.

PAUL. History of the Royal Company of Archers, the Queen's Body-Guard for Scotland. By JAMES BALFOUR PAUL, Advocate of the Scottish Bar. Crown 4to, with Portraits and other Illustrations. £2, 2s.

PEILE. Lawn Tennis as a Game of Skill. By Lieut.-Col. S. C. F. PEILE, B.S.C. Revised Edition, with new Scoring Rules. Fcap. 8vo, cloth, 1s.

PETTIGREW. The Handy Book of Bees, and their Profitable Management. By A. PETTIGREW. Fifth Edition, Enlarged, with Engravings. Crown 8vo, 3s. 6d.

PFLEIDERER. Philosophy and Development of Religion. Being the Edinburgh Gifford Lectures for 1894. By OTTO PFLEIDERER, D.D. Professor of Theology at Berlin University. In 2 vols. post 8vo, 15s. net.

PHILLIPS. The Knight's Tale. By F. EMILY PHILLIPS, Author of 'The Education of Antonia.' Crown 8vo, 3s. 6d.

PHILOSOPHICAL CLASSICS FOR ENGLISH READERS. Edited by WILLIAM KNIGHT, LL.D., Professor of Moral Philosophy, University of St Andrews. In crown 8vo volumes, with Portraits, price 3s. 6d.

[*For List of Volumes, see page 2.*

POLLARD. A Study in Municipal Government: The Corporation of Berlin. By JAMES POLLARD, C.A., Chairman of the Edinburgh Public Health Committee, and Secretary of the Edinburgh Chamber of Commerce. Second Edition, Revised. Crown 8vo, 3s. 6d.

POLLOK. The Course of Time: A Poem. By ROBERT POLLOK, A.M. Cottage Edition, 32mo, 8d. The Same, cloth, gilt edges, 1s. 6d. Another Edition, with Illustrations by Birket Foster and others, fcap., cloth, 3s. 6d., or with edges gilt, 4s.

PORT ROYAL LOGIC. Translated from the French; with Introduction, Notes, and Appendix. By THOMAS SPENCER BAYNES, LL.D., Professor in the University of St Andrews. Tenth Edition, 12mo, 4s.

POTTS AND DARNELL.
Aditus Faciliores: An Easy Latin Construing Book, with Complete Vocabulary By A. W. POTTS, M.A., LL.D., and the Rev. C. DARNELL, M.A., Head-Master of Cargilfield Preparatory School Edinburgh. Tenth Edition, fcap. 8vo, 3s. 6d.

Aditus Faciliores Graeci. An Easy Greek Construing Book, with Complete Vocabulary. Fifth Edition, Revised. Fcap. 8vo, 3s.

POTTS. School Sermons. By the late ALEXANDER WM. POTTS, LL.D., First Head-Master of Fettes College. With a Memoir and Portrait. Crown 8vo, 7s. 6d.

PRINGLE. The Live Stock of the Farm. By ROBERT O. PRINGLE. Third Edition. Revised and Edited by JAMES MACDONALD. Crown 8vo, 7s. 6d.

PRYDE. Pleasant Memories of a Busy Life. By DAVID PRYDE, M.A., LL.D., Author of 'Highways of Literature,' 'Great Men in European History,' 'Biographical Outlines of English Literature,' &c. With a Mezzotint Portrait. Post 8vo, 6s.

PUBLIC GENERAL STATUTES AFFECTING SCOTLAND from 1707 to 1847, with Chronological Table and Index. 3 vols. large 8vo, £3, 3s.

PUBLIC GENERAL STATUTES AFFECTING SCOTLAND, COLLECTION OF. Published Annually, with General Index.

RAMSAY. Scotland and Scotsmen in the Eighteenth Century. Edited from the MSS. of JOHN RAMSAY, Esq. of Ochtertyre, by ALEXANDER ALLARDYCE, Author of 'Memoir of Admiral Lord Keith, K.B.,' &c. 2 vols. 8vo, 31s. 6d.

RANKIN.
A Handbook of the Church of Scotland. By JAMES RANKIN, D.D., Minister of Muthill; Author of 'Character Studies in the Old Testament,' &c. An entirely New and much Enlarged Edition. Crown 8vo, with 2 Maps, 7s. 6d.

The First Saints. Post 8vo, 7s. 6d.

The Creed in Scotland. An Exposition of the Apostles' Creed. With Extracts from Archbishop Hamilton's Catechism of 1552, John Calvin's Catechism of 1556, and a Catena of Ancient Latin and other Hymns. Post 8vo, 7s. 6d.

The Worthy Communicant. A Guide to the Devout Observance of the Lord's Supper. Limp cloth, 1s. 3d.

The Young Churchman. Lessons on the Creed, the Commandments, the Means of Grace, and the Church. Limp cloth, 1s. 3d.

First Communion Lessons. 25th Edition. Paper Cover, 2d.

RANKINE. A Hero of the Dark Continent. Memoir of Rev. Wm. Affleck Scott, M.A., M.B., C.M., Church of Scotland Missionary at Blantyre, British Central Africa. By W. HENRY RANKINE, B.D., Minister at St Boswells. With a Portrait and other Illustrations. Crown 8vo, 5s.

RECORDS OF THE TERCENTENARY FESTIVAL OF THE
UNIVERSITY OF EDINBURGH. Celebrated in April 1884. Published under
the Sanction of the Senatus Academicus. Large 4to, £2, 12s. 6d.

ROBERTSON. The Early Religion of Israel. As set forth by
Biblical Writers and Modern Critical Historians. Being the Baird Lecture for
1888-89. By JAMES ROBERTSON, D.D., Professor of Oriental Languages in the
University of Glasgow. Fourth Edition. Crown 8vo, 10s. 6d.

ROBERTSON.
Orellana, and other Poems. By J. LOGIE ROBERTSON,
M.A. Fcap. 8vo. Printed on hand-made paper. 6s.
A History of English Literature. For Secondary Schools.
With an Introduction by Professor MASSON, Edinburgh University. Cr. 8vo, 3s.
English Verse for Junior Classes. In Two Parts. Part I.—
Chaucer to Coleridge. Part II.—Nineteenth Century Poets. Crown 8vo, each
1s. 6d. net.
Outlines of English Literature for Young Scholars. With
Illustrative Specimens. In 1 vol. crown 8vo. [*In the press.*

ROBINSON. Wild Traits in Tame Animals. Being some
Familiar Studies in Evolution. By LOUIS ROBINSON, M.D. With Illustrations
by STEPHEN J. DADD. In 1 vol. crown 8vo. [*In the press.*

RODGER. Aberdeen Doctors at Home and Abroad. The Story
of a Medical School. By ELLA HILL BURTON RODGER. Demy 8vo, 10s. 6d.

ROSCOE. Rambles with a Fishing-Rod. By E. S. ROSCOE.
Crown 8vo, 4s. 6d.

ROSS AND SOMERVILLE. Beggars on Horseback: A Riding
Tour in North Wales. By MARTIN ROSS and E. Œ. SOMERVILLE. With Illustrations by E. Œ. SOMERVILLE. Crown 8vo, 3s. 6d.

RUTLAND.
Notes of an Irish Tour in 1846. By the DUKE OF RUTLAND,
G.C.B. (Lord JOHN MANNERS). New Edition. Crown 8vo, 2s. 6d.
Correspondence between the Right Honble. William Pitt
and Charles Duke of Rutland, Lord-Lieutenant of Ireland, 1781-1787. With
Introductory Note by JOHN DUKE OF RUTLAND. 8vo, 7s. 6d.

RUTLAND.
Gems of German Poetry. Translated by the DUCHESS OF
RUTLAND (Lady JOHN MANNERS). [*New Edition in preparation.*
Impressions of Bad-Homburg. Comprising a Short Account
of the Women's Associations of Germany under the Red Cross. Crown 8vo, 1s. 6d.
Some Personal Recollections of the Later Years of the Earl
of Beaconsfield, K.G. Sixth Edition. 6d.
Employment of Women in the Public Service. 6d.
Some of the Advantages of Easily Accessible Reading and
Recreation Rooms and Free Libraries. With Remarks on Starting and Main-
taining them. Second Edition. Crown 8vo, 1s.
A Sequel to Rich Men's Dwellings, and other Occasional
Papers. Crown 8vo, 2s. 6d.
Encouraging Experiences of Reading and Recreation Rooms,
Aims of Guilds, Nottingham Social Guide, Existing Institutions, &c., &c.
Crown 8vo, 1s.

SAINTSBURY. The Flourishing of Romance and the Rise of
Allegory (12th and 13th Centuries). By GEORGE SAINTSBURY, M.A., Professor of
Rhetoric and English Literature in Edinburgh University. Being the first vol-
ume issued of "PERIODS OF EUROPEAN LITERATURE." Edited by Professor
SAINTSBURY. Crown 8vo, 5s. net.

SALMON. Songs of a Heart's Surrender, and other Verse. By ARTHUR L. SALMON. Fcap. 8vo, 2s.

SCHEFFEL. The Trumpeter. A Romance of the Rhine. By JOSEPH VICTOR VON SCHEFFEL. Translated from the Two Hundredth German Edition by JESSIE BECK and LOUISA LORIMER. With an Introduction by Sir THEODORE MARTIN, K.C.B. Long 8vo, 3s. 6d.

SCHILLER. Wallenstein. A Dramatic Poem. By FRIEDRICH VON SCHILLER. Translated by C. G. N. LOCKHART. Fcap. 8vo, 7s. 6d.

SCOTT. Tom Cringle's Log. By MICHAEL SCOTT. New Edition. With 19 Full-page Illustrations. Crown 8vo, 3s. 6d.

SCOUGAL. Prisons and their Inmates; or, Scenes from a Silent World. By FRANCIS SCOUGAL. Crown 8vo, boards, 2s.

SELKIRK. Poems. By J. B. SELKIRK, Author of 'Ethics and Æsthetics of Modern Poetry,' 'Bible Truths with Shakespearian Parallels,' &c. New and Enlarged Edition. Crown 8vo, printed on antique paper, 6s.

SELLAR'S Manual of the Acts relating to Education in Scotland. By J. EDWARD GRAHAM, B.A. Oxon., Advocate. Ninth Edition. Demy 8vo, 12s. 6d.

SETH.

Scottish Philosophy. A Comparison of the Scottish and German Answers to Hume. Balfour Philosophical Lectures, University of Edinburgh. By ANDREW SETH, LL.D., Professor of Logic and Metaphysics in Edinburgh University. Second Edition. Crown 8vo, 5s.

Hegelianism and Personality. Balfour Philosophical Lectures. Second Series. Second Edition. Crown 8vo, 5s.

Man's Place in the Cosmos, and other Essays. Post 8vo, 7s. 6d. net.

SETH. A Study of Ethical Principles. By JAMES SETH, M.A., Professor of Philosophy in Cornell University, U.S.A. Second Edition, Revised. Post 8vo, 10s. 6d. net.

SHADWELL. The Life of Colin Campbell, Lord Clyde. Illustrated by Extracts from his Diary and Correspondence. By Lieutenant-General SHADWELL, C.B. With Portrait, Maps, and Plans. 2 vols. 8vo, 36s.

SHAND.

The Life of General Sir Edward Bruce Hamley, K.C.B., K.C.M.G. By ALEX. INNES SHAND, Author of 'Kilcarra,' 'Against Time,' &c. With two Photogravure Portraits and other Illustrations. Cheaper Edition, with a Statement by Mr Edward Hamley. 2 vols. demy 8vo, 10s. 6d.

Half a Century; or, Changes in Men and Manners. Second Edition. 8vo, 12s. 6d.

Letters from the West of Ireland. Reprinted from the 'Times.' Crown 8vo, 5s.

SHARPE. Letters from and to Charles Kirkpatrick Sharpe. Edited by ALEXANDER ALLARDYCE, Author of 'Memoir of Admiral Lord Keith, K.B.,' &c. With a Memoir by the Rev. W. K. R. BEDFORD. In 2 vols. 8vo. Illustrated with Etchings and other Engravings. £2, 12s. 6d.

SIM. Margaret Sim's Cookery. With an Introduction by L. B. WALFORD, Author of 'Mr Smith: A Part of his Life,' &c. Crown 8vo, 5s.

SIMPSON. The Wild Rabbit in a New Aspect; or, Rabbit-Warrens that Pay. A book for Landowners, Sportsmen, Land Agents, Farmers, Gamekeepers, and Allotment Holders. A Record of Recent Experiments conducted on the Estate of the Right Hon. the Earl of Wharncliffe at Wortley Hall. By J. SIMPSON. Second Edition, Enlarged. Small crown 8vo, 5s.

SINCLAIR. Audrey Craven. By MAY SINCLAIR. Crown 8vo, 6s.

SKELTON.

The Table-Talk of Shirley. By JOHN SKELTON, Advocate, C.B., LL.D., Author of 'The Essays of Shirley.' With a Frontispiece. Sixth Edition, Revised and Enlarged. Post 8vo, 7s. 6d.

SKELTON.

The Table-Talk of Shirley. Second Series. Summers and Winters at Balmawhapple. With Illustrations. Two Volumes. Second Edition. Post 8vo, 10s. net.

Maitland of Lethington ; and the Scotland of Mary Stuart. A History. Limited Edition, with Portraits. Demy 8vo, 2 vols., 28s. net.

The Handbook of Public Health. A Complete Edition of the Public Health and other Sanitary Acts relating to Scotland. Annotated, and with the Rules, Instructions, and Decisions of the Board of Supervision brought up to date with relative forms. Second Edition. With Introduction, containing the Administration of the Public Health Act in Counties. 8vo, 8s. 6d.

The Local Government (Scotland) Act in Relation to Public Health. A Handy Guide for County and District Councillors, Medical Officers, Sanitary Inspectors, and Members of Parochial Boards. Second Edition. With a new Preface on appointment of Sanitary Officers. Crown 8vo, 2s.

SKRINE. Columba : A Drama. By JOHN HUNTLEY SKRINE Warden of Glenalmond ; Author of 'A Memory of Edward Thring.' Fcap. 4to, 6s

SMITH.

Thorndale ; or, The Conflict of Opinions. By WILLIAM SMITH, Author of 'A Discourse on Ethics,' &c. New Edition. Crown 8vo, 10s. 6d.

Gravenhurst ; or, Thoughts on Good and Evil. Second Edition. With Memoir and Portrait of the Author. Crown 8vo, 8s.

The Story of William and Lucy Smith. Edited by GEORGE MERRIAM. Large post 8vo, 12s. 6d.

SMITH. Memoir of the Families of M'Combie and Thoms, originally M'Intosh and M'Thomas. Compiled from History and Tradition. By WILLIAM M'COMBIE SMITH. With Illustrations. 8vo, 7s. 6d.

SMITH. Greek Testament Lessons for Colleges, Schools, and Private Students, consisting chiefly of the Sermon on the Mount and the Parables of our Lord. With Notes and Essays. By the Rev. J. HUNTER SMITH, M.A., King Edward's School, Birmingham. Crown 8vo, 6s.

SMITH. The Secretary for Scotland. Being a Statement of the Powers and Duties of the new Scottish Office. With a Short Historical Introduction, and numerous references to important Administrative Documents. By W. C. SMITH, LL.B., Advocate. 8vo, 6s.

"SON OF THE MARSHES, A."

From Spring to Fall ; or, When Life Stirs. By "A SON OF THE MARSHES." Cheap Uniform Edition. Crown 8vo, 3s. 6d.

Within an Hour of London Town : Among Wild Birds and their Haunts. Edited by J. A. OWEN. Cheap Uniform Edition. Crown 8vo, 3s. 6d.

With the Woodlanders and by the Tide. Cheap Uniform Edition. Crown 8vo, 3s. 6d.

On Surrey Hills. Cheap Uniform Edition. Crown 8vo, 3s. 6d.

Annals of a Fishing Village. Cheap Uniform Edition. Crown 8vo, 3s. 6d.

SORLEY. The Ethics of Naturalism. Being the Shaw Fellowship Lectures, 1884. By W. R. SORLEY, M.A., Fellow of Trinity College, Cambridge, Professor of Moral Philosophy in the University of Aberdeen. Crown 8vo, 6s.

SPROTT. The Worship and Offices of the Church of Scotland. By GEORGE W. SPROTT, D.D., Minister of North Berwick. Crown 8vo, 6s.

STATISTICAL ACCOUNT OF SCOTLAND. Complete, with Index. 15 vols. 8vo, £16, 16s.

STEEVENS. The Land of the Dollar. By G. W. STEEVENS, Author of 'Naval Policy,' &c. Crown 8vo, 6s.

STEPHENS.

The Book of the Farm; detailing the Labours of the Farmer,
Farm-Steward, Ploughman, Shepherd, Hedger, Farm-Labourer, Field-Worker,
and Cattle-man. Illustrated with numerous Portraits of Animals and Engravings
of Implements, and Plans of Farm Buildings. Fourth Edition. Revised, and
in great part Re-written, by JAMES MACDONALD, F.R.S.E., Secretary Highland
and Agricultural Society of Scotland. Complete in Six Divisional Volumes,
bound in cloth, each 10s. 6d., or handsomely bound, in 3 volumes, with leather
back and gilt top, £3, 3s.

⁎ Also being issued in 20 monthly Parts, price 2s. 6d. net each.

[Part I. ready.

Catechism of Practical Agriculture. 22d Thousand. Revised
by JAMES MACDONALD, F.R.S.E. With numerous Illustrations. Crown 8vo, 1s.

The Book of Farm Implements and Machines. By J. SLIGHT
and R. SCOTT BURN, Engineers. Edited by HENRY STEPHENS. Large 8vo, £2, 2s.

STEVENSON. British Fungi. (Hymenomycetes.) By Rev.
JOHN STEVENSON, Author of 'Mycologia Scotica,' Hon. Sec. Cryptogamic Society
of Scotland. Vols. I. and II., post 8vo, with Illustrations, price 12s. 6d. net each.

STEWART. Advice to Purchasers of Horses. By JOHN
STEWART, V.S. New Edition. 2s. 6d.

STODDART. Angling Songs. By THOMAS TOD STODDART.
New Edition, with a Memoir by ANNA M. STODDART. Crown 8vo, 7s. 6d.

STODDART.

John Stuart Blackie: A Biography. By ANNA M. STODDART.
With 3 Plates. Third Edition. 2 vols. demy 8vo, 21s.

POPULAR EDITION, with Portrait. Crown 8vo, 6s.

Sir Philip Sidney: Servant of God. Illustrated by MARGARET
L. HUGGINS. With a New Portrait of Sir Philip Sidney. Small 4to, with a
specially designed Cover. 5s.

STORMONTH.

Dictionary of the English Language, Pronouncing, Etymological, and Explanatory. By the Rev. JAMES STORMONTH. Revised by the
Rev. P. H. PHELP. Library Edition. New and Cheaper Edition, with Supplement. Imperial 8vo, handsomely bound in half morocco, 18s. net.

Etymological and Pronouncing Dictionary of the English
Language. Including a very Copious Selection of Scientific Terms. For use in
Schools and Colleges, and as a Book of General Reference. The Pronunciation
carefully revised by the Rev. P. H. PHELP, M.A. Cantab. Thirteenth Edition,
with Supplement. Crown 8vo, pp. 800. 7s. 6d.

The School Dictionary. New Edition, Revised.

[In preparation.

STORY. The Apostolic Ministry in the Scottish Church (The
Baird Lecture for 1897). By ROBERT HERBERT STORY, D.D. (Edin.), F.S.A.
Scot., Professor of Ecclesiastical History in the University of Glasgow; Principal
Clerk of the General Assembly; and Chaplain to the Queen. Crown 8vo, 7s. 6d.

STORY.

Nero; A Historical Play. By W. W. STORY, Author of
'Roba di Roma.' Fcap. 8vo, 6s.

Vallombrosa. Post 8vo, 5s.

Poems. 2 vols., 7s. 6d.

Fiammetta. A Summer Idyl. Crown 8vo, 7s. 6d.

Conversations in a Studio. 2 vols. crown 8vo, 12s. 6d.

Excursions in Art and Letters. Crown 8vo, 7s. 6d.

A Poet's Portfolio: Later Readings. 18mo, 3s. 6d.

STRACHEY. Talk at a Country House. Fact and Fiction.
By Sir EDWARD STRACHEY, Bart. With a Portrait of the Author. Crown 8vo,
4s. 6d. net.

STURGIS. Little Comedies, Old and New. By JULIAN STURGIS.
Crown 8vo, 7s. 6d.

SUTHERLAND. Handbook of Hardy Herbaceous and Alpine
Flowers, for General Garden Decoration. Containing Descriptions of upwards
of 1000 Species of Ornamental Hardy Perennial and Alpine Plants; along with
Concise and Plain Instructions for their Propagation and Culture. By WILLIAM
SUTHERLAND, Landscape Gardener; formerly Manager of the Herbaceous Depart-
ment at Kew. Crown 8vo, 7s. 6d.

TAYLOR. The Story of my Life. By the late Colonel
MEADOWS TAYLOR, Author of 'The Confessions of a Thug,' &c., &c. Edited by
his Daughter. New and Cheaper Edition, being the Fourth. Crown 8vo, 6s.

THOMAS. The Woodland Life. By EDWARD THOMAS. With a
Frontispiece. In 1 vol. square 8vo.   [*In the press.*

THOMSON.
    The Diversions of a Prime Minister. By Basil Thomson.
    With a Map, numerous Illustrations by J. W. Cawston and others, and Repro-
    ductions of Rare Plates from Early Voyages of Sixteenth and Seventeenth Cen-
    turies. Small demy 8vo, 15s.

    South Sea Yarns. With 10 Full-page Illustrations. Cheaper
    Edition. Crown 8vo, 3s. 6d.

THOMSON.
    Handy Book of the Flower-Garden : Being Practical Direc-
    tions for the Propagation, Culture, and Arrangement of Plants in Flower-
    Gardens all the year round. With Engraved Plans. By DAVID THOMSON,
    Gardener to his Grace the Duke of Buccleuch, K.T., at Drumlanrig. Fourth
    and Cheaper Edition. Crown 8vo, 5s.

    The Handy Book of Fruit-Culture under Glass : Being a
    series of Elaborate Practical Treatises on the Cultivation and Forcing of Pines,
    Vines, Peaches, Figs, Melons, Strawberries, and Cucumbers. With Engravings
    of Hothouses, &c. Second Edition, Revised and Enlarged. Crown 8vo, 7s. 6d.

THOMSON. A Practical Treatise on the Cultivation of the
Grape Vine. By WILLIAM THOMSON, Tweed Vineyards. Tenth Edition. 8vo, 5s.

THOMSON. Cookery for the Sick and Convalescent. With
Directions for the Preparation of Poultices, Fomentations, &c. By BARBARA
THOMSON. Fcap. 8vo, 1s. 6d.

THORBURN. Asiatic Neighbours. By S. S. THORBURN, Bengal
Civil Service, Author of 'Bannú; or, Our Afghan Frontier,' 'David Leslie:
A Story of the Afghan Frontier,' 'Musalmans and Money-Lenders in the Pan-
jab.' With Two Maps. Demy 8vo, 10s. 6d. net.

THORNTON. Opposites. A Series of Essays on the Unpopular
Sides of Popular Questions. By LEWIS THORNTON. 8vo, 12s. 6d.

TRANSACTIONS OF THE HIGHLAND AND AGRICUL-
TURAL SOCIETY OF SCOTLAND. Published annually, price 5s.

TRAVERS.
    Mona Maclean, Medical Student. A Novel. By GRAHAM
    TRAVERS. Twelfth Edition. Crown 8vo, 6s.

    Fellow Travellers. Fourth Edition. Crown 8vo, 6s.

TRYON. Life of Vice-Admiral Sir George Tryon, K.C.B. By
Rear-Admiral C. C. PENROSE FITZGERALD. With Two Portraits and numerous
Illustrations. Second Edition. Demy 8vo, 21s.

TULLOCH.
    Rational Theology and Christian Philosophy in England in
    the Seventeenth Century. By JOHN TULLOCH, D.D., Principal of St Mary's Col-
    lege in the University of St Andrews, and one of her Majesty's Chaplains in
    Ordinary in Scotland. Second Edition. 2 vols. 8vo, 16s.

    Modern Theories in Philosophy and Religion. 8vo, 15s.

TULLOCH.
> Luther, and other Leaders of the Reformation. Third Edition, Enlarged. Crown 8vo, 3s. 6d.
>
> Memoir of Principal Tulloch, D.D., LL.D. By Mrs OLIPHANT, Author of 'Life of Edward Irving.' Third and Cheaper Edition. 8vo, with Portrait, 7s. 6d.

TWEEDIE. The Arabian Horse: His Country and People.
> By Major-General W. TWEEDIE, C.S.I., Bengal Staff Corps; for many years H.B.M.'s Consul-General, Baghdad, and Political Resident for the Government of India in Turkish Arabia. In one vol. royal 4to, with Seven Coloured Plates and other Illustrations, and a Map of the Country. Price £3, 3s. net.

TYLER. The Whence and the Whither of Man. A Brief History of his Origin and Development through Conformity to Environment. The Morse Lectures of 1895. By JOHN M. TYLER, Professor of Biology, Amherst College, U.S.A. Post 8vo, 6s. net.

VEITCH.
> Memoir of John Veitch, LL.D., Professor of Logic and Rhetoric, University of Glasgow. By MARY R. L. BRYCE. With Portrait and 3 Photogravure Plates. Demy 8vo, 7s. 6d.
>
> Border Essays. By JOHN VEITCH, LL.D., Professor of Logic and Rhetoric, University of Glasgow. Crown 8vo, 4s. 6d. *net.*
>
> The History and Poetry of the Scottish Border: their Main Features and Relations. New and Enlarged Edition. 2 vols. demy 8vo, 16s.
>
> Institutes of Logic. Post 8vo, 12s. 6d.
>
> The Feeling for Nature in Scottish Poetry. From the Earliest Times to the Present Day. 2 vols. fcap. 8vo, in roxburghe binding, 15s.
>
> Merlin and other Poems. Fcap. 8vo, 4s. 6d.
>
> Knowing and Being. Essays in Philosophy. First Series. Crown 8vo, 5s.
>
> Dualism and Monism; and other Essays. Essays in Philosophy. Second Series. With an Introduction by R. M. Wenley. Crown 8vo, 4s. 6d. net.

VIRGIL. The Æneid of Virgil. Translated in English Blank Verse by G. K. RICKARDS, M.A., and Lord RAVENSWORTH. 2 vols. fcap. 8vo, 10s.

WACE. Christianity and Agnosticism. Reviews of some Recent Attacks on the Christian Faith. By HENRY WACE, D.D., Principal of King's College, London; Preacher of Lincoln's Inn; Chaplain to the Queen. Second Edition. Post 8vo, 10s. 6d. net.

WADDELL. An Old Kirk Chronicle: Being a History of Auldhame, Tyninghame, and Whitekirk, in East Lothian. From Session Records, 1615 to 1850. By Rev. P. HATELY WADDELL, B.D., Minister of the United Parish. Small Paper Edition, 200 Copies. Price £1. Large Paper Edition, 50 Copies. Price £1, 10s.

WALDO. The Ban of the Gubbe. By CEDRIC DANE WALDO. Crown 8vo, 2s. 6d.

WALFORD. Four Biographies from 'Blackwood': Jane Taylor, Hannah More, Elizabeth Fry, Mary Somerville. By L. B. WALFORD. Crown 8vo, 5s.

WARREN'S (SAMUEL) WORKS:—
> Diary of a Late Physician. Cloth, 2s. 6d.; boards, 2s.
>
> Ten Thousand A-Year. Cloth, 3s. 6d.; boards, 2s. 6d.
>
> Now and Then. The Lily and the Bee. Intellectual and Moral Development of the Present Age. 4s. 6d.
>
> Essays: Critical, Imaginative, and Juridical. 5s.

WENLEY.

Socrates and Christ: A Study in the Philosophy of Religion. By R. M. WENLEY, M.A., D.Sc., D.Phil., Professor of Philosophy in the University of Michigan, U.S.A. Crown 8vo, 6s.

Aspects of Pessimism. Crown 8vo, 6s.

WHITE.

The Eighteen Christian Centuries. By the Rev. JAMES WHITE. Seventh Edition. Post 8vo, with Index, 6s.

History of France, from the Earliest Times. Sixth Thousand. Post 8vo, with Index, 6s.

WHITE.

Archæological Sketches in Scotland—Kintyre and Knapdale. By Colonel T. P. WHITE, R.E., of the Ordnance Survey. With numerous Illustrations. 2 vols. folio, £4, 4s. Vol. I., Kintyre, sold separately, £2, 2s.

The Ordnance Survey of the United Kingdom. A Popular Account. Crown 8vo, 5s.

WILLIAMSON. The Horticultural Handbook and Exhibitor's Guide. A Treatise on Cultivating, Exhibiting, and Judging Plants, Flowers, Fruits, and Vegetables. By W. WILLIAMSON, Gardener. Revised by MALCOLM DUNN, Gardener to his Grace the Duke of Buccleuch and Queensberry, Dalkeith Park. New and Cheaper Edition, enlarged. Crown 8vo, paper cover, 2s.; cloth, 2s. 6d.

WILLIAMSON. Poems of Nature and Life. By DAVID R. WILLIAMSON, Minister of Kirkmaiden. Fcap. 8vo, 3s.

WILLS. Behind an Eastern Veil. A Plain Tale of Events occurring in the Experience of a Lady who had a unique opportunity of observing the Inner Life of Ladies of the Upper Class in Persia. By C. J. WILLS, Author of 'In the Land of the Lion and Sun,' 'Persia as it is,' &c., &c. Cheaper Edition. Demy 8vo, 5s.

WILSON.

Works of Professor Wilson. Edited by his Son-in-Law, Professor FERRIER. 12 vols. crown 8vo, £2, 8s.

Christopher in his Sporting-Jacket. 2 vols., 8s.

Isle of Palms, City of the Plague, and other Poems. 4s.

Lights and Shadows of Scottish Life, and other Tales. 4s.

Essays, Critical and Imaginative. 4 vols., 16s.

The Noctes Ambrosianæ. 4 vols., 16s.

Homer and his Translators, and the Greek Drama. Crown 8vo, 4s.

WORSLEY.

Poems and Translations. By PHILIP STANHOPE WORSLEY, M.A. Edited by EDWARD WORSLEY. Second Edition, Enlarged. Fcap. 8vo, 6s.

Homer's Odyssey. Translated into English Verse in the Spenserian Stanza. By P. S. Worsley. New and Cheaper Edition. Post 8vo, 7s. 6d. net.

Homer's Iliad. Translated by P. S. Worsley and Prof. Conington. 2 vols. crown 8vo, 21s.

YATE. England and Russia Face to Face in Asia. A Record of Travel with the Afghan Boundary Commission. By Captain A. C. YATE, Bombay Staff Corps. 8vo, with Maps and Illustrations, 21s.

YATE. Northern Afghanistan; or, Letters from the Afghan Boundary Commission. By Major C. E. YATE, C.S.I., C.M.G., Bombay Staff Corps, F.R.G.S. 8vo, with Maps, 18s.

YULE. Fortification: For the use of Officers in the Army, and Readers of Military History. By Colonel YULE, Bengal Engineers. 8vo, with Numerous Illustrations, 10s.